TOURISM, RECREATION AND
REGIONAL DEVELOPMENT

New Directions in Tourism Analysis

Series Editor: Dimitri Ioannides, E-TOUR, Mid Sweden University, Sweden

Although tourism is becoming increasingly popular as both a taught subject and an area for empirical investigation, the theoretical underpinnings of many approaches have tended to be eclectic and somewhat underdeveloped. However, recent developments indicate that the field of tourism studies is beginning to develop in a more theoretically informed manner, but this has not yet been matched by current publications.

The aim of this series is to fill this gap with high quality monographs or edited collections that seek to develop tourism analysis at both theoretical and substantive levels using approaches which are broadly derived from allied social science disciplines such as Sociology, Social Anthropology, Human and Social Geography, and Cultural Studies. As tourism studies covers a wide range of activities and sub fields, certain areas such as Hospitality Management and Business, which are already well provided for, would be excluded. The series will therefore fill a gap in the current overall pattern of publication.

Suggested themes to be covered by the series, either singly or in combination, include – consumption; cultural change; development; gender; globalisation; political economy; social theory; sustainability.

Also in the series

Tourism and Violence
Edited by Hazel Andrews
ISBN 978-1-4094-3640-9

Volunteer Tourism
Popular Humanitarianism in Neoliberal Times
Mary Mostafanezhad
ISBN 978-1-4094-6953-7

Tourism Destination Development
Turns and Tactics
Edited by Arvid Viken and Brynhild Granås
ISBN 978-1-4724-1658-2

Planning for Ethnic Tourism
Li Yang and Geoffrey Wall
ISBN 978-0-7546-7384-2

Tourism, Recreation and Regional Development
Perspectives from France and Abroad

Edited by

JEAN-CHRISTOPHE DISSART,
Université Grenoble Alpes, France

JEOFFREY DEHEZ
IRSTEA, France

JEAN-BERNARD MARSAT
IRSTEA, France

LONDON AND NEW YORK

First published 2015 by Ashgate Publishing

2 Park Square, Milton Park, Abingdon, Oxon OX14 4RN
711 Third Avenue, New York, NY 10017, USA

Routledge is an imprint of the Taylor & Francis Group, an informa business

First issued in paperback 2017

British Library Cataloguing in Publication Data
A catalogue record for this book is available from the British Library

The Library of Congress has cataloged the printed edition as follows:
Tourism, recreation and regional development : perspectives from France and abroad / edited by Jean-Christophe Dissart, Jeoffrey Dehez and Jean-Bernard Marsat.
    pages cm. — (New directions in tourism analysis)
  Includes bibliographical references and index.
  ISBN 978-1-4724-1622-3 (hardback : alk. paper)
  1. Tourism—France—Planning. 2. Tourism—France—Management. 3. Regional planning—France. 4. Economic development—France.
I. Dissart, Jean-Christophe, editor of compilation. II. Dehez, Jeoffrey, editor of compilation. III. Marsat, Jean-Bernard, editor of compilation.
  G155.F8T66 2015
  338.4'79144--dc23

2014029248

ISBN 978-1-4724-1622-3 (hbk)
ISBN 978-1-138-08384-4 (pbk)

Contents

List of Figures

List of Tables

Notes on Contributors

Salvador Anton Clavé is a full professor of regional geographical analysis at the Rovira i Virgili University. His research focuses on the evolution of mass coastal tourism destinations, the globalisation of leisure facilities and tourism and local development.

Asma Ben Othmen is with the Research Group for Theoretical and Applied Economics (GREThA) at Montesquieu Bordeaux IV University. She teaches economics and, while working on this book's chapter, was conducting her PhD at the National Research Institute of Science and Technology for Environment and Agriculture (Irstea, France).

Philippe Bourdeau is a full professor of cultural geography at the Institute of Alpine Geography (Grenoble University). He conducts research on recreation practices (Pacte research group). He is interested in the meaning of 'elsewhere' in contemporary societies, critical approaches in tourism, and recreational dissent. He co-represents France within the International Scientific Committee on Research in the Alps (ISCAR).

Jean-Marc Callois holds a PhD in economics and currently heads the 'Territories' department at Irstea. He works in the area of regional development, and focuses on the interaction between sociological, institutional and economic mechanisms.

Mary Cawley was formerly a senior lecturer in geography in the School of Geography and Archaeology at the National University of Ireland Galway. Her research relates to rural change and development, including tourism and its impacts. She has participated in and led EU and national research projects on related themes.

Clarisse Cazals is an economist and a researcher with Irstea. Her work focuses mainly on heritage aspects of economic activities. She is interested in stakeholder rationales that contribute to the diversity of heritage forms, particularly their links with tourism, and in coordination mechanisms that make diverging interests compatible.

Gordon Clark was formerly a senior lecturer in geography in the Lancaster Environment Centre, Lancaster University, UK. His research has focused on rural development, including agriculture and tourism. He has led or participated in several EU projects with a tourism focus. He ran an outreach unit to assist small tourism firms in North West England.

Christophe Clivaz is an associate professor of political science at the Institute of Geography and Sustainability of the University of Lausanne, Switzerland. His current research focuses on governance issues in tourism resorts and comparative analysis of tourism development policies.

Jean Corneloup is a senior lecturer at the UFR STAPS (Clermont-Ferrand) and a researcher with the Pacte research group on territories (Grenoble). His research focuses on the analysis of outdoor sport cultures in relation with rural development. He is president of the network of researchers and experts on outdoor sports (http://www.sportnature.org), and editor-in-chief of the *Nature & Récréation* journal (http://www.nature-et-recreation.com).

Isabel Cortés Jiménez is an external researcher at AQR-IREA, University of Barcelona, and has professional experience in Spain, Italy, the UK and France. Her research concentrates on tourism economics with a special focus on applied econometrics for the study of growth and tourism, regional development and tourism demand modelling.

Dominik Cremer-Schulte is a PhD candidate in economics at Irstea, and holds an engineering degree in spatial planning (TU Dortmund). Interested in the impacts of the natural environment on urban and rural development, his PhD work analyses natural amenity effects on socio-spatial configurations in Alpine urban regions in particular.

Jeoffrey Dehez is a senior research fellow at Irstea. He has various interests in the economics of outdoor recreation, including economic evaluation, the monitoring of demand, costs assessment and organisation analysis. In addition to publishing several books and scientific articles in French and in English, he has developed expertise with public institutions, local communities and non-profit organisations.

Jean-Christophe Dissart was formerly a researcher at Irstea (2006–2013), and currently is a full professor at Grenoble Alpes University. He holds a PhD in urban and regional planning from the University of Wisconsin – Madison, USA. He has worked on amenity, tourism, and local development issues for over 15 years, in both European and North American contexts.

Isabelle Frochot completed her PhD at Manchester Metropolitan University and then worked as a tourism marketing lecturer. Since returning to France, Isabelle has moved her research focus to mountain tourism, conducting various studies on its image and exploring customer experience design and the complexity of satisfaction in an experiential context.

Emmanuelle George-Marcelpoil heads the Development of Mountain Territories research unit at Irstea Grenoble. Her research focuses on the tourism economy and governance of mountain destinations, in particular winter sports resorts in the Alps.

Ludovic Ginelli is a study engineer and a PhD candidate in sociology at Irstea and University of Bordeaux. His work focuses on nature-based recreation in several study areas in France (including overseas territories). In particular, he analyses users' stance on environmental norms (ecologisation, disputes) in various contexts (protected or unprotected areas).

France Loubet is an associate researcher with the Pacte (Territories) research group. Her main research topic is the impact of tourism on rural development. She uses the capability approach, in combination with territorial economics perspectives, to assess regional development.

Sandrine Lyser is a statistician and a study engineer at Irstea. Her work focuses on socioeconomic studies in diverse (rural, forested, coastal) areas and on various local issues (tourism, heritage, quality of life) as well as the use of data analysis methods to process results.

Pascal Mao is a senior lecturer in geography at the Institute of Alpine Geography (Grenoble) and a member of the Pacte research group. His research addresses the dynamics of tourism and recreation areas analysed from social, cultural, and public policy perspectives. His key study areas are the Alps, Mediterranean areas as well as the North and South Americas.

David W. Marcouiller is professor and chair of urban and regional planning at the University of Wisconsin – Madison (USA). He has published over 170 manuscripts in a variety of outlets that span tourism and forest economics, outdoor recreation planning, community development planning, regional science, amenity theory, counter-urbanisation, and rural economic development.

Jean-Bernard Marsat is a researcher at Irstea and deputy head of the joint research unit Metafort. He holds a PhD in Environment and Management science. He is interested, from organisational and strategic perspectives, in the coordination of local economic activities (agrifood, tourism) with heritage management and territorial governance, particularly in the context of the French Regional Nature Parks.

Amédée Mollard is an environmental economist and has been a researcher since 1965 at Pierre-Mendès-France University in Grenoble (Inra research institute created in 1976). For 15 years he has been studying the joint valorisation of localised products and services based on an ecodevelopment approach, particularly via the concept of 'basket of goods and services'.

Liliane Perrin-Bensahel holds a PhD and authority to supervise doctoral students in economics. She is a research engineer and the deputy director of the Grenoble urban planning school (Pierre-Mendès-France University). Her main teaching and research interests are in territorial economics with a particular focus on territorial resources, tourism, and social capital.

Tina Rambonilaza is a senior researcher in environmental economics at Irstea. By assigning economic value to environmental goods and services, her research emphasises the application of economic valuation methods as a tool that contributes to decision-making processes in conflict scenarios between the protection vs. the economic use of natural resources and the environment.

Stéphanie Truchet is a researcher at Irstea (Metafort research unit) and holds a PhD in economics. Her research interests include spatial economics, tourism economics, social capital and rural development.

Vincent Vlès, a full professor at the University of Toulouse Jean Jaurès, CERTOP-ISTHIA, has done research in the field of tourism resorts for 30 years. His work focuses on the analysis of stakeholder rationales and associated economic issues through the lens of urban and mountain development projects and in relation with changes in the social space. He is the author of 168 publications in tourism planning.

Dominique Vollet is an economist at Irstea, and the director of the Metafort research unit on territorial dynamics in Clermont-Ferrand (France). His main research interests are the relations between product quality and regional development as well the evaluation of territorial public policies.

Acknowledgements

The editors wish to thank Irstea (Institut National de Recherche en Sciences et Technologies pour l'Environnement et l'Agriculture) for its support, including a financial contribution that made the translation, proofreading and ultimately the publication of this book possible.

We also thank SFR (Structure Fédérative de Recherche) 'Territoires en réseaux', Université Grenoble Alpes, for its financial support.

In addition, we extend our thanks to the people at Ashgate who defended this project and helped us finalise it.

Translation and proofreading were done by Accent Mondial and adjusted by the editors.

Introduction

Blending Perspectives on Tourism and Recreation

Jeoffrey Dehez, Jean-Christophe Dissart and Jean-Bernard Marsat

Which Perspectives to Blend?

Tourism and recreation hardly represent new study topics. In fact, they are the subject of a large number of books, scientific and technical journals, as well as conferences. Most of the social science disciplines have dealt with tourism and recreation at some time or another via research or academic teaching. Analysis tools are also becoming increasingly sophisticated while sources of information are constantly expanded. In this context, the emergence of digital technology and of the Internet opens up new perspectives, the scope of which is yet to be fully grasped (new survey and data collection protocols, refinement of models, geo-location of trips, interactions between researchers and users, and so on). This proliferation of initiatives is an undeniable source of learning, and undoubtedly improves our understanding of the phenomena at play. However, we have to ask ourselves whether these innovations risk artificially isolating the subject of our study by cutting it off – more or less durably – from other social phenomena. Statistical observatories, for example, still sometimes make the distinction between 'tourists' (who spend at least one night away from their homes) and 'day trippers' (who pursue their activities on the same day), whereas a same person may choose freely between these two types of travel.[1] Similarly, concerning analyses in terms of 'industry' (the purpose of which is to retrace the entire 'chain' of stakeholders involved in the creation and supply of a product), there may well be a risk of overlooking the connections between the territories and the 'non-tourism' stakeholders who work on their behalf, such as local authorities, natural area managers, farmers and foresters. That is why we have decided to blend perspectives on the broad topic of tourism and recreation in at least three ways.

Firstly, we will try to (re)-associate tourism and recreation within a more global perspective, that of the use of free time. As mentioned above, tourism and recreation sometimes tend to ignore one another. On the one hand, tourism is often associated with an industry, with a specific economic organisation and with market-based flows that are more or less well identified. It follows that the

---

1   Our aim is not to question the relevance of these monitoring bodies, which are all too often insufficiently developed; quite the contrary.

focus tends to be placed on indicators such as employment, induced expenditures or multiplier effects. On the other hand, the leisure sphere tends to be addressed via the allocation of another scarce resource, namely free time, on the grounds that most leisure activities are supposed to escape any form of payment (walking, resting and meeting friends are all free) and that the choices made are more often based on time constraints than on budget constraints. This brings us to look at developments in terms of household 'time budgets' during the course of a day, a week or a year (OECD 2009). Conversely, tourism and recreation are also sometimes considered to be synonymous given that, after all, a visitor is always a visitor, and that all these activities can be perceived in the more general framework of a choice between work and leisure. One no longer distinguishes between scheduled activities, pursued during the holidays over several weeks (or even over a year in the case of sabbatical leave), and daily leisure activities that have to be squeezed into schedules that are already sufficiently busy. While there are doubtless certain common determinants, these behaviours also respond to expectations and specific constraints (Rulleau et al. 2012). Ultimately, since they are neither distinct nor quite the same, these uses of free time are clearly not detached from one another since constantly changing lifestyles and working conditions encourage toing and froing between them. People increasingly prefer short breaks over long holiday periods spent at the same place, and choices in terms of living environments (both during working lives and retirement) are more and more oriented towards places where they will feel as if they are on holiday 'all year round' (Viard 2006).[2] In fact, many stakeholders, starting with local authorities, have already seized upon the importance of extending the tourist season by developing year-round activities that target new residents. However, the nature of these supposedly virtuous links between tourism and residential activity is far from clear today.

This last reference to residential dynamics prompts us to dig deeper and consider other blends between tourism on the one hand, and other social phenomena (which, on the face of it, have little to do with tourism) on the other hand. Indeed, tourism and recreation interweave tightly with all aspects of the accommodation and activity locations. Tourism and recreation interfere directly with population services, local recreational and cultural activities, or shared access to public goods (outdoor areas, landscapes, built heritage, natural environments). These activities all involve confronting the tourist with certain economic (product prices), social (living conditions) or environmental (pollution, quality of the environment) considerations. In fact, this 'permeability of worlds' is not necessarily confined to the actual locations since, when tourists set out, they take with them an entire system of values and standards that they have carefully established over the course of their existence and during their daily lives. We are already aware that tourism and recreational activities are inclined to embrace environmental concerns,

---

2   Just recently, a public opinion survey conducted in France revealed that, faced with the economic crisis, people were more inclined to reduce their 'holiday' budget than their 'recreation' budget, showing that transfers also concern budgets.

resulting in new expressions such as 'green tourism', 'ecotourism' or even 'responsible tourism'. Today, the concept of equity is increasingly prevalent since, here too, social inequalities have every chance of coming to the fore (Coulangeon et al. 2002).

For their part, the local stakeholders concerned by the accommodation of tourists and their leisure are numerous: inhabitants, businesses that may or may not specialise in tourism, sports, educational, environmental and cultural associations, and finally political leaders for the administration and development of their territories. These stakeholders are involved through their own dynamics in this encounter with the tourist. They individually or collectively combine various rationales, including economic gain or even economic survival, and the integration of environmental, cultural or social values. Local authorities have to deal with the effects of an increased number of visitors. For tourism destinations, coordinating all these skills infers a rapidly changing organisation process. The need for organisation encourages new alliances that are not necessarily self-evident. Moreover, faced with the reality of economic competition, or its increasingly dominant representation, professionalisation and technical requirements now oppose territorial anchoring.

Finally, there is also the blending of perspectives and experiences, which covers the concepts as much as it does the applications. It is obvious (and we by no means claim to be the first to say so) that a single discipline is unable to account for the complexity of the phenomena at work here. Economics must take account of environmental and social motivations, sociology of economic incentives; modelling must integrate spatial and geographical factors and the nature of the various organisations; qualitative analyses must be able to place observations and proposals in the context of global trends, and so on. Similarly, changes in practices and in the issues inherent to tourism and recreation require us to constantly revise our concepts and viewpoints. Such an undertaking can only benefit from a multidisciplinary approach. Moreover, it is acknowledged that the territories and destinations concerned are not entirely neutral either, which quite naturally leads us to put the various experiences and sites into perspective. We will attempt to do so through the diversity of the applications that we have selected in this book.

For the purposes of our research, we will consider the case of France, and then conclude by drawing on foreign perspectives to help us situate France within the global landscape. As the world's leading tourism destination, France recognised tourism as a lever for significant economic development from a very early stage.[3] The administration of tourism first came about at the beginning of the twentieth century with the creation of a national office of tourism in 1910. Since then, it has developed steadily through a highly diverse range of tools and systems (ministries, development plans, events and promotion initiatives, engineering support, taxation, labels, etc.). The development of these tools is part of a recent trend in

---

3 According to the UNWTO (*Tourism Highlights*, 2014 edition), in 2012 France had 83.0 million international tourist arrivals and US$53.6 billion (€41.7 billion) in international tourism receipts.

changing public policies with, among others, a gradual transfer of responsibilities from central authorities such as the State and ministries to local authorities. This may be done in concert with the private sector or even with the users themselves (through the payment of access fees or the delegation of public services). This new allocation of roles is far from easy, and the development of new governance models is by no means straightforward. Similarly, the characteristics that are supposed to define the country's attractiveness are also changing. Thus, while in the post-1960s, efforts were focused mainly on the development of national infrastructure (coastal development in the Mediterranean and in the south west of France, creation of the world's second largest ski area), today there is a tendency to showcase the country's natural assets (a predominantly rural space, 5,500 kilometres of coastline, 15 million hectares of forest, etc.), historical assets (towns, villages, castles, etc.) and cultural assets (since 2010, the gastronomic meal of the French has been listed as a World Intangible Cultural Heritage). While the economic impact of tourism is significant and recognised, not only at a national level, but also in specific areas such as coastal or mountainous regions, its effects are more uneven in inland regions. However, moving from a relatively sector-based definition of tourism to a wider vision of free time allocation still poses problems. In fact, despite the recognition of a certain 'art de vivre' in France, policies for reduced working hours, which could otherwise be perceived as an opportunity for improving people's quality of life and for developing new economic activities oriented towards personal services, continue to inspire heated debate (Maresca 2004). This leads some observers to conclude that the social value of free time is still widely underestimated, and that free time continues to be considered as time that is neither liberated (Viard 2006) nor productive (in the economic sense). Thus in France, unlike Northern European countries in particular, the topic of leisure time (as a fundamental element of the quality of life) does not appear on the political agenda (Sievänen et al. 2008).[4] And yet, a number of changes would seem to be under way. Today, many territories in France are largely oriented towards the so-called 'residential economy' (Davezies 2004). With more than four hours per day on average (Ricroch and Roumier 2011), the French currently have about as much free time as their European or North Americans neighbours (OECD 2009, European Commission 2004). While most of this free time continues to be devoted to television and computers, natural areas are among the places of leisure that are most visited[5]. Also, while the time spent walking outdoors only represents a very

---

4   While there are no regulations or national policy clearly dedicated to the development of leisure and free time in France, this theme nevertheless crops up in certain sector policies. This is particularly the case with laws on sport. In addition, the underlying objective of most natural area classifications (national parks, public forests, etc.) is to maintain the widest possible access to the public. This aspect is far from negligible in a country where private ownership is dominant.

5   For example, it is estimated that the overall number of visits to French forests stands around 500 million visits each year. Moreover, the list of sites such as beaches and forests

limited part of daily routines, it remains the second most enjoyable moment of the day (Ricroch 2011). As a result, stakeholders are turning their attention to new segments such as green tourism, nature sports and urban tourism, while bearing in mind that, in the summer, coastal resorts remain by far the most attractive tourism destination (30.9 per cent of person-nights), and that the preferred activity of the French holidaymaker is still essentially 'to do nothing' (DGCIS 2012).

In France, as elsewhere, permanence and change coexist, whether it be for uses, spatial planning and supply of services, relations with the territory or general organisation. It is the ability to consider and analyse these changes that we are interested in through this book.

Lastly, we also wanted to mention that this book came about through an opportunity and a commitment by a group of French researchers from diverse origins (academic disciplines, organisations and study areas), working in the field of human and social sciences, to exchange views on a stimulating research topic. We have also aimed at illustrating this scientific co-construction approach (with all the challenges and difficulties it entails) in this book.

Content of the Book

In addition to this introduction, the book is divided into four parts: 1) location factors of tourism and recreation; 2) users and stakeholders; 3) local and regional impacts of recreational activities; and 4) foreign perspectives on French tourism and recreation issues.

Part I examines the issue of the actual location of tourism and recreational activities: Why do we observe tourism or recreation in specific places? What factors may explain the location or emergence of leisure activities? This part considers several factors (without comparing their relative impacts) that help to understand why recreation actually emerges or thrives.

In Chapter 1, Truchet and Callois explore the links between social capital and tourism development. In rural areas, the dynamics of tourism development can be explained by traditional location-related factors such as available amenities or accessibility, as well as by sociological factors and the organisational capacity of the stakeholders concerned. This chapter presents an analysis of the second point based on social capital theory. The authors present a summary of the literature dealing with this concept from a territorial perspective, and an analytical framework of the economic mechanisms – collective on the one hand, individual on the other – through which a region's social capital can either promote or hinder tourism development. Then, based on data collected on tourism entrepreneurs, they compare two rural areas located in France's Auvergne region. Overall, the chapter illustrates the influence of individual social capital on tourism development and,

---

(more or less noteworthy) that welcome more than one million visits per year continues to increase (Dehez 2012).

in particular, on tourism entrepreneurship via an empirical analysis. In conclusion, Truchet and Callois underscore both the benefits of this research and its limitations, including issues in terms of measuring the effects of social capital.

In Chapter 2, Cazals and Lyser discuss the connection between local heritage and tourism. Heritage appreciation is not based on universal laws but rests upon social, legal and economic processes that are historically situated. Undoubtedly, tourism contributes to the recognition of heritage, hence its protection, but may also undermine it in certain situations. Consequently, relations between tourism and heritage are complex and paradoxical. In this context, the authors propose an analytical framework for heritage enhancement, which examines the complexity of the economic decisions relating to this aim, highlighting various types of possible and actual economic initiatives and their various meanings. Their approach draws on the economics of conventions in order to understand the various synergies possible between heritage and tourism dynamics within a given territory. The second part of the chapter applies this framework to analyse the tensions between possible trajectories for the specific case of the estuary islands located close to the city of Bordeaux, which are the subject of natural heritage policies while representing important sites of cultural heritage.

Chapter 3 focuses on culture as a factor for the emergence of recreation and its creativity. Corneloup, Bourdeau and Mao argue that culture is central to territorial attractiveness because of the meaning and value attributed to trips, visits or recreational activities. The role of cultural variables in the co-construction of perceptions, practices and tourist places allows them to understand not only their emergence, but also their constant renewal. Therefore, culture appears as an ongoing driver of recreational phenomena. Using the concept of cultural forms, the authors seek to understand the procedures, processes and principles at work in the cultural representation of tourist and recreational areas. After defining the forms and stakes of the 'cultural turn' in recreational areas, their chapter discusses the concepts of territory, culture and development. The authors also use empirical illustrations of these processes in different recreational contexts, before providing elements for discussion and recommendations.

In Chapter 4, Vlès addresses how inter-municipal cooperation constitutes a serious institutional issue for the French tourism industry in Europe, before looking at the benefits cooperation brings to tourism production and management. He explains how the resulting streamlining seems to produce new territorial solidarity and better adjustment to sustainable development. Based on shared governance, inter-municipal governance of tourism would help local authorities adapt to new market demands. However, using the contrasting examples of Spain and Italy, Vlès concludes that French authorities tend to engage inter-municipal tourism groupings at a slow pace. This illustrates the difficulties faced in convincing elected representatives that joining an inter-municipal community would enable a broader, more diversified and more concerted form of tourism production that would in turn benefit visitors and locals alike.

Part II looks at organisational issues, focusing on that which lies at the heart of destinations: users (tourists, day trippers) and stakeholders. The objective is to analyse how the supply of tourism services is managed, and how (actual or potential) user perception is taken into account. Several locations are given as examples, from protected areas to winter sport resorts.

In Chapter 5, Marsat presents a dual perspective on tourism destination management and the strategic action taken by parks to promote sustainable tourism. Indeed, the analysis of destination management must address a complex form of governance, with multiple stakeholders and a certain amount of duality between sectoral versus territorial stakeholders, as well as between public versus private entities. Moreover, Regional Nature Parks must fulfil the dual mission of protecting regional heritage and fostering economic and social development. In this context, how is a strategic project designed, initiated or managed while taking care of day-to-day functioning? Focusing on the role of the stakeholders involved in tourism destination management models, this chapter establishes the legitimacies and roles of both sectoral and territorial stakeholders, as well as those of two unifying stakeholders, the Local Tourism Organisation and the Regional Nature Park. Marsat uses a framework based on the strategic theory of organisations, and focuses on the cases of the two Auvergne regional nature parks to analyse park sustainable tourism strategies and their relation with destination management.

In Chapter 6, Clivaz and George-Marcelpoil analyse mountain tourism development in France and Switzerland, discussing political, administrative and local governance issues. In particular, they look at the various ways in which ski resorts are organised within the institutional framework of the two countries, using the ideal-typical distinction between the corporate model and the community model. Briefly stated, the community model is characterised by the presence of multiple tourism service providers, the lack of a predominant stakeholder and large involvement of public authorities; conversely, in the corporate model, the public stakeholder has a limited presence, while a single private operator controls the operation of the ski area and a significant share of the commercial accommodation. The authors then discuss the ability of current organisation methods to meet the challenges faced by leisure accommodation. Finally, this chapter ends with a comparison of the French and Swiss situations in terms of ski resort governance and how the accommodation issue is addressed. This comparison shows areas of both convergence and divergence between the two countries.

In a very different recreation environment, Chapter 7 analyses the ecologisation of nature-based leisure activities in two coastal areas: the Bassin d'Arcachon on the Atlantic coast, and the Calanques de Marseille on the Mediterranean coast. Indeed, in the current context of the 'ecologisation of thought', it is particularly relevant to study the importance of ecology in outdoor recreation activities. Ginelli looks at the relationship between ecologisation, viewed as a cognitive and normative refocusing, and the nature-based leisure activities that preceded this phenomenon. Are environmental concerns integrated in ecologised practices? Are practices really changing? Identifying the norms and values expressed by nature enthusiasts about their practice seems to be a prerequisite for understanding ambiguities in relation to the environment. This is achieved using a sociological approach inspired by the 'pragmatist' tradition of thought, and selecting an array of activities (from sea kayaking to underwater fishing) that are popular yet debated due to environmental standards.

In Chapter 8, Frochot examines construction mechanisms in the tourism experience. The experience sought by tourists during their vacation is a complex blend between a search for quiet and autonomy, and an expectation of services provided by tourism stakeholders that puts a schedule on daily activities. In fact, the recent literature on marketing services indicates that a holiday may be seen as a succession of encounters where the relationship between the consumer and various providers (both public and private) varies, resulting in a co-construction process of the tourism experience. This chapter aims to investigate these relationships within the tourist resort context. Specifically, it analyses how services are managed within an integrated resort where the offering is totally controlled by the provider, but where consumers are free to choose what they expect from their holiday. Frochot goes on to examine French mountain resorts to understand how this integrated model may be transposed to a situation where the resort is set in a public place, with disjointed public and private service providers.

Part III focuses on the regional impacts of recreation and tourism activities. Do these activities result in local development (irrespective of the dimension considered) through enhanced resource protection or, on the contrary, further damage to the resources that were developed for tourism purposes? In other words, what are the regional effects (regardless of geographic scale) of leisure activities?

Funding for the protection of natural areas is addressed in Chapter 9. Dehez, Ben Othmen and Rambonilaza look at the motivations behind tourists' decision to make a financial contribution to the management of natural sites. In France, public funding of natural area protection relies on two main tools: access fees (paid by the direct users of these areas), or taxes (visitors' tax paid by all tourists; a tax for environmentally sensitive areas paid by 'Département' residents (a NUTS 3 level region)). So far, taxation has been favoured, but implementing a pricing system to access natural areas for recreation purposes is increasingly debated. Emphasising demand analysis, this chapter starts out by presenting the economic principles of pricing access to recreation areas. Next, the authors review the literature on non-economic motivations to explain tourists' willingness to contribute. Using data from a survey conducted in the area of the Gironde estuary (south-western France), an empirical application shows the importance of such motivations in the analysis of tourist behaviour. The authors conclude on the specific character of recreation as a socioeconomic service.

In Chapter 10, Cremer-Schulte and Dissart carry out a quantitative analysis of the socioeconomic situation of resort areas and their neighbouring areas. More specifically, the authors explore associations between local development variables, tourism activity and resort designation in coastal municipalities ('communes') and districts ('cantons'), winter sport resorts, and their respective hinterlands.

The literature review provides key references on the definition of resorts and their socioeconomic impacts, and the methodological approach is mainly based on mapping, descriptive statistics and regression analysis of secondary data. The results underline differences in the spatial distribution of tourism beds (geographically concentrated) and other variable values (more spread out), identify tourism 'poles' and 'holes', and provide evidence of the impact of tourism resort legal recognition on local socioeconomic indicators. Overall, by comparing contrasted situations (seaside tourism versus winter sport tourism; mass tourism versus off-resort tourism), this chapter contributes to the analysis of local spillovers of tourism activity.

In Chapter 11, Loubet and Perrin-Bensahel look at the notion of development and propose an original theoretical framework that combines the capability approach and the territorial economy approach. Indeed, changes in French rural areas and recreation activities over the last decades call rural development strategies into question since, by definition, tourism is an activity that draws on local resources, has both environmental and socioeconomic impacts, and is inherently difficult to relocate. The authors use Sen's capability approach as a multidimensional analysis framework to compare the level of development in terms of capabilities across rural territories in the Rhône-Alpes region. They empirically assess the contribution of tourism to rural development by mixing quantitative and qualitative methods. The results indicate that tourism, by drawing people to work together, facilitates the emergence of local development projects. Therefore, in addition to job and income creation inherent to its activity, tourism also acts as a catalyst for rural development initiatives.

Chapter 12 ends Part III by examining the contribution of amenities to rural development. Indeed, when suitably enhanced, amenities supposedly create jobs and increase revenue. However, the ways in which they contribute to these dynamics are poorly understood. Here, Mollard and Vollet seek to show that the contribution of environmental amenities to regional development can only be effective if these amenities are jointly promoted by local quality products and tourism services. Consequently, the chapter is structured around three successive parts: amenities; the promotion of local quality products and amenities through tourism; and rural tourism as an operating service for enhancing the value of amenities. Using a mixed methods approach, the analysis is based on observations from two cases: the massifs of Bauges (Savoie) and Sancy (Auvergne). Mollard and Vollet conclude on the conditions that are required for amenities to effectively lead to territorial development, including governance issues.

Finally, Part IV reflects on the previous chapters with a foreign perspective on French issues and settings. Indeed, a significant contribution of this book consists in blending North American and European, non-French perspectives on tourism and recreation issues. Do the topics addressed in the first 12 chapters differ when assessed from a non-French perspective? Are other topics relevant when one considers the American, the UK and Irish, or the Spanish tourism and recreation context?

Thus, in Chapter 13, Marcouiller provides an overview of natural amenity-based tourism and outdoor recreation in North America. He discusses counter-urban amenity-driven development, focusing on generic elements reflective of this rapid transition in land use, economic development and social justice. More specifically, the chapter focuses on tourism planning elements that are specific to the development role played by tourism in North American rural regions. Using the example of the US Lake States, Marcouiller addresses core issues related to the factors that contribute to amenity-driven development, the way stakeholders approach public policy and private decision making, or where regions experiencing amenity-driven exurban development are headed in terms of their economic, social, political and demographic structure. Connections are made with the European, and specifically, the French context. The chapter concludes with policy implications to assist in the integrative tourism planning process.

Chapter 14 turns back to Europe and covers two countries, the United Kingdom and Ireland. The UK and Ireland provide a range of experiences that includes cultural and economic similarities and contrasts reviewed with reference to the evidence for France. Overall, Cawley and Clark discuss these comparative experiences with a view to attaining a better understanding of the role of national and international tourism as a use of resources, cultural indicator and contributor to development and sustainability in different rural areas. First, the chapter describes the broad features of tourism in the UK and Ireland and the administrative structures within which tourism operates. Then, the authors discuss similarities and differences with the French experience following the structure of the book: the reasons why tourism and leisure activities are observed in some places and less so in others; the role played by users and stakeholders; and the extent to which tourism and recreation represent opportunities for the places concerned. The conclusion outlines that though geography is not deterministic, it certainly influences some of the dominant types of tourism present. Also, it is likely that the costs and benefits of tourism for rural and regional economies will receive increased attention in future discussion.

Finally, in Chapter 15, Cortés Jiménez and Anton Clavé focus on Spain as an example of southern European countries. The Spanish tourism sector has attracted the attention of scholars and policymakers given the unfaltering expansion of tourism since the 1960s. Like France, Spain is one of the world's leading countries for inbound tourism and this has notably determined the geographic location of leisure activities. This chapter analyses the factors that determine the current map of tourism in Spain from an economic and geographical perspective, the basics of the Spanish tourism model of development, and recent changes in the geographic scope of the activity and its economic performance. The authors explain the shift in the Spanish tourism paradigm and describe the recent economic events that influence tourism and leisure such as low-cost carriers, short and frequent holidays throughout the year, and emerging (and competing) destinations. The chapter begins with a comparative overview of the tourism sector in Spain and France and concludes on more general southern European perspectives.

Conclusion

This rounds off the overview of our work programme. As mentioned earlier, we sought to blend as many approaches and tools as possible in order to guarantee – we hope – the breadth of the analysis. We are already beginning to see that, beyond this blending, perspectives need to be also shifted. We have noticed that researchers are increasingly turning their attention away from 'conventional' tourism destinations (such as coastal or ski resorts, amusement parks, historical monuments, etc.) to focus on other places such as protected sites, natural areas or 'peripheral' areas within which the effects of tourism can also be seen, but whose contours remain vague. The palette of stakeholders concerned is inevitably extended: alongside the sector's private enterprises (restaurants, hotels, etc.) and dedicated public bodies (offices of tourism, ministries, etc.) appear managers of natural sites – either with a productive use (forests) or without it (mountains) – or regional natural parks or administrators of territorial authorities. Similarly, today visitors are given an increasingly important part to play in the production of recreational and tourist services (also referred to as 'co-construction'). This is all the more so given that 'visitors' take on multiple forms. They may be tourists, residents, citizens, members of a local association, donors or second homeowners. Lastly, in a similar shift from convention, the objectives of tourism development are being questioned: there is less focus on the creation of economic wealth (measured by indicators such as GDP) or organisational efficiency, and more on issues such as 'social justice', income redistribution or the ecologisation of activities (which hints at the ambiguity of the relation with the environment). Proof, if it were still needed, that the social time devoted to tourism and recreation is not merely 'residual' time, but time that is socially structuring. This new form of social wealth has yet to reveal the full diversity of its facets.

References

Coulangeon, P., Menger, P.-M. and Roharik, I. 2002. Les loisirs des actifs: un reflet de la stratification sociale. *Economie et Statistique*, (352–53): 39–55.

Davezies, L. 2004. Développement local: le déménagement des Français. La dissociation des lieux de production et de consommation. *Futuribles*, (295): 43–56.

Dehez, J. (ed.). 2012. *L'Ouverture des Forêts au Public. Un Service Récréatif*. Collection Sciences et Techniques Update. Paris: Quae.

DGCIS. 2012. *Memento du Tourisme*. Paris: Direction Générale de la Compétitivité, de l'Industrie et des Services.

European Commission. 2004. *How Europeans Spend their Time – Everyday Life of Women and Men, Data 1998–2002*. Luxembourg: Pocketbooks.

Maresca, B. 2004. *Occupation du Temps Libre: une Norme de Consommation Inégalement Partagée*. Cahier de Recherche, 210. Paris: Credoc.

OECD. 2009. Leisure time, in *OECD Factbook 2009: Economic, Environmental and Social Statistics*. Paris: OECD Publishing, 260–61.

Ricroch, L. 2011. Les moments agréables de la vie quotidienne. Une question d'activités mais aussi de contexte. *INSEE Première*, (1378).

Ricroch, L. and Roumier, B. 2011. Depuis 11 ans, moins de tâches ménagères, plus d'Internet. *INSEE Première*, (1377).

Rulleau, B., Dehez, J. and Point, P. 2012. Recreational value, user heterogeneity and site characteristics in contingent valuation. *Tourism Management*, 33(1): 195–204.

Sievänen, T., Arnberger, A., Dehez, J., Grant, N., Jensen, F.S. and Skov-Petersen, H. (eds.). 2008. *Forest Recreation Monitoring – a European Perspective*. Working Papers of the Finnish Forest Research Institute, 79. Helsinki: METLA.

Viard, J. 2006. *Eloge de la Mobilité. Essai sur le Capital Temps Libre et la Valeur Travail*. La Tour d'Aigues: Editions de l'Aube.

PART I
Tourism and Recreation:
Here and Not Somewhere Else

Chapter 1

Social Capital and Tourism Development in Rural Areas

Stéphanie Truchet and Jean-Marc Callois

Introduction

Traditionally associated with the coastline and mountainous areas, tourism in France now accounts for a considerable share of the economy in some rural areas. Over the past forty years, the number of visitors to these areas has gradually risen, driven in particular by the recent enthusiasm for natural areas and landscapes (Béteille 1996). The countryside now accounts for 30 per cent of person-nights in France's tourism industry, second only to coastal destinations. This development has gone hand in hand with an increase in market accommodation capacity. Between 2001 and 2009, the number of beds available in listed campsites and hotels increased by 0.22 in rural areas, while, over the same period, it dropped by 0.62 per cent in urban areas. Moreover, in addition to traditional lodgings, new forms of accommodation specific to rural destinations have emerged. Between 1976 and 2004,[1] the number of 'gîtes' (country lodges) and 'chambres d'hôtes' (bed and breakfast establishments) increased from 16,000 to 42,000, and from 1,000 to 31,000 respectively. While these figures describe a situation that would generally appear to be favourable to rural tourism, a more extensive analysis means greater caution is in fact required. Indeed, while some rural areas are able to leverage the economic benefits generated by tourism, others do not fare so well. We can thus observe rural areas whose economy benefits greatly from attractive tourist sites, but also a majority of areas where the tourism economy is much less certain and does not create any ripple effect on local economic growth (Dissart et al. 2009). This spatial differentiation in tourism development within rural areas can be explained by differences in terms of resources – natural (e.g. climate), heritage (e.g. châteaux) or recreational (e.g. theme parks), and in terms of geographic position and accessibility. However, it is also due to differences in terms of organisation and collective dynamics.

This chapter will look at the influence of the 'organisation' within a region on its tourism development from the perspective of social capital theories. The first part presents an analytical framework. It starts with a summary of the reference work conducted on social capital, and of the work dealing with this concept

---

1 Source: INSEE, French Ministry of Tourism.

while introducing a territorial aspect. It then goes on to propose transposing this analytical framework to tourism. This framework is based on the economic mechanisms – collective on the one hand, and individual on the other – through which a region's social capital can either promote or hinder tourism development. The rest of the chapter illustrates the influence of individual social capital on tourism development and, in particular, on tourism entrepreneurship via an empirical analysis. The data and methods are presented in the second part of the chapter. The third section presents and discusses the empirical results. Lastly, the conclusion underscores both the benefits of this research and its limitations, before rounding off by opening up new avenues for research.

Social Capital as a Factor for the Development of Tourism

Social Capital and its Various Forms

'Social capital' is a term taken from sociology (Bourdieu 1986) that is now the subject of a wealth of economic literature, and that serves to address non-market phenomena and their origins (Stiglitz 2000). Many studies attempt to understand the role played by sociological characteristics in terms of individual performance or economic development, with social capital providing a relevant angle from which to explain this role. For all that, its very definition raises questions. In this chapter, we use the definition suggested by Nan Lin (1999: 35), according to which 'social capital can be defined as resources embedded in a social structure which are accessed and/or mobilised in purposive actions'. This definition emphasises the fact that social capital does not merely boil down to social relations or networks; it represents all of the resources to which these relations or networks effectively give access.

The Distinction Between Two Forms of Individual Social Capital   Traditionally, we can distinguish two forms of social capital in terms of their respective mechanisms of action. Firstly, social capital can promote economic development or individual success by facilitating the circulation and distribution of information. This effect is based on the existence of *weak links* (mere acquaintance). Research by Granovetter (1973) and Burt (1980) showed that a person with an open social network, i.e. one marked by weak links that connect to people in other social groups, will find employment more easily than others. Weak links allow a person to access information that is more diverse and less redundant than that obtained within one's own social group. The second mechanism of action in relation to social capital rests on values conducive to cooperation such as trust and loyalty. Specific to *strong links* (links of friendship, close links) and dense social networks, these characteristics build economic resources. They help to stabilise market-based relationships or to reduce the risk of opportunist behaviour. They thus promote collective action (Fafchamps 2006) through which collective assets are safeguarded or supplied (e.g. environmental protection) (Adger 2003).

A Regional Form of Social Capital By analogy with this dichotomy between strong and weak links, Putnam (2000) characterises a region's social capital via the following two components: *bonding* and *bridging*. Bonding comes about from strong links between people with similar socio-demographic characteristics (e.g. family, friends). It serves to grasp a region's cohesion and the influence of the community. Bridging corresponds to the social capital generated by weak links between people from different cultural or socio-professional backgrounds. In the case of rural territories, which are sparsely populated and often characterised by a low level of sociological diversity, the weak links that bring with them resources useful to the territory may be relatively limited. Here, links outside the territory are the main source of diversity; bridging thus corresponds more to the extent to which the territory is open to the outside (Callois and Aubert 2007).

The Negative Effects of Bonding and the Radius of Trust Concept There is a wealth of material that underscores the economic virtues of social capital. However, some analyses show that bonding also has some negative effects. In fact, a high level of cohesion in a group is largely dependent on the homogeneity of its members. And yet, this homogeneity may sometimes turn into a need to conform, effectively inhibiting any form of individual initiative and limiting the group's innovative capacity. In addition, while social cohesion within a community may offer certain benefits for its members, it can also bring about certain forms of exclusion and make matters worse for those who are excluded from it. Lastly, bonding alone is not always sufficient to bring about collective action. To better understand this mechanism, Callois (2007) suggests a reinterpretation of the *radius of trust* concept introduced by Fukuyama (2001). He defines an individual's radius of trust as the extent of their relationships of trust within their reference space (sociological or geographical). From a territorial viewpoint, the implementation of collective action is thus constrained by individual variations in the radius of trust within the geographic space. Consequently, even if a territory benefits from considerable bonding, a highly heterogeneous radius of trust will only produce very small cohesive groups that will ultimately be insufficient to implement collective action.

The Influence of Social Capital on Tourism Development

These mechanisms of action in relation to social capital are likely to be particularly present in the case of tourism given the specificities inherent to this sector. We can distinguish between the potential effects of social capital on tourism development according to whether they involve collective or individual phenomena.

Social Capital, Collective Action and Tourism One particularity of a region's tourism development is that it is largely dependent on the existence of collective assets. These may be tangible or intangible. Note that tourists choose their destination based on a set of characteristics in comparison with those of other possible destinations (Papatheodorou 2001). Their choice depends not only on the destination's price index, but also on such factors as accommodation, recreational activities and natural or heritage-related amenities. The latter are often collective assets. Their supply may result from positive externalities or collective action (e.g. landscape). Tourism development also depends on the existence of intangible collective assets (such as reputation or advertising). When tourists choose their destination, they are confronted with the problem of imperfect information. Clearly, tourists will seldom be perfectly knowledgeable about all possible destinations and all the characteristics of these destinations. A given destination's notoriety thus represents an important factor as it ultimately determines whether or not tourists actually come. Such being the case, a destination's notoriety is partly contingent on entrepreneurs' investments and the quality of their services (Claude and Zaccour 2009). Lastly, the information available to tourists can be improved by another collective asset: advertising. As with all collective assets, a given region's tourism entrepreneurs will benefit from the quality of its amenities, its reputation and the advertising of the destination, but none of them will necessarily want to invest in their actual production. Consequently, the public sector and, more specifically, territorial authorities, play a key role in creating or perpetuating these collective assets. However, they rarely fulfil this function alone, and often rely on cooperation between the public and private sectors. As we saw earlier, social capital's bonding component and the radius of trust within a region can promote collective action. In the field of tourism, a number of case studies have been conducted on professional networks. Even if they do not directly involve this concept, these studies provide food for thought regarding the effects of social capital's bonding component. Bhat and Milne (2008) demonstrated that the characteristics of an inter-organisational network had an impact on each member's level of investment in collective dynamics and, as a result, on the creation of a website to promote the destination. Similarly, Scott et al. (2008) showed that the structure of a destination's professional network plays an important role in the effectiveness of both the communication policy and collective decision-making.

Social Capital and Tourism Entrepreneurship Besides its collective effects, social capital can have an impact on the development of tourism via its influence on entrepreneurship (Zhao et al. 2011). This influence may rest on two different mechanisms: access to information and entrepreneurs' economic behaviour.

In tourism, as in many other fields, the emergence and subsequent development of a given economic activity hinge partly on access to information. In order for the tourist service proposed to match demand as closely as possible, an entrepreneur needs access to information concerning prices, tourists' expectations, the market's structure, etc. Furthermore, entrepreneurship requires resources, whether financial or non-financial (e.g. labour, equipment, property). Research by Burt (1980) and Granovetter (1973) leads us to believe that access to this information relies on the presence of weak links and the bridging type of social capital. However, from a geographic viewpoint, we can imagine that the form of bridging involved in passing on information depends on the more or less localised character of the resources sought by the entrepreneur. Thus, if an entrepreneur searches for information on local resources (e.g. labour, regional subsidies), he or she must mobilise the bridging form of social capital, but within the corresponding region. Conversely, if the information concerns resources that are not local (such as information on quality labels), an entrepreneur's extra-territorial bridging may well compensate for the region's weak internal bridging, a trait typical of rural areas.

Social capital may also promote tourism entrepreneurship by influencing entrepreneurs' economic and strategic behaviour. Firstly, entrepreneurs who produce the same type of tourist service within a region are likely to be in competition with one another. The existence of strong links between these entrepreneurs and a bonding type of social capital may encourage them to adopt a more cooperative, altruistic form of behaviour (Von Friedrichs Grängsjo and Gummesson 2006). This may result in agreements concerning prices or the quality of services, sometimes to the detriment of the tourists themselves. Secondly, the bonding type of social capital may have negative effects on entrepreneurship. This situation typically involves cases in which an entrepreneur who does not belong to the community decides to create his or her business within that region regardless. The dense network formed by the region's entrepreneurs may result in higher 'entry costs' for the newcomer, whether tangible (e.g. property) or intangible (e.g. hostility, social cost), and may ultimately dissuade them from creating their business (Kneafsey 2001).

Data and Methods

In this section, we will illustrate the influence of social capital on a region's tourism entrepreneurship via a case study.

Areas of Study and Data Collection

This study was conducted with owners of tourist accommodation facilities within two territories in the Auvergne region in central France (Figure 1.1). These areas are known as the 'Pays[2] de Lafayette' and the 'Pays des Combrailles'. These two territories, marked by rural tourism, were chosen for their similar characteristics (e.g. amenities, accessibility, institutional framework) and in order to control for the geographic effect. Situated in the northwest of France's Puy de Dôme

---

2 'Pays': French administrative category corresponding to a territory that is intermediate in size between the 'département' and the 'canton'.

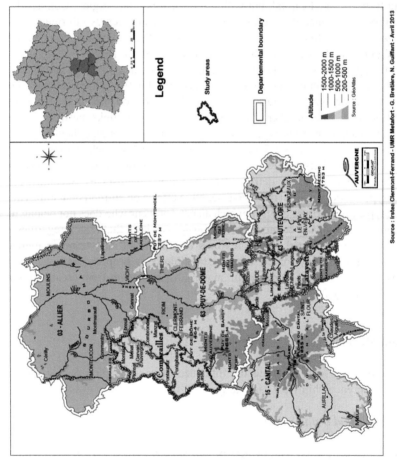

Figure 1.1 Location of the two case study areas. Reproduced by permission of the creators G. Bretière and N. Guiffant, both at IRSTEA

'département', the 'Pays des Combrailles' includes three tourism sub-units associated with different landscapes: the 'vallée de la Sioule' (Sioule valley), which crosses the area from north to south, the 'chaîne des Puys' (Puys mountain range) to the east, and the 'secteur des étangs' (ponds area) in the southwest. The river system represents an important source of amenities, and is particularly used for various water sports. The area also benefits from a certain cultural heritage (e.g. Manoir de Veygoux, Château de Chazeron) and from its proximity to a major tourist site, the Vulcania theme park. Located to the west of the Haute-Loire 'département', the 'Pays de Lafayette' area is notably defined by the river Allier. According to experts, this river is the area's primary asset, around which sporting and leisure activities (such as fishing and white water sports) are organised. However, the area also boasts a considerable cultural and architectural heritage, and enjoys a certain notoriety (e.g. the 'Chaise Dieu' site, the villages of Blesle and Lavaudieu). While the area's tourism employment cannot really be compared with that of the ski resorts in Auvergne, these sources of amenities nevertheless represent a not insignificant share of jobs, accounting for 4.8 per cent of overall employment in the Combrailles, and 5.5 per cent in the Pays de Lafayette, which is above the regional average (4.4 per cent).[3]

The data are taken from a survey conducted via questionnaire in 2007 of a sample of tourist accommodation owners in each of the two territories. The purpose of these surveys was not so much to gain a representative image of a given territory, as to be able to compare the situation of entrepreneurs within the two territories and among France's four tourist accommodation categories: 'chambres d'hôtes' (bed and breakfast), 'hôtels', 'gîtes ruraux' (country lodges) and 'meublés de tourisme' (furnished tourist accommodation). The two samples were thus assembled based on tourist accommodation files provided in one instance by the Departmental Tourism Committee ('Comité Départemental du Tourisme' – CDT) of the Haute-Loire, and in the other instance by the Combrailles Joint association for regional planning and development ('Syndicat Mixte pour l'Aménagement et le Développement des Combrailles' – SMADC), through stratified random sampling for each type of accommodation, rather than through quota sampling. The final sample comprises 73 tourist accommodation owners: 37 in the Pays des Combrailles area, and 36 in the Pays de Lafayette area. Among them are 10 owners of 'chambres d'hôtes', 'gîtes ruraux' and 'meublés de tourisme' in each area studied. Given a higher rate of non-response by hotel owners, hotels are represented less in both areas, albeit at an equivalent level (7 in the Combrailles, and 6 in the Pays de Lafayette). Conducted over the phone, the questionnaire comprised 77 questions concerning the characteristics of the entrepreneur and his or her accommodation structure on the one hand and the social capital of the entrepreneur on the other hand.

---

3   Source: INSEE, DADS (2007).

Social Capital Metrics

The issue of a tourist accommodation owner's social relations is a vast topic. We decided to focus our analysis on the owner's relations with other tourist entrepreneurs, distinguishing relations established within the territory from those established outside it. Moreover, we segregated relations with tourist accommodation owners from those with other types of tourist entrepreneurs (e.g. restaurant owners, leisure facility owners). In the empirical literature, two aspects of social capital are typically distinguished: the structural aspect corresponding to the characteristics of the social relations and the social network, and the cognitive aspect relating to standards and individual representations (Uphoff 2000). Via closed-ended questions, we broached the social capital issue from these two perspectives. From the structural perspective, we took account of the network's size as well as the frequency of family ties, friendship ties or mere acquaintances within this network. From the cognitive perspective, we sought to observe an entrepreneur's radius of trust via his or her relations with other entrepreneurs, depending on their geographic location. To simplify the answers to the questions, each of these social capital variables was evaluated based on a four-point Likert scale. We ultimately established 11 social capital variables (Table 1.1):

- Three variables concern the number of links with tourist accommodation owners inside the territory, outside the territory, and with other tourist entrepreneurs within the territory. These variables range from 0 to 3 depending on whether the entrepreneur does not know anyone among these categories (0), knows less than 5 people (1), knows between 5 and 10 people (2), or knows more than 10 people (3).
- Four variables concern the frequency of friendship ties or mere acquaintances among the relations with accommodation owners and with other tourist entrepreneurs. None of the owners polled had any family ties with these social relations in the territory. This frequency was evaluated according to a scale of 0 to 3, where 0 corresponds to never, 1 corresponds to rarely, 2 corresponds to sometimes, and 3 corresponds to often.
- To account for the influence of more formal professional networks, we integrated one variable linked to the number of quality labels with which the entrepreneur is affiliated.
- Lastly, three variables measure the entrepreneurs' radius of trust and evaluate the geographic scope of his or her relations within the territory. This point concerns the location of other accommodation owners/tourist entrepreneurs with whom the entrepreneurs have close relations – whether friendship or family-based, or the location of tourist accommodation owners to whom the entrepreneur refers or transfers customers. The values of the radiuses of trust were defined based on exploratory surveys. The variable corresponds to 1 if the location is within a radius of 10 km, 2 if it

is within a radius of 25 km, 3 if it is within a radius of 50 km, and 4 if it is within a radius of more than 50 km.

Table 1.1   Descriptive statistics

Variables	Abbreviation	Obs	Mean	Sd	Min.	Max.
Number of links:						
- with tourist accommodation owners inside the territory	Nb. links accom.	67	1.84	0.88	0	3
- with other tourist entrepreneurs within the territory	Nb. links entr.	67	1.51	1.05	0	3
- with tourist accommodation owners outside the territory	Nb. links out.	67	1.01	1.08	0	3
Frequency of:						
- friendship with local tourist accommodation owners	Friends accom.	67	3.10	1.33	0	4
- friendship with other local tourist entrepreneurs	Friends entr.	67	1.90	1.54	0	4
- mere acquaintance with local tourist accommodation owners	Acqu. accom.	67	2.69	1.48	0	4
- mere acquaintance with other local tourist entrepreneurs	Acqu. entr.	67	2.78	1.69	0	4
Formal professional networks: number of quality labels	Nb. labels	67	0.94	0.67	0	2
Radius of trust:						
- geo. scope of relations with local owners of accommodation	RT geo accom.	67	1.46	0.99	0	3

continued

Table 1.1   *concluded*

Variables	Abbreviation	Obs	Mean	Sd	Min.	Max.
- geo. scope of relations with other local tourist entrepreneurs	RT geo entr.	67	1.21	1.07	0	3
- transfer of customers	RT transfer	67	1.16	0.88	0	3
Age of entrepreneur	Age	67	52.87	9.84	32	70
Capacity (number of beds)	Capacity	67	10.46	8.61	2	45
Turnover per bed	Turnover	65	1,356.25	863.68	63	3,333.33
Quality level (number of stars)	Quality	67	2.34	0.93	0	4
Occupancy rate	Occupancy	65	32.08	16.22	5.26	79.37
Age of accommodation	Structure age	67	8.68	7.65	0	35
Subsidies	Subsidies	62	18,313.71	27,082.46	0	115,000
Price per bed and per night	Price	67	15.56	5.68	6.14	29.25

Other Variables

In addition to the social capital variables, other variables were calculated on the one hand to describe the entrepreneurs (age) and their accommodation structures (age of the structure, capacity in terms of number of beds, level of quality), and on the other hand to evaluate the results of their activity (occupancy rate, turnover per bed, price per bed and per person-night) and their access to financial support (subsidies).

Results and Discussion

Based on these data, we characterised the entrepreneurs according to their social capital, then analysed the social capital's influence on access to certain financial resources (subsidies).

Analysis of the Types of Entrepreneurs

To characterise the entrepreneurs, we created a typology using ascending hierarchical classification based on the social capital variables. After eliminating outliers, the classification concerned 67 individuals out of 73. The most relevant breakdown shows two main entrepreneur profiles (Table 1.2). By comparing the mean values of the social capital variables and of certain illustrative variables, we can identify areas of convergence or divergence between these two profiles. Both types of entrepreneur have approximately the same number and type of relations with other tourist accommodation owners within the territory.

However, the minority category (cluster 2) has a less diversified network since its entrepreneurs are less oriented towards other tourist entrepreneurs, both inside and outside the territory. In addition, these entrepreneurs tend to have a smaller radius of trust. An analysis of the illustrative variables shows that, for structures

Table 1.2   Descriptive statistics by cluster and comparison of mean values

Variables	Cluster 1 (N=53)	Cluster 2 (N=14)	Comparison of means (t-test)
Social capital variables			
Nb. links accom.	1.89	1.64	No difference
Nb. links entr.	1.91	0.00	Difference
Nb. links out.	1.11	0.64	Difference
Friends accom.	3.09	3.14	No difference
Friends entr.	2.40	0.00	Difference
Acqu. accom.	2.74	2.50	No difference
Acqu. entr.	3.51	0.00	Difference
Nb. labels	0.92	1.00	No difference
RT geo accom.	1.53	1.21	No difference
RT transfer	1.23	0.93	No difference
RT geo entr.	1.53	0.00	Difference
Illustrative variables			
Age	53.09	52.00	No difference
Capacity	10.83	9.07	No difference
Turnover	1,400.86	1,193.73	No difference
Quality	2.34	2.36	No difference
Occupancy	31.33	34.80	No difference
Structure age	9.42	5.89	Different
Subsidies	20,045.92	11,784.62	No difference
Price	16.31	12.74	Different

Note: Test comparing mean values with a significance threshold of 10 per cent.

that are equivalent in terms of quality, these entrepreneurs apply higher prices. This initial analysis thus suggests that a diverse local professional network and a geographically open approach are likely to help entrepreneurs enhance the value of their business activity.

Estimation Results

Our next step was to test the influence of the entrepreneurs' social capital on their access to financial resources (amount of subsidies received). The analysis framework suggests that it is mainly the bridging form of social capital which, by promoting the circulation and transmission of information, facilitates access to new resources. We carried out four series of simple regression analyses, integrating variables on the different forms of social capital (Table 1.3). Insofar as the bonding form of social capital is concerned, we evaluated the influence of strong links within the territory by incorporating two indicators relating firstly to ties with tourist accommodation owners, and secondly to ties with other tourist entrepreneurs. These indicators were obtained by cross-tabulating the variables concerning the size of the network and the frequency of friendship relations. Similarly, we obtained two territorial bridging indicators by cross-tabulating the variables concerning the size of the network and the frequency of mere acquaintances. In every case, the cross-tabulated variables were not correlated with one another. Extraterritorial bridging was dealt with by integrating two variables: the variable concerning the number of quality labels with which the entrepreneur is affiliated, and that concerning the number of links with tourist accommodation owners outside the territory. Given problems of multicollinearity, only two of the three variables associated with the radius of trust were integrated in the fourth series of estimates. The variable relating to the referral or transfer of customers was excluded. Lastly, to control for the territorial effect, we added dummy variables relative to the study areas.

The estimates show that the amount of subsidies received by a tourist accommodation owner is positively and significantly associated with the bridging type of social capital within the territory, whereas no relationship with the bonding variables is established. Furthermore, in model 3, we can see that the amount of subsidies received is positively associated with links to tourist accommodation owners, even when located outside the territory. Lastly, the fourth series of estimates shows that the amount of subsidies received increases with the geographic radius in which the entrepreneur has trustful relations with other tourist accommodation owners. These results would thus seem to corroborate the hypotheses formulated regarding the role of the bridging form of social capital in access to new resources, in particular financial, and regarding the importance for an entrepreneur of maintaining diverse professional relations within a given territory. Similarly, they seem to indicate that insufficient territorial bridging can be compensated for, at least in part, by extraterritorial bridging.

Table 1.3   Estimation results: amount of subsidies received

Variables	Model 1	Model 2	Model 3	Model 4
Intercept	-1,469.27	-9,144.87	-1,836.27	-1,407.32
Control variables				
Age	-381.49	-330.18	-78.77	-388.86
Capacity	***1,399.34	***1,292.22	1,084.54	***1,381.54
Structure age	-260.62	-413.42	-677.15	-162.22
Quality	***8,762.79	****9,504.13	**6,720.96	***8,996.18
Area: Combrailles	-6,214.77	-5,663.73	-7,722.08	-3,630.90
Area: Lafayette	—	—	—	—
Bonding variables				
Nb. links accom. x Friends accom.	989.27			
Nb. links entr. x Friends entr.	1,096.67			
Internal bridging variables				
Nb. links accom. x Acqu. accom.		*1,589.46		
Nb. links entr. x Acqu. entr.		*1,489.16		
External bridging variables				
Nb. labels			-3,889.87	
Nb. links out.			**9,847.90	
Radius of trust variables				
RT geo accom.				*5,764.11
RT geo entr.				-429.01
N	62	62	62	62
R²	0.320	0.383	0.370	0.312
R² adjusted	0.232	0.303	0.289	0.223

Note: *** 1 per cent significance; ** 5 per cent significance; * 10 per cent significance.

Discussion

This analysis nevertheless presents two methodological limitations. The first limitation concerns the actual measurement of social capital. Indeed, to facilitate the answers to the questionnaire and the collection of data, the social capital variables were established based on declarations made by entrepreneurs and evaluated using a Likert scale. These variables were then processed as scores and as discrete quantitative variables. However, the level of these variables is particularly sensitive to the way in which we define the classes proposed to the respondents. One way of improving the variables concerning the structural aspect of the social capital would be to identify the entrepreneurs' relations via network analysis methods, such as the name generator (Burt 1997), and to deduce exact measurements concerning the size of the entrepreneur's network and the importance of the different types of relations. This method requires a large amount of data per individual, however. The second limitation concerns the difficulty in establishing a causal relationship between the phenomenon studied and social capital. Given its very definition, social capital cannot be directly measured; it can only ever be dealt with in an imperfect way. Endogeneity problems may thus occur as a result of the existence of unobserved variables, thereby leading to bias in the estimates (Durlauf 2002). In our case, the effect of the entrepreneur's social relations that we ascribe to social capital may actually hide the effect of another aspect: that of the entrepreneur's sociable and open nature, which affects both his social relations and his ability to defend his project and thus obtain subsidies. This kind of bias can be corrected using the instrumental variable method, provided that relevant instrumental variables are used to take into account the effect of the entrepreneurs' personalities.

Conclusion and Perspectives

A great deal of research has been carried out on the influence of social capital on the economic performance of entrepreneurs, on the search for employment by individuals, or on collective action. However, analyses that apply these questions to the tourism sector are still relatively few and far between. Moreover, the spatial and territorial aspect of social capital is rarely addressed. And yet, throughout this chapter, we have seen that differences in social capital within territories can contribute to their differentiation in terms of economic development, by influencing collective or individual phenomena. This brief overview also reveals some interesting avenues for research.

Firstly, in this chapter we gave an empirical, individual analysis of social capital. In fact, an analysis of social capital's influence on collective dynamics is an important issue given that the development of tourism within a territory is largely dependent on collective assets (e.g. amenities, reputation, marketing) and on the organisation of tourism supply. Here, two types of empirical analysis may be conducted. The first consists in considering, much like Scott et al. (2008), the entrepreneurs and various tourism organisations within a territory as forming a network, and then analysing this network's characteristics. This type of analysis produces a considerable amount of food for thought in terms of the mechanisms involved. But, as we saw earlier, a large amount of data is required in order to analyse a network properly. An econometric approach would mean producing this type of analysis in many territories, however, this would be difficult to achieve. The alternative would be to establish proxies for the social capital specific to a territory's tourism organisations and businesses, and to link them up to variables concerning the presence or amount of collective action, or the overall dynamics of tourism development.

Secondly, we saw that a territory's social capital can concurrently promote and hinder tourism entrepreneurship. In this respect, our empirical analysis allowed us to illustrate the influence of social capital on an entrepreneur's access to resources, in particular financial. However, based on interviews with some tourist accommodation owners, conducted in parallel to our surveys, we believe that the negative effect of social capital (e.g. exclusion of new entrepreneurs who come from elsewhere) can be particularly pronounced in some territories. This effect, just like the positive effect of social capital, is felt especially when the activity is in its starting phase. Consequently, it would be worthwhile analysing the influence of social capital on the actual process of creating the business, for example by comparing the social capital of entrepreneurs who have failed in their activity with those who have succeeded, like Davidsson and Honig (2003). Gaining a better understanding of the influence of social capital, both individually and collectively, is of both scientific and political importance. Firstly, this knowledge can help to better understand the conditions – and in particular the sociological context – in which policies intended to foster tourism development can effectively achieve their objectives. Secondly, it can determine exactly which forms of social capital policies need to be focused on in order to promote tourism development.

References

Adger, N. 2003. Social capital, collective action, and adaptation to climate change. *Economic Geography*, 79(4), 387–404.

Béteille, R. 1996. *Le Tourisme Vert*. Collection Que Sais-Je? Paris: Presses Universitaires de France.

Bhat, S.S. and Milne, S. 2008. Network effects on cooperation in destination website development. *Tourism Management*, 29(6), 1131–40.

Bourdieu, P. 1986. The forms of capital, in *Handbook of Theory and Research for the Sociology of Education*, edited by J. Richardson. New-York: Greenwood Press, 241–58.

Burt, R. 1997. A note on social capital and network content. *Social Networks*, 19(4), 355–73.

—. 1980. Models of network structure. *Annual Review of Sociology*, (6), 79–141.

Callois, J.-M. 2007. Les limites du territoire: une application de la notion de rayon de confiance au développement territorial. *Revue d'Economie Régionale et Urbaine*, (5), 811–30.

Callois, J.-M. and Aubert, F. 2007. Towards indicators of social capital for regional development issues: the case of French rural areas. *Regional Studies*, 41(6), 809–21.

Claude, D. and Zaccour, G. 2009. Investment in tourism market and reputation. *Journal of Public Economic Theory*, 11(5), 797–817.

Dasgupta, P. and Serageldin, I. (eds.) 2000. *Social Capital: a Multifaceted Perspective*. Washington, DC: The World Bank.

Davidsson, P. and Honig, B. 2003. The role of social and human capital among nascent entrepreneurs. *Journal of Business Venturing*, 18(3), 301–31.

Dissart, J.-C., Aubert, F. and Truchet, S. 2009. An estimation of tourism dependence in French rural areas, in *Advances in Tourism Economics: New developments*, edited by Á. Matias et al. Heidelberg: Physica-Verlag/Springer, 273–94.

Durlauf, S.N. 2002. On the empirics of social capital. *The Economic Journal*, 112(483), 459–79.

Fafchamps, M. 2006. Development and social capital. *The Journal of Development Studies*, 42(7), 1180–98.

Fukuyama, F. 2001. Social capital, civil society and development. *Third World Quarterly*, 22(1), 7–20.

Granovetter, M. 1973. The strength of weak ties. *The American Journal of Sociology*, 78(6), 1360–80.

Kneafsey, M. 2001. Rural cultural economy: tourism and social relations. *Annals of Tourism Research*, 28(3), 762–83.

Lin, N. 1999. Building a network theory of social capital. *Connections*, 22(1), 28–51.

Papatheodorou, A. 2001. Why people travel to different places. *Annals of Tourism Research*, 28(1), 164–79.

Putnam, R.D. 2000. *Bowling Alone: the Collapse and Revival of American Community*. New York: Simon & Schuster.

Scott, N., Cooper, C. and Baggio, R. 2008. Destination networks: four Australian cases. *Annals of Tourism Research*, 35(1), 169–88.

Uphoff, N. 2000. Understanding social capital: learning from the analysis and experience of participation, in *Social Capital: a Multifaceted Perspective*, edited by P. Dasgupta and I. Serageldin. Washington, DC: The World Bank, 215–49.

Von Friedrichs Grängsjö, Y. and Gummesson, E. 2006. Hotel networks and social capital in destination marketing. *International Journal of Service Industry Management*, 17(1), 58–75.

Zhao, W., Ritchie, J.R.B. and Echtner, C.M. 2011. Social capital and tourism entrepreneurship. *Annals of Tourism Research*, 38(4), 1570–93.

Chapter 2

What Middle Way Is Possible Between a Tourist Site and Natural Heritage? The Case of the Gironde Estuary's Islands

Clarisse Cazals and Sandrine Lyser

Introduction

An estuary may be defined as the mouth of a river leading to the open sea where the movement of the tides can be felt. Under this definition it is not easy to clearly delineate the geographical borders of these areas 'between land and sea'. That said, they are currently largely recognised for the diversity of the issues that they raise and the complexity of their management. They are in fact marked by major, historical economic issues linked to the development of port activities and more recent environmental issues relating to the preservation of the ecosystems that they represent. However, aside from these general characteristics, each estuary is set apart by the combination of its particular ecological, geographic, historic and social features.

This means that these particular areas, described as 'rural' if they have remained on the margins of metropolisation phenomena or other forms of population agglomerations, in principle have no unity or coherence. However, they benefit from an extensive heritage which is of growing interest to private- and public-sector stakeholders given that this heritage raises issues concerning protection, preservation, and rural and tourism development. However, combining diverse economic activities in areas of great ecological importance like estuaries is not possible without conflicts over environmental and heritage uses. Against this backdrop, marked both by competing territories and collective awareness of environmental issues, some stakeholders are coming together to institutionalise the enhancement of natural (landscapes, remarkable ecosystems) and/or cultural heritage, architectural heritage or even know-how specific to their territory. Given the weight of the tourism sector in the French economy, both nationally and regionally, tourism should be viewed as the appropriate intermediate operator between the 'territory and the market' (François et al. 2006). Although coastal and mountain tourism remain the pillars of the French tourism sector, thanks to the national development plans dedicated to them in the 1970–80s, the 1990s were marked by the emergence of rural tourism that developed based on diverse regional policies. This form of tourism, which currently accounts for 28.5 per cent of overnight stays, has prompted new practices linked to productive, natural or cultural local specificities. This trend lies at the intersection of two changes. Firstly, the development of eco-tourism followed by sustainable tourism, which is reflected in various formal expressions of its principles (1995 WTO Charter for Sustainable Tourism, 1999 Global Code of Ethics for Tourism, etc.). Secondly, the importance of heritage concerns both worldwide and locally, which is concomitant with the widening of the heritage scope (Benhamou 2012). Consequently, tourism-heritage relations currently seem to be marked by the virtuous circle of sustainable tourism development. However, this positive perception should not mask the complexity of relations between a 'unique' and 'fragile' heritage, which should always be preserved, and tourism development that all too often brings with it the negative effects of mass tourism. This is all the more true considering that all the research conducted on heritage and heritage tourism stresses their multi-faceted character and the socially constructed aspect (Poria et al. 2003). This is the complex relationship that we seek to clarify via an original analytical framework and a methodology to render it operational by applying it to an area of the Gironde estuary, the estuarine archipelago. This area has the advantage of presenting many natural and cultural heritage aspects in keeping with expectations in terms of 'untamed nature' and 'authenticity', characteristics of a demand that is tending towards eco-tourism.

The first part proposes an analytical framework for the tourism enhancement of the heritage, which deals with the complexity of the economic decisions relating to this aim, highlighting various types of possible and actual economic initiatives and their various meanings. Our approach draws on the economics of conventions in order to understand the various synergies possible between the heritage and tourism dynamics within a given territory. The second part presents an analysis of the tensions between the various possible trajectories for the specific case of the estuary islands which are the subject of natural heritage policies, while representing an important site of cultural heritage.

The Economics of Conventions and the Tourism Enhancement of Heritage

Institutionalised Heritage

In both geography and economics, the last twenty years have been marked by the development of research on the subject of heritage, attesting to the fact that this issue has been taken beyond the historical and cultural fields alone (Tengberg et al. 2012, Swensen and Jerpåsen 2008). However, the appropriation of this category by economists long predates this enthusiasm for heritage, and has been largely influenced by the legal categories inherited from the French Civil Code and by the categories of economic theory focused on capitalisation and individual market logics. Indeed, in traditional legal and economic theories, heritage is made up of assets that can be assigned monetary value which are owned by individuals, and constitute a form of capital. In the current environment of widening heritagisation, we have gone beyond this restrictive perception, as capital and heritage obey clearly differentiated management rules (Godard 1990). Indeed, the aim of managing capital is to increase it, while heritage management is based on a compromise between interdependent but often opposing logics: preservation and use. This compromise is a vehicle for collective identity and ensures the transmission of heritage. This means that today, any type of asset or institution (tangible/intangible, natural/cultural) may be described as 'heritage'. In addition, the unavoidable consideration of environmental issues and the weight of local development concerns have prompted economists to revise the way they see heritage by underscoring its 'condensed value' (Benhamou 2010). From an institutionalist viewpoint, this overhaul highlights the need to integrate the dual market and non-market aspect of heritage, the primary function of which is to be transmitted. Based on these works, we can see that heritage does not merely involve public assets whose levels and forms of protection are, in principle, determined. Various types of appropriation or non-appropriation are possible depending on the stakeholder networks organising the construction of heritages. In this respect, the introduction of the 'natural heritage' concept in France at the end of the 1960s, now shared by both economists and political decision-makers, has been far from neutral in the process of extending the heritage field. Indeed, this category testifies to the recognition of a particular link (not merely market-based) that is established in the long term between natural objects, whose preservation and longevity must be respectively organised and ensured, and a local community whose identity is tied to these objects (Calvo-Mendieta et al. 2011). The components of the said category are varied but are expressed or, to a certain extent, materialised through sites, landscapes or natural curiosities. While market tourism services may be associated with these particular features, they are often reductive of the ecological services provided.

In this respect, many questions may be raised about the relationships between tourism and heritage, since these relationships are ambivalent, or even contradictory. On the one hand, tourism serves to enhance heritage sites and avoids the risk of them being forgotten. Indeed, the tourism experience is the source of a relationship between places and visitors that gives a territory meaning (Heritier 2013). Tourism is therefore a vital means for transmitting heritage, all the more so as the current development of heritage tourism has led to a diversified demand and varied forms of tourism (Nuryanti 1996). On the other hand, the increasing numbers of tourists and the resulting congestion phenomena are a non-negligible threat to the preservation of sites, particularly natural sites (Russo 2002). The infrastructures that are nevertheless necessary to accommodate the public tend to challenge the authenticity of sites and often signify a decline in heritage quality.

Heritage Conventions

Heritage is therefore very much the result of a compromise between preservation, use and enhancement that changes with the development of society. The institutional economic analysis offers various analyses of the rules in their capacity as institutional constraints. We believe that this approach is a relevant starting point for the analysis of heritage, which is built up and evolves in line with the conjunction of many rules, such as those relating to the preservation of monuments and natural sites both nationally and internationally. In addition, on a local level, heritagisation leads to the emergence of projects that are based on commitments in terms of heritage, but also in terms of environment and economic development. Accordingly, while being omnipresent in economic and social practices, the paths leading to this process are multiple, and are developing in an environment of uncertainty, described as radical (Knight 1921). Indeed, this heritagisation is the result of circumstances that are unique, since they depend on collective action established on the basis of agreements whose outlines may be continually redefined by stakeholders. This research is therefore based on the assumption that acquiring heritage status and the decisions relating to its enhancement do not depend on universal laws, but on social mechanisms described as 'conventions' (Vecco 2010).

This places our work within the field of the French movement referred to as the 'economics of conventions', which is intended to study the various methods used to coordinate economic stakeholders, and the decisive role of conventions in the success and sustainability of these methods (Favereau 2008, Salais and Storper 1992). The conventions, which are composed of references shared by stakeholders, allow uncertainty to be reduced. The convention, which is both external to the stakeholders and shaped by their decisions, may therefore be defined as 'a system of mutual expectations with respect to the competences and behaviour of others, conceived as being self-evident, so as to be self-evident' (Salais 1989: 213). As an extension of these works, this analytical framework has already been applied in France and abroad to deal with issues relating to the emergence of compromises between the various methods for preserving and using resources. They stress the diversity of the possible 'arrangements' between different legitimacy principles, enhancement methods and methods for appropriating formal rules, whether in the productive field (Cazals 2012) or in the field of resource management (Baron and Isla 2006). Regarding the consideration of environmental justifications, which has prompted a major debate within this theoretical movement, the diversity of opinions referring to nature leads to, rather than specifying one natural heritage convention, enumerate the various natural heritage conventions, in order to reflect this diversity.

Based on these factors and on previous work applied to other coastal territories (Cazals et al. 2011), we can identify four types of conventions: universal heritage, collective heritage, domestic heritage and market heritage. These are presented in Table 2.1.

Table 2.1   Heritage conventions

Convention	Higher principle	Assessment model	Ownership	Protection method	Enhancement method
Universal heritage	Universal value/ well-known heritage	Formal system of judgement	Public/ private	Supranational with national implementation	International tourism between mass and elite tourism, towards ecotourism?
Collective heritage	Community value	Impersonal system of judgement	Collective	Localised participative management	Non-market development. Limited tourism
Domestic heritage	Traditional value	Personal system of judgement	Public/ private	Local management	The tourism cluster
Market heritage	Market value	Impersonal system of judgement	Private	Market exchanges	Sustainable tourism

Source: Authors.

The universal heritage convention is suited to unique assets or sites whose exceptional value requires international recognition warranting specific protection measures. Formalised assessment criteria are used to select 'applicant' assets. Protection is organised at a national level and may therefore infer different perceptions of preservation (Benhamou 2010). The control of tourism is a major issue for the protection of this type of heritage, which tends to be resolved in the development of ecotourism (Weaver and Lawton 2007).

The collective heritage convention corresponds to the recognition and qualification of collective assets that may be consumed by a more or less broad community of individuals at the local level. The role of localised collective action structures is to organise protection. While such resources are attractive, which justifies the desire to develop their market value in some territories, the development of a tourism sector is not immediately compatible with the objectives of protecting these resources (Milian 2003).

The domestic heritage convention depends on the integration, within the heritage field, of the traditions that comprise cultural diversity. Their preservation, which is mainly managed by local stakeholders, is a priority, although some see this as a lever for local development. In this context, the development of a tourism cluster seems consistent with this objective of preserving tradition while promoting territorial development (Alberti and Giusti 2012).

The market heritage convention rests on the market-based enhancement of heritage resources using a tourism model that dominated the tourism sector in the 1970s, based on profitability through economies of scale and the consumption of identical products in large quantities, but that has since had to adapt to changes in demand. Indeed, the emergence of a demand for diversified products, including heritage-related expectations, is tending to force the predominant model to evolve towards a sustainable tourism model justifying the 'market heritage' convention label.

These various heritage conventions are not models to be met, but rather ideal models whose components have served to shape the semi-structured interview grids and the qualitative survey questionnaire. The results are also interpreted with regard to these ideal models.

What is the Possible Path for the Heritagisation of the Gironde Estuary's Islands?

The Islands: An Area at the Heart of the Gironde Estuary's Heritage

The Gironde estuary is the largest in Europe, but shares the many features of other estuary areas that make their management problematic. However, it is distinctive in that it has avoided industrial development, and thus maintains a preserved aspect that may meet the current expectations of urban populations, while raising the problematic issue of the implementation of a harmonious economic development policy.

From the natural heritage viewpoint, the resources are varied. This is due to large variations in their hydrological and sedimentary properties, which allow them to harbour 75 species.[1] Well-known fish species co-exist with less well-known planktonic and phytoplanktonic organisms, which interact with each other.

The estuary is also characterised by varied natural landscapes linked to the movement of the water, the presence of marshlands, which are neither land nor water, the various wine-producing activities between the Charente and the Gironde, the hills and cliffs, and of course the islands. These attributes are not isolated, but are combined – or even reinforced – by elements that constitute monumental and cultural heritage.

Remarkable sites, which boast a built and architectural heritage, are sources of tourist activities:

- The Cordouan lighthouse, the last inhabited lighthouse in France;
- The village of Talmont with its church on the rocky spur; and
- The Blaye Citadel

---

1   This number, which varies according to the area and the season, is high for an estuary.

- The vineyards of the foremost Médoc appellations, notably the famous Château de Beychevelle, which faces onto the estuary.

In addition, the specific features of this area between river and land convey a specific human history which can be brought back to life through the various archaeological and historical sites. On the Gironde estuary there is no shortage of cultural specificities linked to river traffic and the traditional activities of hunting, fishing and wine production, exhibited by the estuary dwellers as a source of identity, all the more so as local artists are helping to perpetuate them. Furthermore, such a territory benefits from the gradual consideration of environmental issues at local, national and also European levels. These various resources contribute to the attractiveness of this territory and the emergence of a certain political will to structure its development around tourism. However, to implement such a policy, the territory's stakeholders must deal with the sheer extent and administrative fragmentation of the territory, and with a consensus-building process that goes hand in hand with the implementation of these policy systems. Various tourism strategies are therefore possible, all the more so since the results of our survey (see below) show that tourists' knowledge of tourist sites is structured by the geography of the territory, with two groups of sites that effectively emerge (Figure 2.1).

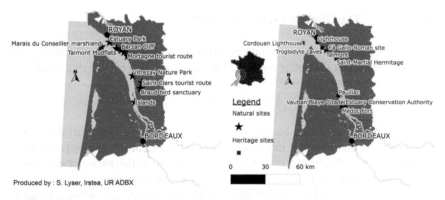

Produced by : S. Lyser, Irstea, UR ADBX

Source: Authors.

Figure 2.1   The natural, cultural and heritage sites of the Gironde Estuary

Firstly, there is a set of natural and cultural sites that are located in the northern part of the estuary and on its right bank, and secondly a group that corresponds to the sites in the 'upstream' part of the estuary, close to the point where the Dordogne and the Garonne meet. Given the above, it would seem appropriate to continue the analysis by focusing on the islands. These islands form an archipelago in the middle of the Gironde estuary (Figure 2.2) and depend on sediments carried by the Dordogne and the Garonne, the swell and the tides. They have the particular feature of being little known even by residents of the Gironde and Charente-Maritime regions. From their location at the heart of the estuary, they offer a panoramic view

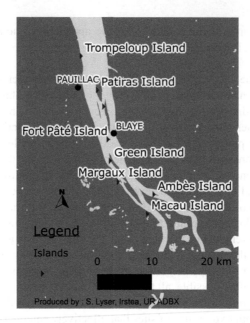

Source: Authors.

Figure 2.2   The Gironde Estuary's islands

of the diversity of the territory's natural and architectural heritage and their central position means that they offer potential for exchanges between the river banks.

Qualitative and Quantitative Methodologies

In line with the convention-based analytical framework, our empirical work aims to account for and interpret individuals' understanding of the spaces (economic, environmental, political, etc.) that they are engaged in. On this basis, we developed a methodology that led us to build instruments able to produce information on the meaning conferred by stakeholders on their practices, behavioural patterns and the institutional support that they attract. The construction of the empirical part therefore rests on a strong interaction between theory and reality based on a comprehensive approach that answers the question of 'how' a given event occurred: which stakeholders and which institutions are involved, and what are the principles of justification? Starting from this choice, we identified the stakeholders able to answer these questions. Using the analytical framework presented in the first section, we produced a three-point interview grid:

- Your part in the enhancement of the estuarine islands;
- Which stakeholders are involved alongside you in enhancing the heritage? and
- What is your assessment and your outlook concerning these projects?

Eleven semi-structured interviews were therefore conducted between 2010 and 2011 with private-sector stakeholders (tourism businesses and associations, environmental associations) and public-sector stakeholders ('Conservatoire du littoral' (French coastline conservation authority) and representatives of the 'Conseil Général' (General Council) and the 'Conseil Régional' (Regional Council)). Each interview, lasting on average two hours, was fully transcribed for a close analysis of the responses. The results produced from this sample are not intended to draw general conclusions, but rather to show the operationality of the analysis grid with a view to understanding the heritagisation process – regularly redefined by the stakeholders – undergone by the Gironde estuary's archipelago.

The qualitative study of heritage supply was completed by a quantitative study of the demand conducted from July 2010 to June 2011 via an online questionnaire with tourists and potential visitors to the estuary. Intended to account for the specific features of tourist demand within this territory, this online survey includes a section dedicated to a particular area: the estuary's archipelago. The aim is to study the number of visitors to the islands, the activities carried out and the motivations and expectations of visitors or potential visitors.

Online surveys, whose use has grown sharply over the past fifteen years, raise questions about the representativeness of samples thus obtained. In our case study, as the parent population is unknown, carrying out sampling is not feasible. Our results are thus undermined by self-selection and coverage bias, which are impossible to correct retrospectively. However, the coverage bias is reduced as the rate of home internet connection availability was nearly 80 per cent in mainland France in 2012 (according to the information and communication technology survey conducted by INSEE – the French national statistics office). Used to survey a given population, the Internet allows responses to be obtained quickly, but suffers both from a low response rate and poor quality responses. For our survey, there are no or few partial non-responses, but questions may legitimately be asked about the low response rate. Indeed, although it involved tourism stakeholders from the area being studied (tourist offices, 'Conseil Départemental du Tourisme' (Departmental Tourist Board)), the trade and local press, various environmental institutions and social networks (restricted to the tourism field: tourist offices, holiday rentals, holiday homes, campsites), our sample comprises only 127 usable responses. In the absence of data on tourism demand for the estuary, where tourism on the islands remains limited and highly regulated, we believe, without wishing to draw general conclusions, that our results constitute initial exploratory work, especially given that, ultimately, no survey, regardless of the sampling and surveying methods, can claim to be free of bias.

A brief description of the sample obtained is given in Table 2.2 below.

Table 2.2   Socio-economic characteristics of the sample

Socio-economic characteristics	Number	Percentage
Sex		
Men	54	42.52
Women	73	57.48
Age		
Under 30	28	22.22
30–44	43	34.13
45–59	41	32.54
60–74	13	10.32
75 and +	1	0.79
Household type		
Single without children	25	20.00
Single with children	7	5.60
In a couple without children	48	38.40
In a couple with children	45	36.00
Educational attainment		
No qualifications	1	0.79
Vocational qualifications, Secondary school certificate	17	13.49
Baccalaureate	15	11.90
Baccalaureate +1 year to Baccalaureate +2 years	26	20.63
Bachelor's or Master's degree	57	45.24
Higher	10	7.94
Socio-professional category		
Other	2	1.59
Farmer	2	1.59
Craftsman, merchant, business owner	3	2.38
Executive, higher level intellectual profession	39	30.95
Intermediate profession	13	10.32
Office worker	31	24.60
Manual worker	1	0.79
No professional activity	35	27.78
Of which		
(Pre)Retiree	13	10.32
Job-seeker	8	6.35

Socio-economic characteristics	Number	Percentage
Student	10	7.94
Housewife/husband	4	3.18
Hours worked per week		
Statutory regime (35/39h)	61	66.30
Less than the statutory regime	9	9.78
More than the statutory regime	22	23.91
Household's total net monthly income		
<€1,000	10	7.94
[€1,000;€1,300[	14	11.11
[€1,300,€2,000[	32	25.40
[€2,000;€4,000[	48	38.10
≥€4,000	22	17.46
Place of residence		
Rural	49	38.89
Urban	77	61.11
Visits to the Gironde estuary		
Yes, I come regularly	43	33.86
Yes, I've already been	62	48.82
No, I've never been before. This is my first visit	22	17.32

Source: Authors.

Heritage and Tourism Enhancement of the Estuarine Archipelago

The archipelago is mostly fragmented into different privately-owned areas. The 'Conservatoire du littoral', a public body responsible for coastal protection since 1975, only owns two parts of this archipelago (one on the New Island and another on the North Island). In this context, these islands have been, and still are, the site of various economic activities (farming, animal husbandry and hunting activities) which contribute to the economic and social life specific to this territory. Indeed, six of these islands have been inhabited and, according to a former inhabitant, the population across all six reached a peak of 500 inhabitants at the start of the twentieth century. The private owners who succeeded each other on these islands developed traditional economic uses – wine production and cattle grazing. These evolved in line with the advantages and disadvantages of the 'island nature' inherent in these territories. These economic activities structured an island lifestyle which, according to a former inhabitant's account, was 'quite a remote lifestyle as there were few visitors to the continent … but when you're right there on the river bank it's hard to give it up'. The traditional way of living revolved around three key figures: the steward, who organised the work, the teacher, who represented knowledge and relations with the State, and the sailor, who provided links to the continent. However, as of the 1970s, the continuously declining population further threatened this traditional society. As a result, by the end of the 1980s, the protection of what is now recognised as 'heritage' was driven by private initiatives, notably sponsored by stakeholders in the voluntary sector sharing the traditional values that form the foundations of this society, in line with a logic similar to that which we described as the domestic heritage convention. This consisted of former 'islanders' (former inhabitants of the islands) or individuals with a strong attachment to the estuary and its islands coming together to promote this territory's riches, which constitute a heritage to be protected and transmitted. In this context, some stakeholders tried to implement a strategy involving the economic enhancement of this heritage, as illustrated by this extract from an interview with a private sector stakeholder: 'He grew up on the islands and went to school there and knows all of the islands very well. So when he decided to create his own service company, he also developed the boat tour aspect ...' (Interview No. 2).

It wasn't until the early 1990s that public-sector stakeholders took action to protect the heritage of the estuarine island territory which, according to one public-sector stakeholder, is 'a territory that has been overlooked by development policies, and also by protection policies' (Interview No. 5). The purchase by the 'Conservatoire du Littoral' of part of the New Island in 1991, with a view to protecting its ornithological potential, therefore branched off from the heritage strategy to take into account the natural heritage, but with an additional cultural aspect. The area's management, which is entrusted to the 'Conseil Général' under its 'Espaces Naturels Sensibles' (ENS) (Sensitive Natural Areas) policy, forms the basis of a project which, from our viewpoint, is in keeping with the collective heritage convention logic. Indeed, this project has two parts. The first relates to the northern three-quarters of the Island, which are subject to a policy of depolderisation characterised by a decision not to repair dikes each time that there is a breach, consistent with an objective for restoring the natural environment. This area is therefore closed to the public so as not to disturb the avifauna's peace. The second part relates to the area of the island that is accessible to the public and is aimed at enhancing the natural and cultural heritage. Tours by nature guides and 'island history' projects in which artistic events are offered drawing on the island's specific natural and cultural features are the operational component of this collective heritage enhancement. As a result, the 'Conseil Général' has built a jetty to accommodate the public, as well as working in partnership with private-sector stakeholders (businesses and associations) to organise the transport of visitors. Although this project is helping to develop nature tourism on the estuary, its access to the public remains very limited and does not yet allow transport operators to develop any profitable economic activity, especially since much of the archipelago is all but closed to the public due to private ownership. However, for some, this method of enhancement is compliant with their values: 'the fact that it is restricted is good as this is a thought-out model for tourism development, which is reasonable because this isn't a funfair or a theme park; this is a slightly more gentle and respectful exploration' (Interview No. 1). The quantitative survey effectively shows that tourism on the islands remains highly limited, as only 17 per cent of the individuals questioned had already visited one of the archipelago's islands.

However, on the basis of this private ownership along with the maintaining of certain productive uses, such as wine production, hunting and the emergence of an handful of targeted tourist offers, some stakeholders would like to see a form of heritage protection based on market values while maintaining – or even developing – these economic uses. This position is also upheld by a public-sector stakeholder involved in a heritage inventory policy: 'a better way to preserve heritage is to maintain its uses and activities ... and there have always been activities on these islands' (Interview No. 7). This stance which, on the face of it, hardly seems compatible with a policy of depolderisation, limiting the possibilities for access by the public and the potential for economic development, and which may ultimately result in the disappearance of part of the island, is therefore not specific to private-sector stakeholders. However, according to our framework, this perception is in keeping with a market heritage convention, whereby the islands are part of an estuarine tourism trajectory: 'there needs to be more contact with local residents (...) there need to be more jetties so that people can come and go freely (...) the islands should be bridges or stepping stones for crossing the estuary' (Interview No. 3).

In line with the broader perception of heritage that is gradually gaining traction, it is possible to see a consensus around the recognition and protection of the estuarine island heritage. That said, the stakeholders in this heritage do not share the same conception of its enhancement. This diversity reflects the tensions between the various approaches to protection and use, and the resulting compromises, which are the basis of any heritagisation process and of the heritage conventions. For the estuarine islands, this process is marked by the diversity of possible avenues between prioritising non-market relationships and traditional values on the one hand, and focusing on market-based enhancement on the other. These dynamics thus leave plenty of room for innovation and diversity rather than for a single heritage-oriented strategy based on synergy between natural heritage, cultural heritage and tourism development.

The Tourists' Perception

The results of the survey with tourists are a further step in the analysis of heritage conventions. Consumers also contribute to the sustainability and predominant character of a convention-based system. Indeed, the stabilisation of a heritage convention results from an alignment of expectations in terms of heritage supply and demand. Given these factors, the study of how tourists and probable future tourists perceive the estuary is a key step in the analysis of heritage in terms of conventions.

The results of the survey show that only four islands are visited, chiefly on passenger boats (62 per cent). The activities pursued are mainly related to nature tourism, consisting of walking tours as part of day-long excursions whose main purpose is to 'visit a protected site that is relatively free of developments', which basically complies with the framework of the collective heritage convention. However, 'the two-day cruise with a stopover on the islands' represents the third type of activity, which offers prospects tending towards a form of market enhancement of these islands. Given the limited number of visitors to these islands, we focused on the larger sub-sample of non-visitors (103 individuals) who were able to answer the questions about their expectations regarding a possible visit to the islands. These answers provide information useful for identifying prospects for enhancing the archipelago's heritage. The two-stage analysis (multiple correspondence analysis then ascending hierarchical classification) of the variables 'Reason for visiting the islands' and 'activities probably carried out on the islands' allowed us to identify 6 categories of tourists. Only two groups, accounting for 30 per cent and 10 per cent of the sub-sample of non-visitors respectively, are interested in the natural aspect, whether this relates to water-based or walking activities. The other four groups, accounting for 60 per cent of the sample of non-visitors to the islands, state that they would be interested in learning about traditional cultural activities and culinary, regional specialities; some of them (8 per cent) would visit the islands to support the local way of life. Although they represent statements of potential actions, the results reveal certain expectations by tourists in terms of the enhancement of traditional cultural heritage with, for some, a certain sensitivity in terms of prices. These results would appear to fall within the domestic heritage convention.

Conclusion

The various studies on tourism tend to tackle the issues of territorial governance and consumer expectations separately. For its part, the conventionalist approach that we have adopted in this work underscores the importance of market and non-market references shared by stakeholders involved in supply and demand with a view to studying the development potential of specific activities. We applied this approach to analyse how the heritage represented by the Gironde estuary islands can be enhanced. Our empirical work thus sought to grasp both the issues relating to the structuring of the heritage supply, and tourists' expectations. This prompted us to develop work aimed at identifying the meaning of actions, and also behavioural patterns, by combining qualitative and quantitative approaches. However, the use of a variety of methods means that the scope of the two surveys, which were created simultaneously, had to be restricted. While this limits the scope of the results, it opens up avenues for applying a combination of methodologies in subsequent work.

Despite these limitations, the results of this empirical work clearly show the diversity of possible paths in terms of the strategy for tourism enhancement of the estuarine archipelago. This characteristic is not specific to the Gironde estuary. Indeed, while not focusing exclusively on the subject of tourism development, work underway in the Arcachon Bay reveals the coexistence of a number of heritage conventions. This plurality opens the door to a dynamic analysis of how stakeholders coordinate their activity around heritage enhancement.

Thus, for the islands of the Gironde estuary, the current form of enhancement, which is mainly structured around the emblematic character of the natural heritage, tends to meet the expectations of the few tourists who have visited the islands. While this policy may seem relevant, the operations effectively implemented do not create the possibility of developing economically profitable tourism activities. However, our survey also shows that there is some potential for enhancing the islands' cultural and traditional heritage. Indeed, whether from the supply perspective, where some public-sector stakeholders have made an inventory of heritage resources that private-sector stakeholders wish to develop, or from the demand perspective, where estuary tourists have expressed an interest in this heritage, there are some noticeable development prospects. However, exploiting this potential remains at the mercy of both political divergences accentuated by the administrative fragmentation of this territory, and the difficulty in creating sustainable synergies between natural, cultural and traditional heritage.

References

Alberti, F.G. and Giusti, J.D. 2012. Cultural heritage, tourism and regional competitiveness: the Motor Valley cluster. *City, Culture and Society*, 3(4), 261–73.

Baron, C. and Isla, A. 2006. Marchandisation de l'eau et convention d'accessibilité à la ressource. Le cas des métropoles sub-sahariennes, in *L'économie des Conventions*, edited by F. Eymard-Duvernay. Paris: La Découverte, 369–82.

Benhamou, F. 2010. L'inscription au patrimoine mondial de l'humanité. La force d'un langage à l'appui d'une promesse de développement. *Revue Tiers Monde*, 2(202), 113–30.

—. 2012. *Economie du Patrimoine Culturel*. Paris: La Découverte.

Calvo-Mendieta, I., Petit, O. and Vivien, F.-D. 2011. The patrimonial value of water: how to approach water management while avoiding an exclusively market perspective. *Policy and Society*, 30(4), 301–10.

Cazals, C. 2012. Examining the conventions of voluntary environmental approaches in French agriculture. *Cambridge Journal of Economics*, 36, 1181–98.

Cazals, C., Dachary-Bernard, J. and Lemarié, M. 2011. Land uses and environmental conflicts in the Arcachon Bay coastal area: an analysis in term of heritage. *European Planning Studies* (in press).

Favereau, O. 2008. The unconventional, but conventionalist, legacy of lewis's 'Convention'. *Topoi*, 27, 115–26.

François, H., Hirczak, M. and Senil, N. 2006. Territoire et patrimoine: la co-construction d'une dynamique et de ses ressources. *Revue d'Economie Régionale et Urbaine*, 5, 683–700.

Godard, O. 1990. Environnement, modes de coordination et systèmes de légitimité: analyse de la catégorie de patrimoine naturel. *Revue Economique*, 41(2), 215–41.

Heritier, S. 2013. Le patrimoine comme chronogenèse? Réflexions sur l'espace et le temps. *Annales de Géographie*, 1(689), 3–23.

Knight, F. 1921. *Risk, Uncertainty and Profit.* New York: A.H. Kelly.

Milian, J. 2003. Politiques publiques de protection de la nature: l'exemple des espaces naturels protégés. *Ecologie et Politique*, 1(27), 179–92.

Nuryanti, W. 1996. Heritage and postmodern tourism. *Annals of Tourism Research*, 23(2), 249–60.

Poria, Y., Butler, R. and Airey, D. 2003. The core of heritage tourism. *Annals of Tourism Research*, 30(1), 238–54.

Russo, A.P. 2002. The 'vicious circle' of tourism development in heritage cities. *Annals of Tourism Research*, 29(1), 165–82.

Salais, R. 1989. L'analyse économique des conventions du travail. *Revue Economique*, 40(2), 199–220.

Salais, R. and Storper, M. 1992. The four worlds of contemporary industry. *Cambridge Journal of Economics*, 16, 169–83.

Swensen, G. and Jerpåsen, G.B. 2008. Cultural heritage in suburban landscape planning: a case study in Southern Norway. *Landscape and urban planning*, 87(4), 289–300.

Tengberg, A., Fredholm, S., Eliasson, I., Knez, I., Saltzman, K. and Wetterberg, O. 2012. Cultural ecosystem services provided by landscapes: assessment of heritage values and identity. *Ecosystem Services*, 2, 14–26.

Vecco, M. 2010. A definition of cultural heritage: from the tangible to the intangible. *Journal of Cultural Heritage*, 11(3), 321–24.

Weaver, D.B. and Lawton, L.J. 2007. Twenty years on: the state of contemporary ecotourism research. *Tourism Management*, 28(5), 1168–79.

Chapter 3

Culture, a Factor for Recreation Emergence and Creativity

Jean Corneloup, Philippe Bourdeau and Pascal Mao

Introduction

For the past decade, culture has come to represent a legitimate and unavoidable factor in discussions addressing the development of tourist and sports-related territories. Representing the focal point of this chapter, the concept of 'cultural forms' provides an insight into how tourism objects are shaped and developed to participate in the development of sites and areas of activity, in particular outdoor leisure activities.

The economic, social and political value inherent in the shaping and cultural labelling of recreational sites is however not obvious, and does not equate with the same criteria as those used to gauge and appreciate territorial attractiveness. Very often, tourism stakeholders prefer to use criteria such as customer flows, prices, quality assurance procedures, product positioning in relation to the competition, customer portfolios and services, almost as if the cultural entry point were secondary. On the contrary, we see it as being central: tourism is first and foremost about culture, precisely because of the construction of meaning and value associated with a trip, with travelling, visiting or pursuing recreational activities. The weight of cultural variables in the co-construction of perceptions, practices and tourism places allows us to understand not only their emergence, but also their constant renewal. Representing more than just a geohistorical activator in the assertion of a territory's attractiveness, culture appears as an ongoing driver of recreational phenomena. By using this viewpoint, we seek to understand the procedures, processes and principles at work in the cultural representation of tourism and sports areas. Thus, after presenting the forms and issues of the 'cultural turn' in recreation areas, this chapter re-examines the concepts of territory, culture and development. It then goes on to provide empirical illustrations that help to observe these processes in different recreational contexts, before wrapping up with elements for discussion and recommendations.

Culture in Motion

One of the reasons why the issue of recreation's cultural foundations is the focus of attention today is the fact that the international and local situation is marked by increasing competition among tourism destinations, which is becoming more global with the internationalisation of tourism and tourist practices. A vast global movement can be observed, underpinned by the emergence of new means of communication that are changing the interpretation of destinations, the vision of markets and consumption patterns. France is additionally the subject of decentralisation movements which are effectively promoting local competition and dynamics in terms of establishing territorial attractiveness. Faced with the escalation of offerings, often combined with a degree of standardisation, each tourist entity must leverage the value of its cultural capital more shrewdly in order to strengthen its specificities, differences and 'labellings'.

This requirement is all the more clearer given that recreational activities – the vectors of this attractiveness – have increased in number and diversity, dragging each destination into an endless race to produce a never-ending stream of innovations and to redefine services and offerings. In the case of mountain and outdoor sports, our research (Corneloup et al. 2004) has notably shown an increasingly prevalent geographic fragmentation of the spaces, sites and routes in which activities are pursued. We can thus see that nature – that of the wilderness or the great outdoors – is no longer the only place for these activities; the natural areas surrounding resorts and towns are now increasingly used (for *aroundoor*[1] activities: canyoning, mountain-biking, rambling, via ferrata, climbing, etc.), and even intra-resort spaces, suited to all typically urban *indoor* activities: team sports, fitness, combat sports, skateboarding, etc. Taking into account this constant reshaping, set against a backdrop of diversified activities, geographical openness and increased competition, the questions of territorial positioning and identity require that territorial stakeholders and tourism operators define a coherent, shared development policy.

Concerning tourist services and facilities, the long-neglected and hitherto unthinkable intertwining of culture and sport now seems to be an increasingly indisputable fact. The increased popularity of 'geocaching'[2] (literally, geohiding), hiking, theme parks, incentives, cultural treks or even the success of heritage, religious and ecological tours all help to consolidate symbolic, informational and technological mediations between those who pursue these activities, and the territories in which they are pursued. Significant innovations are underway in terms of how to conceive links between culture, heritage, technology and sport which have the effect of strengthening the place of culture in territorial management.

Added to these observations is the emergence of new economic and management approaches that change how we perceive the links between economy and sociology,

1   'Aroundoor' (Corneloup 2002) can be defined as a recreational space on the outskirts of towns, resorts and massifs that represents an intermediary between the complete artificiality of 'indoor' sports and leisure activities (such as artificial climbing walls), and the still essentially natural state of 'outdoor' activities (where nature is still relatively wild).

2   A treasure hunting game using a GPS device that is one of the forms of M-tourism (tourism based on local or networked mobile technologies: smartphone, GPS, Internet etc.).

and between culture and business. The cultural models of organisations (Deal and Kennedy 1982) bypass the rationalist and functionalist models of the firm in classic microeconomic theory. In the field of tourism and sport, work by Chantelat (2004) and Bouhaouala (2001) stresses, for example, the importance of socio-cultural entry points in order to understand the sport economy, entrepreneurship and the operation of tourist activities.

To complete this interpretation of a new, emerging recreation world, we must examine the profound socio-cultural changes that drive tourist behaviour and practices. The emergence of interactivity, the ageing of populations, aesthetic awareness, the diversification of styles or the upheaval in values, attitudes and sporting cultures all redefine tourist expectations (Bourdeau et al. 2004). The tourist enters into an anthropo-cultural relationship with his or her place of visit or stay, in search of an emblematic touristic/social identity. Consequently, we can no longer underestimate the value given to 'the spirit of a place', nor to the experiences to be made that position the tourist inside a cultural universe within which symbolic and social integration is established. While tourism destinations are places of consumption, they are also, more importantly, cultural places and living spaces that go beyond the commonly accepted instrumental and utilitarian vision.

Theoretical Detour via the Concepts of Territory, Culture and Development

The Concept of Territory: From the Functional to the Symbolic

According to various research works (Gumuchian et al. 2003), we can perceive the territory as a social space that is more or less formal and structured. The recreation territory is specific in that it is rather like a hybrid organisation comprising public and private aspects, endogenous and exogenous forces, associative and entrepreneurial practices, free and paid activities, etc. The issues at stake in these territorial dynamics concern the definition of game rules, of legitimate practices or of the system's general orientation. Power plays are perceptible between the different stakeholders who participate in blurring the rationality of decision-making procedures. Our detour via the Localised Tourism System concept (Marcelpoil and Perret 1996) helps to show the limits of an entry point via the market economy model. Similarly, territorial effects must be considered to understand how the territorial economy actually operates, just as references to concepts such as industrial districts or innovative environments prompt us to place importance on professional cultures, local expertise, relational capital and endogenous cooperation (Terluin 2003).

In reference to regulationist approaches, the presence of territorial labelling implies considering the destination's management. This brings us to the problem of governance in terms of how a collective stakeholder imagines its composition, bearing in mind that territorial anchoring – as a process for developing common knowledge and shared reflexivity – appears as a fundamental resource for governing the future of the territory (Nonaka 1991).

However, a territory is also a space that produces symbolic reference points which serve to define the place's symbolic labelling, co-established between the different exogenous and endogenous forces involved locally. The attractiveness of a place is the product of this labelling, which helps to define the mood, atmosphere and images that convey meaning and value. This local alchemy, combining a host of insignificant events, proximity interactions and little places alongside more established practices (organised events, communication, etc.) helps to create a destination's 'spirit'. It thus appears increasingly necessary to look into the issue of the symbolic attractiveness of tourism sites. The concept of inhabiting a destination (Stock 2004) opens up the perspective of the place's practical use, thus giving renewed importance to the understanding of activities in terms of how they are practised as part of the place's daily life.

Cultural Dynamics

Contrary to a fairly common vision, culture not only concerns the public but all those – public and stakeholders alike – involved in a tourism territory. This culture produces a social, material, spatial and symbolic orientation of the practices that generate differences, common usages and traits, particularities and historical labellings. In the approach of a territory in which recreation practices are pursued, this perspective is concerned with the various elements – tangible and intangible, human and non-human, individual and collective – that will help to define a cultural form that leaves its mark on the place. The question does not merely boil down to knowing whether there is a rich local heritage, good ski slopes or a cinema (these are objects), it also involves the types of experiences, practices and the actual consumption of these objects.

We can thus define a cultural form as a set of social and sport practices, uses of the body and symbolic representations of a period; it is part of an organisation that is more or less formalised. This cultural form is the product of social forces (internal and/or external) on the recreation system which, at a given moment in the history of the activities, participate in its emergence. Once activated, this cultural form continues to develop in line with economic cycles, stakeholder dynamics and its capacity to attract audiences. On a structural level, we can identify four major historical forms (traditional, modern, post-modern and trans-modern) that organise the relationship with nature and with recreational practices (Corneloup 2009).

In this approach, two cultural processes are the focus of attention. The first consists in examining the spirit and experience of the place. A place delivers an atmosphere, action situations, links and proximity interactions. This kind of labelling is often observed via ethnographic approaches. The second process seeks to understand the recreational styles and the cultural universes present locally. The styles describe a coherent structure within which the users 'live' their practice based on different variables: social logic (profession, gender, area of residence, income, etc.), sporting logic (methods of participating, technical level, etc.), social usages (sociability, reading matter, clothing, food, social codes, etc.) and representations (images, views, conceptions, values, emotions, etc.). The cultural universe concept serves to describe – in a more flexible manner – the orientations of the recreational cultures according to symbolic and tangible polarities that organise the relationship with the actual practice (freerider universe, sportsperson universe, adventurer universe, etc.).

What Development?

The relationship between culture and territory raises the question of the considered type of development. The vision of change and of territorial dynamics is not conceived in the same way, depending on whether we are talking about planning, growth, action, local development, soft tourism, sustainable development or alternative development. Similarly, what criteria are to be used to evaluate a territory's development: companies' sales figures, customer flows, volume of refuse, reservations, customer satisfaction, local opinion, local well-being, profitability, etc.? By going further, we must bear in mind that the development concept refers to the way in which the action carried out acts on the place's ecological, social, economic or political situation, and how it forms part of a defined tourism conception. Values and conceptions of the world are well established, and must take into account this reality and look at the effect of the (positive or negative) externalities of the actions carried out as part of localised development. It is therefore important to understand how this development process is built from the territorial resources activated (tangible and intangible), the networks of relevant stakeholders, the strategic assets enhanced and the given evaluative and regulatory procedures: governance, impacts, management, strategy, legitimate or acceptable orientation. Our work on the forms of development (Mao and Corneloup 2005) has enabled us to identify – in the case of France – a typology of forms (republican, educational, marketing, heritage, local, libertine-libertarian etc.) from which the connection with the tourism site is established.

The Elements of Territorial and Territorialised Culture

If culture is truly a vector for the development of tourist and sporting territories, the approach is then to observe the way in which this culture works and how it is built locally. The field study must thus observe significant elements of the localised action: the media, cultural interactions, meeting places, identifiable practice areas and local markers (posters, music, various cultural or commercial labelling, logos, atmosphere, etc.) are the indicators of these elements. Similarly, based on the study of the cultural forms to be found locally (stories, epics, driving forces, game rules, sporting and tourist styles, cultural points of reference), the cultural universes that symbolise the place can be identified. These two polarities (local dynamics and cultural universes) participate in the construction of territorial attraction and labelling. Their power hinges on the value of the strategic assets determined from the evaluation of the local cultural capital.

However, a number of problems arise when qualifying this value. On the one hand, the presence of an independent form of cultural dynamics may be recognised (one that is internal and/or external to the territory) which partly escapes the place's stakeholders. Similarly, the social aspect itself produces a grey area, manipulates labellings and constantly rebuilds its relations with the places of practice. In some cases, there may even be contradictions between the interests of the territory and those of the tourists when the latter become rebels, strategists, disloyal, libertarian, etc. Cultural 'wear' may also be observable and may undermine the attractiveness of a place, to say nothing of social conflicts and games for gaining distinction and position that partly escape the logic of the market and of the territory. On the other hand, it must be acknowledged that from a methodological viewpoint, evaluating the process remains a complex matter. Which benchmark variable should be used to gauge the territorial value of this local cultural capital: opinions, accidents, attendance in the places of practice, visitor satisfaction, the success of events? While it is easy to assess the commercial value of some form of historical heritage or of a ski area based on attendance figures and satisfaction surveys, how do we go about assessing the value of a cultural universe or a local atmosphere? A good deal of research remains to be carried out to qualify the value of this labelling, either by continuing the work carried out in sensory marketing (Rieunier 2002), or based on the 'basket of goods' model developed by Pecqueur (2001).

One possible evaluative entry point consists in observing this labelling via studies on sporting styles. A quantitative survey can demonstrate the existence of tourism site cultural labelling. The results of research on summer mountain sports cultures have thus shown the summertime cultural differences between three tourism resorts in the French Alps: Chamonix (Haute-Savoie), Les Arcs (Savoie) and Vallouise-Pelvoux (Hautes-Alpes). The sporting styles that significantly mark the practice territories in these resorts differ. In Chamonix, so-called 'extreme adventurers' are over-represented, as opposed to Les Arcs where there are numerous 'contemplative' sportspersons, and Vallouise-Pelvoux where active 'hedo sportspersons' tend to dominate (Corneloup 2004). Going further, our detour via sporting styles shows the presence of a political labelling of tourism sites in relation to the sporting opinions expressed by those who practice these sports, who do not share the same vision of legitimate practice and do not see the management and development of these places in the same way. The study of cultures also concerns the observation of views, conflicts and positions on the basis of which participation in local decisions by tourists can be considered. Lastly, the study of the Localised Cultural System (LCS) would appear necessary to account for the level of development and its control. In fact, whether formally or informally, stakeholders and the public – brought together within an economy of roles – participate in producing this territorialised cultural action. The LCS approach serves to find out how this organisation and the various elements that are involved in producing a specific system and its territorial anchoring work.

The Study of the Cultural Territory and of its Action System

The next step in the approach is to understand how this LCS is positioned in the Localised Tourism System (LTS), which means considering the local and social interactions that participate in the organisation of the cultural form and in the production of localised cultural capital. It thus seems necessary to interpret this cultural action through the creation of a set of action forces that are integrated in identifiable structuring poles (Figure 3.1).

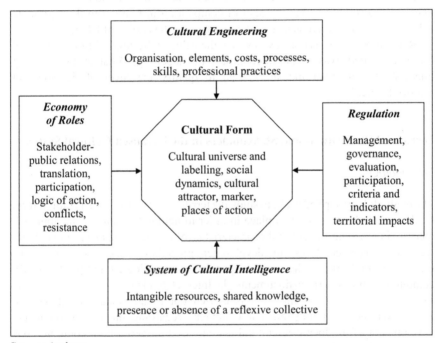

Source: Authors.

Figure 3.1   Cultural territory and poles that structure the Localised Cultural System

The purpose of Cultural Engineering (CE) is to ensure that the cultural form defined beforehand becomes operational. This involves defining the various materials, the physical, intangible and human resources, and the financial means used to develop this localised form.

The System of Cultural Intelligence (SCI) concerns the reflexive and meta-reflexive aspects that participate in producing shared knowledge. How do local stakeholders conceive and represent the cultural form? How do they use the various informational resources to devise the resulting concept? What are the reference interpretations? Do they consult experts? Do they conduct surveys?

Do they produce documents for local distribution? Who is invited to participate in the creation of these documents?, etc.

The economy of roles regards the link between the cultural form that develops in a given place (and the accompanying LCS) and the stakeholders and public present locally. The involvement of locals may infer 'translation' operations to promote public support and to convince the decision-makers of the usefulness and relevance of this positioning. Relations may be strained between the various local stakeholders and power plays may be observed, raising the issue of justification and forms of agreement and negotiation to strive towards an acceptable cultural form. There may also be a certain amount of competition in relation to the legitimate cultural form when there is a lack of consensus on the choice of labelling.

Regulation concerns the way in which the value of the cultural form concerned can be evaluated. Was it right to commit to this labelling? What are the resulting impacts? Are relevant indicators used to qualify the level of development achieved?, etc.

Territorial Illustrations and Stakeholders in the Localised Cultural System

Methodology

The methodology applied seeks to study the territorial production of a cultural form by the stakeholders of a given place in order to define its content. The approach consists in grasping the cultural characteristics of this form (sporting logic, body techniques, representations), the development procedure (stakeholders, materials, financial resources) and the social responsiveness considered and produced. By combining sources (written documents, the Internet, field observations, interviews, surveys), an analysis of the LCS is carried out to understand its dynamics. Three examples will illustrate our comments regarding the management and development of the localised cultural action based on geo-tourist configurations that are symbolic of rural tourism and mountain tourism in France.

'Les Sentiers de l'Imaginaire' (Literally, the Trails of the Imagination), the Mur-de-Barrez Community of Municipalities (Aveyron)

The first example concerns the cultural development actions implemented in the 'Communauté de Communes' (joint local authority) of Mur-de-Barrez (Aveyron 'département') in order to establish the 'trails of the imagination' within this territory. The local stakeholders decided to develop this action by inviting the inhabitants of the various member municipalities to participate in the conceptualisation and creation of these trails. A de facto SCI was implemented in local meetings to guide the project based on the identity and culture of the place. Debates were held within the local economy of roles to validate this project (translation, negotiation and justification), a form of cultural engineering emerged to create the various elements associated with this trail (map, objects, text, plan, joint manufacture of elements, etc.). Regulation was necessary to evaluate the project's results, maintain the trails and find out what the public's opinion and its level of satisfaction were in order to improve the LCS. Here, we are dealing with the overall approach of a localised cultural action resulting in new tourist practices and local dynamics likely to transform how the place is imagined and used. A labelling and a cultural attractor were established to boost local tourism.

The Development of a System of Cultural Intelligence in Chamonix Mont-Blanc (Haute-Savoie)

The second example regards the town of Chamonix where, since 2000, the tourist office has sought to consolidate relations between the various tourism stakeholders in order to influence the local economy of roles and the LCS, and to regulate it. After starting a think-tank made up of various local stakeholders, an SCI was established to build collective knowledge and a shared identity to better understand the characteristics of the localised cultural capital. The creation of this group and its subsequent debates, discussions and reflexivities brought about a collective sense of belonging to a territory project, helping to better define what the operators have in common, and what differentiates them from other resorts. Following these various actions, a first brochure was published and forwarded to the different local stakeholders to raise the community's awareness of this cultural labelling, and of the shared, common heritage that underpins local tourism. The challenge was also to encourage everyone to appreciate that this labelling is a fragile undertaking, and that it rests on a historic and context-sensitive construction that is explained and analysed. Based on this initial work, a marketing agency was contacted to draw up a report to understand the identity and values of Chamonix in greater detail. Here, we are dealing with an approach based on an intervention in the production of the localised cultural action that grants a key role to the system of cultural intelligence, and which seeks to intervene participatively in the local dynamics.

The Freeride-Freestyle Positioning in the Deux-Alpes (Isère)

The third example is the resort of Les Deux Alpes, where the 'Deux-Alpes Loisirs' company, responsible for the domain's ski lifts, decided to establish a dominant cultural form and labelling around the freeride-freestyle universe. A thought process (SCI) was developed on the role and characteristics of the gliding/sliding culture to justify this positioning. An engineering of the cultural action subsequently emerged with different technicians and consulting firms to design the different recreational spaces, communication and events (Cultural Engineering). Lastly, a regulation system was set up to assess the value of this action and its media impact and general attraction. The challenge was to be able to justify the approach initiated in relation to the company's shareholders and local elected representatives (for example: 'We have observed an increase in the number of young people in the resort, extensive media coverage'). However, tensions arose within the local economy of roles between the tourist office, elected representatives and other service providers who were not all necessarily convinced that this positioning was appropriate. We can thus observe tensions between two forms of development that do not have the same vision of territorial development: on the one hand the form of local development focused on a territorial rationale (the municipalities of Venosc and Mont-de-Lans), and on the other hand the entrepreneurial form focused on the industrial exploitation of winter sports (the Deux-Alpes Loisirs company). In this other type of development of a localised cultural action, only one stakeholder is involved in enhancing the value of the resort through the promotion and development of a specific cultural universe that it seeks to impose on the entire local community (Figure 3.2). It must be noted that this stakeholder justifies its action by explaining that this cultural process initially

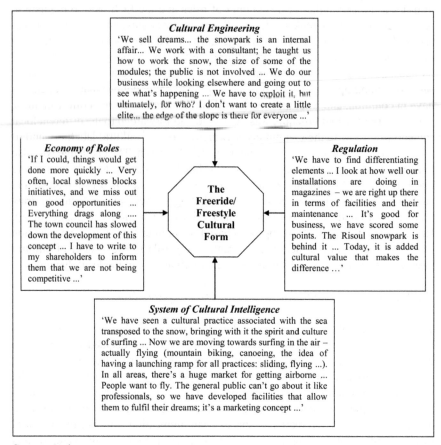

Source: Authors.

Figure 3.2   Operating rationale of the designer of the LCS in the Deux-Alpes (France)

came about from the sporting community in the town of Grenoble (associations and 'tribes' of enthusiasts). Apparently, this community was responsible for initiating this labelling and activating this cultural force in the Deux-Alpes resort; the resort merely contented itself with pursuing, maintaining, enhancing and marketing it.

Elements for Discussion and Recommendations

Having progressed from a localised, makeshift activity to a global industry in just a few decades, and from ingenuity to engineering, hasn't tourism lost some of its capacity to renew itself and deal with the uncertainties that lie ahead? How can we devise other models that are more flexible, diversified, creative and sustainable faced with the 'triple crunch' of the climate, energy and economic crises? (Bourdeau 2009). Are recreation territories able to project themselves in the sphere of cultural creativity, to seize openings, to create cycles and alternatives, and to invite consumers to become actors and citizens once more? Can these territories see themselves as areas of transition, and even invent themselves as permanent or temporary places to live, embracing notions such as habitability and amenity migration?

On the basis of these questions, the challenge of innovation in tourism is not limited merely to establishing tools for marketing, managing or engineering communication and events. It also rests on successfully combining geocultural ingenuity and engineering to place the singularities of each destination at the heart of the relation it builds with its visitors. This implies a sidestep in relation to the conventions of tourism engineering and management:

- rethinking the role of visitors in the experience that they live;
- reconsidering the place of culture in relation to the facilities;
- restoring importance to non-tradable processes as social practices and factors for creativity;
- raising the question of limits (definition, management, etc.) in relation to the normalisation, standardisation and commoditisation of recreational spaces; and
- extending the spatial representation of tourism beyond resorts towards travelling, diffuse practices, etc.

To support this perspective, we point out that the history of leisure, tourism and sport ties in substantially with creative diversions, turnarounds and circumventions all related to micro-social practices and micro-spatial situations that are neglected or ignored, and experienced outside any economic framework, but nevertheless drivers for recreational activities and destinations. In recent times, we can refer to innovative technological improvisations (paragliding, hydrospeed, snowboarding, mountain biking), revivals and reinventions (telemark skiing, snowshoeing, sledding, snowkiting), transgressions (road jumping, night-time skiing, bivouacking), the use of makeshift, self-built or converted supports (rocks, trees, barn doors or walls of buildings), the revival of intuitive, low-tech practices (sledges, snowbags), and so on.

In the symbolic case of winter sports, the concept of the resort as a unity of place, time and action based on the functional coherence of the 'accommodation-lifts-slopes' triptych can thus be circumvented or diverted by new interpretations of the mountain playground. A striking contrast can be observed, for example, between the race toward gigantic proportions in the interconnection of skiing areas, and the spatial micro-scale on which the emerging activities of young sliders seem to thrive. A snowpark's bump module, but also a simple slope, an 'improved' hump, a rock, a tree trunk, a snow-covered stairway or the door of a building have all become possible media for an expression centred on body language and shared emotions in which the 'tailored' shaping and tinkering of the terrain using simple tools (hands, snow shovels, etc.) hold a place of their own, while the use of ski lifts is avoided and even frowned upon as secondary or superfluous. These selective or alternative activities using standardised resources offered by the resorts, which promote proximity, simplicity or 'making do', and for which insufficient snow is not a problem, are also reflected in the aspirations of many visitors to go beyond the slopes or to find new forms of fun and expression beside the slope, whether by ski, snowshoe or simply on foot.

It is the tourists, mountaineers, skiers, climbers, hikers, paragliders, kayakers, and so on who have invented and who constantly reinvent their activities, their 'codes' and the associated meaning on the ground, so long as the geographic, economic and legal possibilities allow them to do so. Whatever their concerns in terms of safety or environmental control and economic value enhancement, institutional operators and professionals would clearly benefit from catering to the independent side of recreational culture, which produces 'practices' more than it does actual 'products', since it is essentially an ongoing creative process. In this perspective, the primary objective of any action – or inaction – by tourism operators should be to create and allow the creation of 'situations' in the situationist sense of the word, i.e. '*a moment of life concretely and deliberately constructed by the collective organisation of a unitary ambiance and a game of events*' (Internationale Situationniste 1958: 13). This reference helps to understand the demand and the recreational experience in terms of practices and psycho-geographic experiences rather than in terms of consumption and show performance. It thus confers upon the visitor the role of an independent player in relation to this experience, rather than merely being the consumer of a landscape or the spectator of a 'show' that diminishes the meaning of recreational situations.

Conclusion

A tourist location does not merely boil down to geographic characteristics (landscape, climate, etc.), infrastructure facts and figures (accommodation, ski lifts, slopes, etc.), and organisational and functional qualities (reception services, ski schools, etc.). It is also shaped by history, by epics and myths, by its attachment to a territory, by the interplay of cooperation and tension that involves its inhabitants, professionals and visitors. It is based on an 'ambiance' which gives it an identity. Intangible tourism resources do not therefore merely equate with a form of heritage that is recognised as such, whether tangible or intangible. The examples presented herein and the proposed topics of discussion illustrate the weight of cultural labelling in the shaping of tourism destinations. Implementing this type of approach opens up promising prospects for greater familiarity with tourist practices. Thus, while culture has long been involved in the construction of tourism destinations, all too often the approaches taken remain descriptive. They are rarely interested in examining this aspect of 'inhabiting' a destination in terms of how culture is presented, developed and practised in recreational areas. Work that involves constructing and considering territorial identities must thus be undertaken to better control the selected form of development and local anchoring. A tourism destination's cultural labelling cannot merely be limited to presenting the number of kilometres of ski slopes or ski lifts, highlighting the events proposed, the quality of the tourist services available or the destination's architectural or historic heritage. The cultural experiences that can be considered locally must be formulated and enhanced in order to understand how to integrate tourist places within a given atmosphere, style and identity, based on a form of cultural and historical consistency that underscores the value and attractiveness of the place. Alongside this type of approach, it would also be beneficial to better establish the link between the structural and local approaches of cultural dynamics. Indeed, territories are increasingly part of sociocultural networks that combine urban influences, advertising scenarios, virtual practices and societal dynamics which influence and reconstruct the map of territorialised cultural practices. Similarly, we cannot underestimate the role of alternative activities, of disagreements and cultural socialities that emerge from local exchange, social tinkering and interaction with new technologies, all of which help to redefine a given territory's cultural attractions and repulsions. Territories are thus part of exogenous and global cultural networks. Knowing how to deal with these networks by drawing on innovative resources to refine and rethink the cultural labelling of a recreational site is therefore important. Part of the elements from which tourists' territorial attractions are shaped can be found at the intersection of these considerations. We must therefore recognise the importance of understanding and interpreting the cultural networks that fashion, renew and revitalise tourist practices.

References

Bouhaouala, M. 2001. Relations inter-entreprises dans le marché local. *Espaces et sociétés*, (105–106), 229–51.

Bourdeau, P. 2009. Mountain tourism in a climate of change, in *Global Change and Sustainable Development in Mountain Regions*, edited by R. Jandl et al. Innsbruck: Innsbruck University Press, 39–52.

Bourdeau, P., Corneloup, J., Mao, P. 2004. Outdoor sports and tourism in French mountains: towards a sustainable development?, in *Sport Tourism: Interrelationships, Impacts and Issues*, edited by B.W. Ritchie and D. Adair. Clevedon: Channel View Publications, 101–16.

Chantelat, P. 2004. La Nouvelle Sociologie Economique et le lien marchand: des relations personnelles à l'impersonnalité des relations. *Revue Française de Sociologie*, 43(3), 521–56.

Corneloup, J. 2002. *Les Théories Sociologiques de la Pratique Sportive*. Paris: Presses Universitaires de France.

——. 2004. L'enquête d'opinion dans l'étude des pratiques sportives de montagne. *Bulletin de Méthodologie Sociologique*, 83, 19–42.

——. 2009. Dynamique culturelle et loisirs sportifs de nature, in *Tourisme et Société*, edited by G. Ferréol and A.-M. Mamontoff. Bruxelles: InterCommunications and E.M.E, 177–93.

Corneloup, J., Bourdeau, P., Mao, P. 2004. The cultural labelling of natural tourist areas. *Journal of Alpine Research*, 92(4), 21–32.

Deal, T.E., Kennedy, A.A. 1982. *Corporate Cultures*. Reading, MA: Addison-Wesley.

Gumuchian, H., Grasset, E., Lajarge, R., Roux, E. 2003. *Les Acteurs, ces Oubliés du Territoire*. Paris: Economica.

Internationale Situationniste. 1958. *Bulletin n°1*. Paris: Librairie Arthème Fayard.

Mao, P., Corneloup, J. 2005. Approche géo-historique des formes de développement d'un territoire touristique et sportif de nature: la construction du haut lieu 'Gorges de l'Ardèche' durant le XXe siècle. *Loisir et Société*, 28(1), 117–40.

Marcelpoil, E., Perret, J. 1999. Le poids conceptuel des districts industriels dans la construction des territoires, in *Utopie pour le Territoire*, edited by F. Gerbaux. La Tour d'Aigues: L'Aube, 15–34.

Nonaka, I. 1991. The knowledge-creating company. *Harvard Business Review*, 69(6), 96–104.

Pecqueur, B. 2001. Qualité et développement territorial: l'hypothèse du panier de biens et de services territorialisés. *Economie Rurale*, (261), 37–49.

Rieunier, S. 2002. *Le Marketing Sensoriel du Point de Vente*. Paris: Dunod.

Stock, M. 2004. L'habiter comme pratique des lieux géographiques. *EspacesTemps.net*, Travaux [Online]. Available at: http://www.espacestemps.net/articles/lrsquohabiter-comme-pratique-des-lieux-geographiques/ [accessed: 18 December 2004].

Terluin, I.J. 2003. Differences in economic development in rural regions of advanced countries: an overview and critical analysis of theories. *Journal of Rural Studies*, 19(3), 327–44.

Chapter 4
Inter-Municipal Cooperation and Tourism: New Local Roots

Vincent Vlès

Introduction

In France, tourism has undoubtedly become an inescapable inter-municipal issue in the last ten years. A survey conducted by the Assembly of district communities in 2010 showed that 85 per cent of inter-municipal councils had included this competence in their bylaws. This very recent phenomenon transfers the local organisation of tourism from the municipality level to the district level, reflecting the fundamental break-away from the undertaking of tourism-related assignments, which the country has traditionally left to municipalities, ever since the creation of tourism in the nineteenth century. This symbolic break-away is even stronger, as the regrouping of municipalities into wider political and administrative instances has taken a long time in France, unlike other major tourist countries in Europe. The issue was settled over a century ago in the UK and after the Second World War in Germany, in Belgium and in Italy. In Spain, the issue was addressed after the Franco period. Why, and how, has France managed to catch up with such delay? How is it expressed, and what are the first results? This chapter is a synthetic presentation of the research which was conducted and published on this issue within an area that has been rather neglected by most researchers. Because of its institutional complexity and the many multidisciplinary skills involved, the scientists who deal with these issues are involved in the following areas: planning, law, geography, political science, sociology of organisations and management sciences. The purpose of this chapter is to summarise, for the first time, inter-municipal tourism in France. This summary presents demonstrations originating from the research work we have published on a variety of geographical areas (on the coast, in the mountain and in cities), as well as more in-depth comparisons between experiments in France – where municipalities have chosen to work together – and Spain, the world's second largest tourist destination, where regrouping was imposed by the autonomous regions. This comparison, initiated by Clarimont (2006), has shown that the inter-municipality issue is crucial for this sector, as it restructures and makes the production and marketing of tourism more effective (Clarimont and Vlès 2009, Vlès 2012).

We will successively see 1) how inter-municipal cooperation constitutes a significant institutional challenge for the French tourist industry in Europe, 2) what the advantages are that scientists agree it brings to its production and management, 3) and finally, how the streamlining it results in seems to produce new territorial solidarities and better adjustment to sustainable development.

Inter-Municipal Anchoring of Tourism, a New Challenge for France, Well-Tried in Europe

France often considers itself as quite a centralised country even though it is actually decentralised: with over 560,000 elective mandates within local autonomous authorities, devolved State constituencies and electoral constituencies. Of the 43,000 municipalities created in 1790, 36,779 still are still active today and 92 per cent of them count less than 3,500 inhabitants. Municipalities in France represent 49 per cent of the total number of municipalities in Europe, even though they only account for 16 per cent of the population and 14 per cent of the European Union surface area. At a higher geographical level, France is divided into 101 counties or 'départements' and 26 regions are over this network of 'départements', without however replacing them or interfering in their policies. Each one of these three territorial levels (municipalities, 'départements' and regions) has its own tourism-related policy. Locally, this results in at least 36,826 different potential policies structuring this major tourist destination. Paradoxically, France is a unitary state and its local communities do not have any legislative power, even at the regional level, unlike Germany, Italy in the 1970s and Spain in the 1980s. Since there are many local authorities involved in tourism in France, each one ends up with very few resources. A region like Alsace, for example, has a budget of only 700 million euros, whereas its neighbour, the German State of Baden-Württemberg has a budget of 37 billion euros. In Spain, the constitutional reform of 1978 entrusted autonomous regions with the organisation of tourism, as in Italy. In Catalonia and in Aragon, this role (among others) has been entirely transferred to inter-municipal structures called 'comarcas', imposed on municipalities (Clarimont 2006). The 'comarca' is a small territory (the equivalent of the French 'pays'), which is geographically and economically uniform, covering an uninterrupted area. It is a new administrative unit separate from the municipality, with its own, autonomous legal personality and financial character. However, unlike France, a municipality can only belong to one 'comarca', and to a large extent, regions have delegated their tourism-related functions to these municipalities. For example, in Aragon, 'comarcas' now have a general competence in tourism, exceeding by far the scope of marketing: they can play a role in the creation and the management of leisure or tourism facilities as well as in their own development and the regulation of their entire activity. In about ten years, 'comarcas' such as Alto Gállego, Sobrarbe, Ribagorza in the Aragonian Pyrenees, Somontano in the south of the Sierra de Guara, Alt Urgell or Cerdanya in Catalonia have become tourist destinations that are totally autonomous in their organisation. They have adopted very aggressive territorial marketing strategies to create a network of public and private tourism operators.

In France, to remedy this municipal fragmentation, for a long time the State proposed inter-municipal regroupings (the first ones, 'pays touristiques', created in 1976, were short-lived) that were gradually added to municipalities that only wished to take up specific assignments. Until recent years, tourism remained a forced choice because it was not considered as very strategic. These multiple groups (municipalities can join several types of groupings depending on the competences they choose to transfer to them) have taken the form of municipal associations,[1] joint entities,[2] district communities or integrated area councils[3] that have overlapping roles. In 2013, there were 2,581 districts communities in France (each with its own independent tax system) covering 35,303 municipalities regrouped around a common project of economic development and planning. These groupings currently cover the whole of France, but do not necessarily deal with tourism. There are also no resources available for conducting a scientific investigation to obtain a reliable assessment. Research works that have been undertaken clearly show that some municipalities do not have any competence in the tourism area but nevertheless exercise it, while others who have included it in their bylaws do not exercise it, or if they do, very little and very partially.

This is because, unlike Spanish autonomous communities, local governance of tourism in France is experiencing the difficulties of inter-municipal implementation. First of all because the 'tourism' competence to be transferred is already in itself not very clearly defined for the municipality: 75 per cent of inter-municipalities declared that they find it difficult to define community interest when it comes to tourism (Dupuy and Lewy 2004). It is usually reduced to promotion, or at best, marketing of services. Yet we know that 70 per cent of local investments

---

1   The 'Syndicat de communes' (inter-municipal association) is an association of municipalities created to run services with inter-municipal significance. The 'Syndicat Intercommunal à Vocation Unique' (single-purpose inter-municipal association – SIVU) was created in 1890; the 'Syndicat Intercommunal à Vocations Multiples' (multiple-purpose inter-municipal association – SIVOM) was created in 1959 to provide several services transferred to it by the different municipalities as well as its financing. Today it is gradually being replaced by the 'Communauté de communes' (district community), which has a more comprehensive legal and financial status, is more autonomous and has extended possibilities in terms of competence.

2   The 'Syndicat Mixte', created in 1935, brings together continuities of different types, municipalities and an urban community or a 'département', for example, or a public institution of inter-municipal cooperation (EPCI), a region and a 'département'.

3   After the Urban Community (1966), which does not handle tourism, the District or Urban Community was created in 1992. The law of 12 July 1999 clearly stated that the purpose of inter-municipal cooperation is to create 'project territories'. The concept of 'solidarity area' introduces the objective of equalisation through new financing procedures (independent tax regime) and through joint investments and policies that have become mandatory.

in tourism apply to development and the creation of facilities. To make things even more complex, unlike in Spain or Italy, French 'départements' and regions continue to exert 'tourism-related' competences of the same content by virtue of a 'clause of general competence' allowing them to deal with nearly all the areas of their economic and social life. Tourism is considered at all levels as an economic sector requiring organisation, and this mission is even recognised as a 'public service' (Council of State, 1985). France has made no distinction in allocating this role to municipalities or their groupings, 'départements' and regions. In Spain and in Italy, two other major international destinations, the regionalisation of tourism has made it possible to transfer all power, most of the time as a whole and without fragmentation, in any case without overlapping the powers belonging to regions and inter-municipalities. The Italian agency in charge of local tourism and the Spanish 'comarca' systematically structure the tourism of resorts together with their hinterland, connect tourist towns to the surrounding countryside and ensure that supply matches destination. Efficient management of the supply-demand balance means that the territory of production and supply management is adapted to that of demand, the destination. This is all the more so since significant synergies and economies of scale are to be gained from this broad-based territorial management.

Benefits of Inter-Municipal Cooperation for the Production and Management of Tourism

Nationally, tourism is the leading economic sector in France, representing over 7 per cent of gross domestic product, i.e. three times the volume of business of the automotive industry and two million direct and indirect jobs. Locally, this economic sector is recognised as a producer of 'solidarity spaces' (laws of 1992 and 1997 on inter-municipality) and pressures, an area that far exceeds the scope of the municipality or the resort. The ever-increasing mobility of modern tourists generates increasingly complex flows and spatial dynamics beyond the municipal territory and falling within the larger area of the destination.

Why is Tourism Supply Management by Inter-municipality an Advantage?

Within a context of increasing competition, tourism in resorts, cities and villages in southern Europe has now been confronted with globalised challenges for about 20 years, questioning the relevance of the local level as an adapted solution:

- The accelerated growth of global tourism and the political opening of countries that position themselves on the new low-cost 'sunny' destinations market and compete with the traditional French products including the 'snow' product (Central Europe, North Africa, Asia),

- The development, through requalification, of high-quality and very competitive products of tourism with the main competitors, and the enhancement of their value through a very aggressive and ambitious promotion policy (Spanish *Quality plan, Italia* brand in Italy, low-cost destinations in North Africa, etc.), endowed with very large budgets that France has never had before at a similar level of investment,
- The industrialisation of production and distribution networks linked to the globalisation of tourism and direct marketing on the Internet, which now concerns over 60 per cent of the customer base (2013),
- The reorganisation of working hours with the resulting new mobility, facilitated by the setting up of high-speed and/or low-cost transportation, which redefine the forms of traditional resorts on which French tourism was historically built,
- The need for ethics and sustainability which increasingly determines the choice of tourism infrastructure and development, marked by the search for stronger communities of interest between visitors and inhabitants.

Confronted with these challenges, which are linked to the globalisation of the economy, all the research being carried out on France shows the divergence between the geographic municipality scale, where traditional tourism development and management policies are prepared, and much larger territories where the economic flows of tourists who benefit from these policies take place (Clarimont and Vlès 2009). Inter-municipality offers four types of advantages to match these two scales:

1. With respect to leisure products, only inter-municipal solidarity can provide sufficient tourism opportunities in areas of low population density and services (mountainside, countryside and rural coast), a rich and diverse production of sites and events (by grouping and drawing on the complementary nature of supply) that are more in line with sustainable development requirements. Here, pooling, sharing and the complementary space are excellent ways of uniting, building and offering a complete range of products and activities, which can be the determining factor and the reason for loyalty to a holiday destination. This pooling rationale enables resorts, towns and host sites to find a specific positioning and a differentiation logic to give them a head start or, at least, a complementarity that will set them apart from competing destinations. In 2013, being part of the tourism market means offering a variety of services and activities (for example, a heritage and cycling complement in the hinterland for a beach destination, after-ski activities, hot baths, nature hikes, pleasure carriage rides or horse-related tourism, etc.) all year round. This will reduce pressure in terms of carrying capacity. A better foothold[4] of tourism in the local economy and society involves bringing

---

4   The *territorial anchoring* of tourism is determined by the relationships maintained by the organising authority with the economic sphere and civil society. These relationships depend on the genesis of the resort and the creation of a local productive system (Georges-

together leisure products that are often fragmented in space and organisation. All research works prove that producers who remain isolated are uninformed. Inter-municipal cooperation makes it possible to unite beaches, snowfields, to create a network of ski lifts, to diversify the landscape, to increase attractiveness, to manage complementary activities of diversification and facilities within seaside resorts with inland areas, valleys and countryside. This *multiple community interconnection* generates a more communicative coordinated pool of tourism activities. It connects leisure products that are very scattered across municipalities sometimes far from one another, thus creating the links of a marketable offering as well as broadening and diversifying the customer base.

2. The pricing policy plays a significant role in boosting demand, by proposing cheaper costs of access to leisure activities than that of competing destinations. In the area of tourism development and infrastructure, it is financially difficult for a small municipality to carry out a large-scale local economic action on its own. The small population of most tourist municipalities (in France, 92 per cent of them count less than 3,500 inhabitants) makes them vulnerable when it comes to negotiating costs and fixing prices with financial institutions. Conversely, the pooling of their resources makes it possible to play with the price elasticity of demand and reach competitive thresholds in the market. This is because, although inter-municipal cooperation has no impact on fixed costs (which do not change regardless of the level of production), some variable costs can be significantly reduced through the sharing of infrastructure management charges (promotion or rental of accommodation, etc.) or operating costs (wages).

3. Building a common identity is also an asset for sustainable development if objectives, image and reputation are shared. When governance is shared over a wider territory, it can fit better into the long-term because of the consultations and the necessary debates between more diverse positions on shared objectives. The assumption that inter-municipal actions promote more sustainable products of tourism than municipal actions was demonstrated in 2005 (Clarimont and Vlès 2007, Vlès 2005). *Project inter-municipality* makes it possible to take account of social challenges and local employment, new forms of governance involving the local population *upstream* of operations, and biodiversity protection

---

Marcelpoil 2002). Anchoring in France was originally usually determined by a system of established stakeholders in a municipality. It is this pattern that is now rapidly evolving, like in Spain and Italy, into a system of stakeholders extending to several municipalities. This transformation results in changes in the local political landscape, tourism activities and local finance and heritage promotion strategies. In this context therefore, the term 'territorial anchoring' means the creation of a network, by the participants and thanks to inter-municipality, of modern leisure products, often very fragmented in terms of space and their organisation (except at some very organised and reputable sites), which the producers are ignorant of when they remain isolated.

or its reinforcement. This form of sustainable tourism depends on factors such as dialogue and communication that are better controlled by inter-municipality because of its size and its measured distance from citizens. Economic factors give it a better position in the long-term: sustainable tourism must match supply (local development needs) and demand (customer needs). It is therefore accessible to all operators and tourists and offers quality products that are created and marketed from the various local resources. It meets political and social communication criteria (it promotes local democracy as it is totally controlled by local stakeholders) and environmental protection criteria (it takes primarily into account environmental factors, the reinforcement of biological diversity and the balanced use of resources) paying greater attention to local societies.

4. Finally, distributing local products and leisure activities involves assessing catchment areas and networks, as well as training, informing, stimulating and helping producers through a sales force. As it is more visible and better equipped, grouping makes it possible, via the backing of the regional authority, to fit into an international distribution network and to gain access to the global market. On the international market, inter-municipal cooperation is a facilitating process that makes the destination more visible and enhances its reputation. Very often, the size of a resort will not enable it to achieve this function on its own.

Customers will thus find it easier to obtain a diversified, complementary offer at the destination level, which is labelled and marketed under a unifying banner and with a higher level of organisation. With the inter-municipal project, it becomes possible to reach a critical size to define and carry out interconnected tourism projects. It provides a destination territory with more visibility than an isolated municipality. It provides the human and financial resources to develop an integrated and strategic vision (Chateau 2004). Inter-municipalities involved in tourism streamline expenses by avoiding double expenditure. They place their resources within a network and can obtain a more rounded expertise. And finally, it increases the negotiating power of the local territory thanks to the reinforcement of legitimacy of a federation as compared with an isolated municipality. In short, it makes it possible to make public action more effective by sharing supply resources.

A Management of Interdependencies that Takes Long to Define

However, tourism-related inter-municipality has developed more slowly in France than in neighbouring countries having similar challenges, such as Spain and Italy.

This is because in France, the power transferred to the communities by the municipalities often continues to be limited to intermediation or promotion assignments (in 70 per cent of communities, according to Chateau). It must be pointed out that in France, unlike Spain, the transfer of tourism-related powers is optional. And yet tourism depends on many spheres of intervention that municipalities deem strategic: studies, infrastructure, building and operation of facilities, enhancement of natural or architectural heritage, modernisation or embellishment of public areas in towns and villages, town planning which is a necessary stage for changing tourism supply. Except in very large metropolitan areas where they were under obligation to give up these functions, most municipalities refused to do so, because these functions are the essence of their power. Loaded with symbols, they mark the municipal initiative, express the legitimacy of local elected representatives, and give them the power to mark the life of the community with their seal. Once the powers have been transferred to the inter-municipality, the municipality can no longer exercise these functions.

Therefore, for a municipality, transferring the 'tourism' competence means sharing tourism assets, products, stakeholders and professionals. It also means waiving the power of deciding alone and becoming part of a collective process. Defining an inter-municipal tourism project means reaching a compromise between local interests that are sometimes divergent. An increasing number of inter-municipalities write this into their bylaws. For the Communauté de Communes de la Haute Tarentaise (district community) in the Alps, the Communauté d'agglomération (urban community) of Pau (urban tourism), the southern coast of the Landes or the Gulf of Saint-Tropez (coastal tourism), competence in tourism-related areas concerns the development and maintenance of paths between resorts, villages and the countryside, enhancing their heritage (architecture, sceneries), very different traditional know-how, creating and promoting tourist products (hiking, cycling, local cuisine, visits of towns), management of customer services and organisation of cultural or sports events. To obtain this result, the inter-municipal territorial management focused on the management of interdependencies (Mayntz 1997) and committed itself to accommodate diverse interests. The transfer of competence produced an organised system of action, and established contacts between stakeholders who used to be remote or unknown in most groupings (Catlla 2007).

The establishment of inter-municipal cooperation in tourism is therefore a progressive territorial regulation tool, where boundaries between the public and private sphere blur and where alliances contribute to the increased sharing of solidarities (Simoulin 2007). If this movement, which has been compulsory in Italy and in Spain for the last three decades, is now inevitable in France, it is more due to market pressure than national laws and regulations. Admittedly, European, national and regional standards and policies have a part to play by granting more aid to inter-municipalities for tourism. More often than not, international competition weakens scattered operators and forces them to regroup. Roundtables of complex financial arrangements for projects also require public-private tourism joint funding that fall under the mandatory scope of inter-municipal communities[5] (Vlès 2012). Economic constraints are undoubtedly the real reason behind the

---

5   The creation of a facility or simple tourist development depends on the 'spatial planning' competence which has now been transferred by law to inter-municipalities. Moreover, 42 per cent of groupings now consider the 'tourism' competence as mandatory (CNT 2005).

acceleration of such restructuring rather than national political incentives, which in France are not binding.

Question in Debate: Does the Streamlining of Tourism within Inter-Municipalities Really Generate Local Solidarity and Activity Diversification?

The French management of local tourism is thus confronted with its interdependencies with the natural environment, farming, local social organisation, residentiality and new forms of 'inhabiting'.

Ongoing changes in these areas may question the concept traditionally grounded on the search to increase visitor traffic. New phenomena have emerged in recent years: the lack of a positive image of rural, mountain and sometimes coastal tourism municipalities among tourists in general and young people in particular, especially with respect to the summer or end of the season; changes in behaviour (decrease or diversification of board-sports – coast and mountain, exponential expansion of the offer, etc.), in consumption modes (day tripping, short stays, etc.); climate change which threatens the level, duration and distribution of wet periods on the coast and snow conditions in the mountain, and therefore the projects of resorts, currently based on high-season tourist activity; the sharp increase in urban tourism at the expense of the other spaces. Research is being conducted on all these changes, the results of which make it possible to state the assumption of a productive territorial system that is being recreated.

Will Inter-Municipal Cooperation Enable the Emergence of a Multifaceted Tourism?

In this societal context of global change, at a time when people are becoming aware of the impacts of their activities on the earth's balance, the idea of restructuring the modern tourism development model is gradually emerging in France (Bourdeau 2009). After about 50 years of fast socio-economic success and progress based on an ideal of growth in specific locations, the non-sustainability of the traditional productive process implemented by municipalities and traditional resorts has shown many cases of deterioration and systemic dependencies, denounced in public debates (for example, regarding the mountain or the coast: unpredictable snow or weather conditions à increased debt à an already obsolete real estate that is not sufficient to stagger the season à stagnant number of visitors à drop in revenue, increased energy and operating costs à operating losses à increased debt, etc.). This is all the more so since the repeated and increasingly frequent crises have resulted in the idea of a profound transformation that challenges the definition of new, more sustainable development policies. The model of a single tourist activity is entirely questioned by scientists of all disciplines (for the mountain, for example, by D'Amico et al. 2013). Everyone agrees that to resist international competition, this model, which is fragmented between many territorial stakeholders, is not suited to the necessary diversification of tourism supply.

These perspectives have therefore created a new scope of public action: they impose on public authorities a new and more comprehensive approach to governance of polarised tourism areas (resorts and related municipalities) (Vlès 2012). We have seen how inter-municipality cooperation makes it possible to attain this diversification of tourism and the conditions for implementing it, by examining tourist areas through a broader systemic approach that includes other economic activities such as the Italian tourist information boards (APT in Florence for example).[6] These new and larger forms of tourism anchoring redefine the productive system of mountain, coastal, countryside and urban areas, and in particular small, ageing seaside resorts and mid-mountain ski resorts, which may or may not be faced with problems of product obsolescence and climate change phenomena, for example on the Mediterranean coast, the North Sea or the Atlantic, which will be the most exposed.

This ongoing remapping of the territories of tourism, which is slow but continuous, undeniably raises the question of the choice of the development process of territories, between the old approach, fragmented into seasonal areas, urban islands and resorts, and a more structured approach between hubs functioning in networks. This new movement to create a tourism foundation comes with an inter-municipal structuring and directly questions the outlines of the extended scopes of tourism organisation, how they function, the relationship between operators and elected representatives, and therefore the governance of tourism activity as an object of public policy, which is better identified locally (Vlès 2012).

The diversification of activities (which requires an extension of the territorial tourism management space in order to increase the diversity and complementarity of the forms of tourism supply) favours the search for a model to adapt to a new form of modernity that is neither 'all ski', 'all beach', 'all rural' or all 'urban centre'. Inter-municipalities are engaging their tourism development on resources other than real estate and land development linked to initial specialisation in a single activity. They are integrating the culture, identity and heritage dimensions into their new competence. For example, national or regional parks (inter-municipal joint associations made up of municipalities, 'départements' and regions) combine heritage enhancement and agro-pastoralism to control tourism. These inter-municipal entities wish to prevent tourism from damaging the unity of the 'tourism area'[7] in time and space.

---

6   The Florence Tourist Information Board, formerly *Azienda di promozione turistica di Firenze*, promotes and operates tourism services at the provincial level, not only of the town or metropolitan area. The 'urbs-rus' interconnection has been a tradition in Italy since ancient Rome.

7   In an initial analysis, the tourism area may be understood as the economic, social and political territory marked by a strong relationship between the resort and its hinterland.

The process consists in regulating tourism by integrating it into a comprehensive, social, environmental and anthropic system (controlling the virtuous feedback loops between the elements of the system with which it has links of dependency), by setting up eco-systemic services. By drawing on tourism activities enhancing the value of heritage in the broad sense of the word (landscape, nature, architecture, agro-pastoral, industrial, forest, etc.) of a wider area, the inter-municipal approach enables current destinations (municipalities) to expand their activity to new tourism segments corresponding to a more diverse positioning of tourism, which is spread out and softer (sustainable). This movement is being implemented, not only in the mountains and in rural areas, but also on the coast, as seen in the recent actions of GIP Littoral Aquitain (Aquitaine coast public interest group). It repositions the Fordian resorts (specialising in a single activity) into a progressive requalification rationale. This perspective gradually defines a local anthropo-system[8] that integrates tourism, this new element of modern life that appeared in the second half of the twentieth century, into traditional society.

Does Inter-Municipal Cooperation Lead to New Forms of Local
Tourism Governance?

A whole series of research work have demonstrated the significance of governance for tourism development. Inter-municipal governance, defined as 'all situations of cooperation not arranged by hierarchy that correspond to the building, management and representation of territories, in particular in relation to their economic or institutional environment' is more adapted to the cultural, agricultural, land and real estate implications than municipal policies alone (Simoulin 2007: 15–32). In it, we observe that a series of factors contribute to the increasingly hybrid nature, not only of public action and private intervention, but also activity sectors and stakeholders. This is the main symptom, together with the trend towards contracts, of the territorial governance of tourism, which creates an increasingly marked porosity between territorial levels: the traditional stay clientele is gradually giving way to a residential clientele that gives preference to second homes, and thereby a unique form of 'urban sprawl' in the mountain, on the coast, even in rural areas. This phenomenon leads to transformations of property and land (Vlès 2012). In the mountain and on the coastline, customers have become increasingly demanding and responsive to living conditions, quality of the habitat and urban services and facilities. Many resorts must therefore deal with the management (and debt repayment) of the sometimes heavy legacy of the Fordist-Taylorist model of the post-war boom years. In the hope of finding (or retaining) customers

---

8   By drawing on the systemic approach, Lévêque et al. (2003) suggested the concept of anthropo-system, which includes in the definition of local development issues not only the maintenance of agro-systems (man + agrosystem), but also the economy of services represented by tourism, which leads to profound transformations in the local environment as a results of the meeting between the urban world and the rural world.

who are attracted by the increasingly varied nature-based activities, water games, and heritage discovery, municipalities hosting small-sized resorts come together to pool the costs of modernising their infrastructure. They have understood that municipal fragmentation was creating a compartmentalised management of the territory rather than the integrated development of tourism all year round. However, as long as the legal frameworks and procedures for transferring tourism competences in France remain vague, there is, for the moment, no guarantee that they will enable economic/and or business streamlining and create true local economic and social systems.

To conclude, we must return to the Italian and especially the Spanish experiences that show the importance of clarifying the competences of each local authority: the Spanish regional autonomous communities avoid becoming entangled in the local political web because they clearly define the content of the set of competences in tourism attributed to each administrative level without any overlapping (Clarimont 2006). What Spain achieved through its laws in the period between 1990 and 2005 is currently happening in France, driven by the economic constraints linked to the globalisation of the tourism market. It is by expanding their foothold,[9] through the inter-municipal governance of tourism that local authorities will adapt to new market requests. This is because the new governance scopes of local tourism policies result in a redefinition of local solidarities. Although these are admittedly based on a political agreement, they are also conditioned by interdependencies among stakeholders, economic sectors and (agro-forestry, pastoral, residential, etc.) systems. We have seen how this transformation of traditional anchorings appears to pay more attention to sustainable development, in search of a better long-term balance between anthropo-systems and in search of an inter-municipal political consensus. In any case, it is based on shared governance. The slow course taken by the French authorities in adopting this inter-municipal tourism grouping shows the difficulty in convincing elected representatives that joining an inter-municipal community would enable redeployments beneficial to visitors and locals alike. However, in the end, France will maybe manage to implement, a few decades later, what its two major tourism neighbours, Spain and Italy, have already achieved: a renewed, expanded, diversified and organised foothold of its tourism production, a percolation of tourism governance into the productive space.

References

Bourdeau, P. 2009. From après-ski to après-tourism: the Alps in transition? *Journal of Alpine Research* [Online], 97(3). Available at: http://rga.revues.org/1049 [accessed: 9 December 2009].

---

9   See footnote 4.

Cattla, M. 2007. De la genèse d'une régulation territorialisée à l'émergence d'une gouvernance territoriale, in *La Gouvernance Territoriale. Pratiques, Discours et Théories*, edited by R. Pasquier et al. Paris: LGDJ, 89–109.

Chateau, L. 2004. *Intercommunalité et Tourisme*. Etude KPMG, Assemblée des Communautés de France.

Clarimont, S. 2006. Partage de la compétence tourisme. L'expérience aragonaise. *Cahiers Espaces*, (91) 'Intercommunalité et tourisme', 116–21.

Clarimont, S., Vlès, V. 2007. El turismo en los Pirineos: ¿un instrumento de desarollo sostenible ?, in *Ecología Política de los Pirineos. Estado, Historia y Paisaje*, edited by I. Vaccaro and O. Beltran. Barcelona: Garsineu Edicions, 77–99.

— . 2009. Pyrenean tourism confronted with sustainable development: partial and hesitant integration. *Journal of Alpine research* [Online], 97(3). Available at: http://rga.revues.org/index978.html [accessed: 9 December 2009].

Conseil National du Tourisme. 2005. *Tourisme et Intercommunalité*. Section 'Politiques Territoriales Touristiques'. Paris: CNT.

D'Amico, F., Bardonnet, A., Delzon, S., Michalet, R., Vlès, V. 2013. L'impact du changement climatique sur l'activité touristique en montagne aquitaine, in *Changement Climatique en Aquitaine*, edited by Conseil régional d'Aquitaine, Bordeaux: CRA, 1–28.

Dupuy, K., Lewy, R. 2004. *Tourisme et Intercommunalité*. Rapport du Conseil National du Tourisme, session 2004–2005.

George-Marcelpoil, E. 2002. Les systèmes d'acteurs dans les stations françaises, in *Perspectives pour un Nouveau Siècle de Sports d'Hiver*. Chambéry: FACIM, Comp'Act, 189–98.

Lévêque, C., Muxart, T., Abbadie, L., Weil, A., van der Leeuw, S. 2003. L'anthroposystème: entité structurelle et fonctionnelle des interactions sociétés-milieux, in *Quelles natures voulons-nous?*, edited by C. Lévêque and S. van der Leeuw. Paris: Elsevier, 110–29.

Mayntz, R. 1997. *Soziale Dynamik und Politische Steuerung*. Francfort/Main, New York: Campus Verlag.

Simoulin, V. 2007. La gouvernance territoriale: dynamiques discursives, stratégiques et organisationnelles, in *La Gouvernance Territoriale. Pratiques, Discours et Théories*, edited by R. Pasquier et al. Paris: LGDJ, 15–32.

Vlès, V. 2012. Ski resorts in crisis and territorial construction in French Catalonia. *Journal of Alpine Research* [Online], 100(2). Available at: http://rga.revues.org/1824 [accessed: 28 December 2012].

—. 2014. *Métastations: Mutations Urbaines des Stations de Montagne. Un Regard Pyrénéen*. Pessac: PUB (Presses Universitaires de Bordeaux).

PART II
At the Heart of Destinations:
Users and Stakeholders

Chapter 5

Strategic Management of Tourism Destinations Within Territories: Key Stakeholders and the Example of 'Parcs Naturels Régionaux' (Regional Natural Parks)

Jean-Bernard Marsat

Introduction

The cross-cutting nature of tourism makes it a prime field for examining the relationships between a socio-economic (multi-)sector activity and territorial regulations. A tourism destination is a complete package combining a supply of accommodation, recreation, transport and other services. It involves a large and highly diverse range of stakeholders. Some of them are important for the activity, for example because of a resource that they control, although they do not have a specific tourism rationale. The purpose of this chapter is to give a managerial view of this complex system, i.e., focused on issues of action, organisation and strategy: how to design and manage collective and integrated action in this field of destination operation?

This chapter focuses on the place of stakeholders in tourism destination management models in general. It also places special emphasis on the territorial aspects of tourism and the way in which sectoral and territorial stakeholders interact. It establishes the respective legitimacies and roles of these two types of stakeholders as well as that of a unifying stakeholder, the 'Organisme Local de Tourisme' (OLT, Local Tourism Organisation). The French 'Parcs Naturels Régionaux' (PNR, Regional Natural Parks), in their role as territorial organisations with specific, multi-sector tasks, are also unifying bodies, and we will systematically examine how they contribute to tourism destination management.

The chapter proposes and uses a framework based on the strategic theory of organisations, which calls on several major approaches. These are positioning (Porter 1980), resources and competencies (Barney 1991, Wernerfelt 1984) and stakeholders (Freeman 1984, Martinet 1984).

The Strategic Management of Tourism Destinations Within Territories

The Strategic Management of Tourism Destinations (SMTD)

A tourism destination, viewed as a supply-side system, operates through interdependent stakeholders around a supply of numerous goods and services, which creates a need for coordination. An analogy is therefore possible between this supply-side system and a company. Is it possible to construct a strategic management approach to tourism destinations and if so how? The first defining feature is that the destination seen as a company includes a large number of specialist tourism stakeholders in both the private and public sectors. The second defining feature is that destinations seen as territories also involve a large number of other stakeholders, who are important for tourism activity in one way or another, sometimes unintentionally, for example with respect to the environment, landscapes, culture or local services (Marsat et al. 2009).

Tourism Destination Management (TDM) Models

Models have been proposed for Tourism Destination Management. We will use their strategic aspects. The Ritchie and Crouch model (2003) proposes a map of the components that make up a destination and the functions that the TDM must perform. These are divided between simple management (resource stewardship, marketing, organisation, etc.) and so-called 'political' functions, which we will suggest linking to the strategic aspect. These consist of defining the scope of the system, establishing a shared vision, defining a positioning and making strategic development choices and cooperation-competition decisions. For reasons explained further on we will also assume that some functions referred to by the authors above as 'operational' (resource stewardship, human resource development, etc.) are linked to a necessary strategic counterpart.

The major approaches of corporate strategy are explicitly used by Flagestad and Hope (2001), particularly 'positioning' and 'resources and competencies'. While noting that the latter are usually considered to be competing approaches, they suggest combining them, for example by using positioning to identify which resources are relevant. Also note that, for these authors, what structures the organisation of a destination is the interplay between forces oriented towards the satisfaction of residents and those oriented towards economic performance. Finally, they also believe that recognition of the multiple externalities within a destination must be incorporated, making it useful to draw on the 'stakeholder' approach (see specific section below).

A Focus on Resources and Competencies

The strategic Model of Resources and Competencies (MRC) asserts that the main performance factor for a company is the owning and operation of so-called 'core' resources and competencies, in other words those that are both useful and difficult to imitate or transfer by the competition (Barney 1991, Wernerfelt 1984). We will take two examples of issues being researched in the area that we are exploring for which this approach seems to be relevant.

1. The fragmentation of the supply-side system into a multitude of Very Small Enterprises (VSE) raises the question of the management of these VSEs' individual competencies and of their coordination viewed as a collective competency.
2. Our previous work on the relationships between tourism and environmental management led us into the field of desirable methods of coordination around collective or public goods, which are tourism resources (Marsat 2008). Being able to protect and develop these resources and make them accessible for tourism activity is strategic for destination management (Simao 2010).

The MRC approach has been used in tourism: Van der Yeught (2007) proposes a typology of resources as a tool for strategic analysis. MRC may also be a guiding light for tackling relationship issues within destinations: Sainaghi (2006) puts stakeholders into categories (the local tourism organisation, local government bodies and associations, and companies), and proposes a typology of the power relationships between them, depending on whether or not they control the resource on which they operate. Denicolai et al. (2010) believe that the coordination of stakeholders within a network stems from 'core competencies' within the destination.

The 'Stakeholder' Approach

Stakeholder Theory (ST) postulates the value of recognising stakeholder diversity, being able to analyse stakeholders and acting so as to deal with them according to the various priorities identified. Some of the priorities in question have no relation to economics and still less so to economic competition. This makes this approach particularly suitable for looking at the numerous relationships between tourism and local populations.

ST focuses on identifying and understanding stakeholders. Mitchell et al. (1997) use three attributes to assess the importance of a stakeholder. These are the 'power' and 'legitimacy'[1] of the stakeholder for the issue at hand, and the 'urgency' of the stakeholder's claim for the focal stakeholder.[2]

This approach is already used in the tourism field: tourism system models call on stakeholder pre-typologies, as established by Perdue (2004) based on the

---

1   They adopt the definition of legitimacy given by Suchman (1995: 574): 'a generalized perception or assumption that the actions of an entity are desirable, proper, or appropriate within some socially constructed system of norms, values, beliefs, and definitions'

2   The stakeholder who performs the analysis on its own behalf

service triangle (three groups of relevant stakeholders: consumers, interacting staff and residents). This is the angle from which Stokes (2008) looks at the two alternative models of tourism destinations: the market-oriented 'corporate' type (around a dominant company), and the stakeholder-oriented 'community' type. The contribution of Peters et al. (2011) combines the 'resource' and 'market' approaches in a stakeholder type analysis. The authors used cognitive maps to identify the existence of two clearly separate sets of representations depending on whether the respondent stakeholder was close to the market view or the resource view.

A Concise Presentation of the Territorial Aspect and the Regional Natural Parks

Both the MRC and ST approaches encourage a better understanding of 'host communities' and their relationships with tourism and tourists. Similarly, access to resources that are not controlled by tourism and the effects of tourism on local life are linked to issues of general interest. Tourism is therefore embedded in territories, but to varying degrees. The 'integrated tourism' model developed by the European research program SPRITE (2001–2004) explains this embeddedness according to seven dimensions (Oliver and Jenkins 2003): scale, endogeneity, sustainability, embeddedness, complementarity, networking and local control.

Territorial governance brings private (people, companies and associations) and public stakeholders into play, particularly local authorities (and their groupings). In France, the latter hold an important position in the tourism system in several respects. Legally, they determine the tourism policy for their territory and the provision of functions of public interest such as accommodation and visitor information. They may be seen as the managers of a common good, which is the territory's image. A large number of local authorities perform de facto tourism production functions directly, often following the failure of the private sector to do so. Their public regulation and policing functions play a significant role in the access of tourism stakeholders to resources, and the interferences between the various local activities. They are also the driving force behind territorial strategies and projects that add the quest for a global synergy to the previous points.

The Regional Natural Parks ('Parcs Naturels Régionaux', PNR) represent a particular form of public, local, territorial and sectoral public action. These are territories recognised for their rich and vulnerable heritage and for their sustainable development programs set out in a PNR Charter. PNRs are regional initiatives but the label is awarded by the French Ministry for the Environment. The structure that manages PNRs is a partnership bringing together the relevant municipalities, 'Départements' and Regions. These PNR organisations have their own strategies while undergoing remote monitoring in connection with their statutory remits. There are five remits, which notably include heritage protection and contributing to the economic and social development of the territory. They may all deal with or interfere with tourism, while operating within a territorial framework. Finally, the protection and development tasks may go hand in hand or be (viewed as) conflicting, which makes PNRs particularly worth analysing.

Method

Approach and Proposals

The issues tackled in this chapter are expressed by the following questions: does tourism destination management exist and if so in what forms and with what stakeholders? How do specialist tourism stakeholders (sector stakeholders) and territorial stakeholders interact? For example, what is the place and role of PNRs in tourism destination management? Based on an action-research approach, our contribution aims to construct an analysis tool for mapping the relevant strategic competencies in relation to the stakeholders central to these competencies, and to suggest interaction and consistency issues.

We have adopted a general inductive study approach based on case studies. Under this approach, the following working hypotheses will govern our observation and analysis:

- It is possible to compare the strategic management of organisations and what we refer to as the 'Strategic Management of Tourism Destinations' (SMTD).
- This SMTD may be broken down into major connected strategic functions (see below).
- This SMTD does not depend on a single manager. We see it as a form of 'distributed management' involving various 'key stakeholders' who have the legitimacy to participate and contribute different views.

Case Studies

The SMTD study was part of a research component of the MODINTOUR[3] program, a component dedicated to the organisation, governance and management of tourism.

The case studies were conducted following a comprehensive methodology (Yin 2003, David 2002). The empirical data were collected through face-to-face, open-ended, semi-structured interviews, as well as the mining of numerous documents, and lastly, participation in various public and private meetings (participant observation). The interviews were recorded, fully transcribed and then processed through a content analysis procedure (selecting of terms and counting of occurrences).

---

3 Interdisciplinary research program on 'tourism models', conducted from 2008 to 2011 in the Auvergne (France) region, as part of the national program known as PSDR.

Eleven destinations, located in the Auvergne region, formed the basis for the cases studied. The Auvergne region is in the centre of France, in a mainly mid-mountain region. The tourism activities practiced there are varied. The sampling took into account diversity criteria for the following aspects: tourism density, nature of the activities, location (across the whole of the Auvergne), size of the destination (from 10 to 150 municipalities) and territorial organisation (municipalities and their different forms of groupings: joint local communities ('communautés de communes') and public partnerships). The tourism resources ranged from natural heritage (lakes and rivers, forest, mountain) to cultural heritage (villages, monuments, music festival, terroir) and specific infrastructure (ski areas, spas, etc.).

Regarding the analysis of the PNRs' role in the SMTD, we based our observations on several studies. We took part in the European research programme SPRITE dedicated to 'integrated (rural) tourism'. The French fields of study of the programme were two PNRs (Cawley et al. 2007). We directly participated in the works of PNR teams leading strategic tourism projects on several scales: the defining of a tourism strategy for the whole of the French PNR network, the methodological development of the 'European Charter for Sustainable Tourism in Protected areas' (ECSTPA), the signing of this charter by the Livradois-Forez PNR and the Auvergne Volcano PNR and its implementation in both parks. All the above research fall within the scope of action-based research according to the expanded definition proposed by David (2002).

Interpretation Framework

We have produced an interpretation framework cross-tabulating the various cases:

- a list of types of stakeholders or groups of stakeholders (e.g. local authorities, tourism offices, service providers); and
- a list of strategic functions based on the literature review.

The cross-tabulation therefore shows who participates in distributed strategic management and through which functions. When necessary, we may also specify how stakeholders participate. Table 5.1 presents the substance of the framework.

Results

The analysis of the results of our observations and the scope of this chapter provide the following:

- a comparison between two types of stakeholders (territorial stakeholders; specialist tourism service stakeholders);

- the definition of a third type of stakeholder that combines a lot of the features of the first two, the 'Organisme Local de Tourisme'[4] (OLT); and
- and the systematic examination of the role of PNRs.

We chose four functions from the table to illustrate this point: strategic marketing, other resource (natural and cultural, not dedicated to tourism) management, general organisation, and competency management (human resources) functions.

Table 5.1   Distributed strategic management interpretation framework (simplified version)

Strategic school focused on functions	Strategic functions	Stakeholder i	Stakeholder j
All	Shared view, vision for the destination		
Positioning	Strategic marketing		
Resources, competencies	General organisation Management of competencies Management of other resources: • specific tourism assets • other resources: natural, cultural		
Stakeholders	Social embeddedness: the local population's claim		

Source: Author.

Strategic Marketing Function

This function consists of choosing and/or defining product/market couples, competitive positioning and marketing mix policies. In our research we chose a type of tourism destination comparable to a political and administrative territory. The tourism marketing looked at is therefore similar to territorial marketing, which is a multi-sector form of marketing where the territorial stakeholder is central.

The Local Authorities (LA) studied have little contact with tourism customers and their political and technical staff are not very well informed about this issue. The main input from LAs is an internal analysis of the territory's identity and its resources. However, the local population is recognised as one of the customer groups for local tourism, giving legitimacy to the role of elected representatives through their privileged relationship with the public. Another factor lending legitimacy to territorial stakeholders in terms of marketing is the assumed synergy

---

4   This is the legal name for what most commonly takes the form of a Tourism Office.

between tourism appeal and attracting new populations and companies (territorial marketing), as recalled by the regional tourism plan for the Auvergne.

Companies have their own marketing strategies. In our case studies, these are mostly Very Small Enterprises (VSE), which rarely formalise these strategies; they have little influence on the marketing of the destination. When they form part of a network, they play a more noticeable strategic role, particularly in terms of marketing. These local networks are often created with the goal of performing operational marketing functions. More broadly, several of them express the aim of contributing to tourism governance and its strategic processes. National networks (of companies or destinations) play an indirect role in this area, in proportion to the local response (partnerships, proposing of Charters, new brands).

Finally, the OLT is at the heart of the marketing function, firstly at an operational level, and potentially also at a strategic level. At the operational level, its tasks enhance knowledge of the market. It usually recruits staff with a marketing background and the degree of technical expertise required of them continues to increase. When a decision is made to define a marketing strategy, the OLT is, in most cases, responsible for managing the process.

Regarding the regulators, in the Auvergne region, the influence of the Region[5] and of the 'Comité Régional du Tourisme' (CRT, Regional Tourism Committee)[6] on marketing is strong. For example, they have decided to address a lack of accommodation in the medium-top end segment, with specific focuses (naturalness, presence of water, etc.); the 'Nattitude' policy therefore consisting in channelling regional assistance towards this 'rebalancing'. The regional strategy testifies to a strong concern for listening to markets and their operators. Marketing effectiveness is one of the two arguments that led to the regional policy of grouping together OLTs.

Without bringing it into conflict with 'demand marketing', which focuses on consumer expectations, PNRs are inspired by the identity of the supply: their objective is to promote 'sustainable tourism' and more precisely to find a positioning in activities and customer groups close to the natural and cultural heritage and open to the desired practices.

Within their jurisdiction, the PNR Charters are approved by the local authorities; the latter and the destinations linked to them are therefore committed to the Charters. This commitment covers principles, guidelines and some actions, but it is not exhaustive depending on local situations and activities: PNRs have little involvement in the marketing strategy of ski resorts, for example.

Aside from the recurring activity of their territory's specific promotion, the PNRs have more recently carried out work on marketing tools and channels: branding systems (including a 'park brand'), the Ecotourism website of the Massif Central's PNRs with an offering of hiking products, a national catalogue of stay packages (sold by the operator Smartbox) and a partnership planned by

5   Politico-administrative entity, local authority of European level NUTS II
6   The CRT is the regional equivalent of the OLT

the ECSTPA with willing tour operators (currently being finalised). Some of these initiatives are under development, others have had limited success or have been short lived. Finally, the Livradois-Forez PNR offers willing ECSTPA service providers marketing training focused both on knowledge of the markets and marketing channels and how to define and propose an identity-based offering.

Use of Resources Not Dedicated to Tourism, Shared with Other Activities

Tourism resources that are shared with other uses vary greatly, in both the natural and cultural fields. Being able to identify them as potential resources, evaluate them and use them as tourism assets, maintain them or even create them and manage them, are a competency that may be 'core' under the Model of Resources and Competencies (MRC).

By definition, these non-dedicated resources are shared and/or controlled by other stakeholders, who we will refer to as 'resource operators'. A direct relationship may be established between specialist tourism stakeholders and these resource operators. However, the latter may have no reason to be interested in tourism and there may be all kinds of conflicts of use or other forms of rivalry between their activities and tourism, as shown by Candau and Deuffic (2012) in the field of forestry. In this case the role of the regulator and/or territorial stakeholder, which has an inter-sector remit, comes into play.

Our observations showed that local authorities were effectively in the front line, in both operational and strategic terms. They manage pathways and traffic and participate in the management of water quality, environmental quality and landscapes and town planning. All of the cases of tourism destination strategies observed feature proactive projects to manage a given type of heritage with a tourism purpose; many large projects rely on a shared resource (a forest, a lake, an abbey or a railway). The resource operators in question vary greatly and have their own logic, even though they may be open to enhancing the value of these resources through tourism. Also note that the geography of the resource may be very different from the geography of tourism. The strategic priority of the relationship with all resource operators is to reassure them about the risks that they sometimes fear when it comes to tourism, to resolve antagonisms and to interest them in joint management.

The purpose of PNRs is to encourage and assist with the most effective possible management of heritage. They work on getting to know the environment (research, inventories, etc.). They support national protection policies and may assume their local management (agri-environmental measures, water development and management schemes, Natura 2000 management programs, and so on). They are resource operators. In their task of supporting economic development, they have promoted a large number of business niches based on the showcasing of natural or cultural local resources. In the tourism field they have a preference for nature-based tourism, in other words ecotourism. They foster the use of resources (creation of routes, cultural guides, etc.). This is how PNRs combine the management of heritage with its enhancement.

That said, the two tasks remain separate. 'Creating heritage for tourism development' is rarely considered. Although PNR staff are open to overlaps between tasks – this is a recruitment criterion – in practice, distances between teams are sometime observed. Finally, note that the theory of resources and competencies was developed within a very competitive view of development. Transposing this view to competition between territories would go against the fifth task of PNRs, which is to innovate and experiment to transfer their knowledge to other territories.

General Organisation and Structuring Function of the Tourism System

This involves ensuring a process of stabilised cooperation, which takes place through the creation of structures or through traditional cooperation. Organisation is a resource and organisational ability is a competency: both are potentially 'core'.

The general organisation function consists of several possible actions:

- creating groupings of Local Authorities (LA) themselves, depending on tourism activity, as has happened with the Massif du Sancy joint Local Authority;
- creating Tourism Offices,[7] as associations or public organisations and defining their optional tasks;
- creating specialist stakeholders for town planning or management (such as local private-private partnerships); and
- and/or organising tourism by agreements (particularly via public-service delegations).

Local Authorities are driving forces, at various levels (grouping together when necessary) depending on the geographical characteristics of the targeted tourism. The Regional (council) regulator has pushed for a structural concentration of OLTs and constantly intervenes in this function. Except in the case of one PNR (see below), the territories observed had no other stakeholder, whether companies, networks of companies or resource operators, able to influence this structuring.

A major outcome of this function is the (re)structuring of the 'Organismes Locaux de Tourisme' (OLT): these (most commonly Tourism Offices) are places for public/private cooperation and local/sectoral cooperation. One priority is to provide destination territories with OLTs that are appropriate in terms of the scale of tourism. An upscaling rationale is developing (Bieger et al. 2009) and one of the main objectives of regional policy is the merging of OLTs.

PNRs are themselves a grouping of local authorities. Their task does not usually include the general structuring of tourism (they may nevertheless be given

---

7   The common form of OLTs.

responsibility for tourism) but they may encourage and assist with structuring throughout the park or on the scale of more local destinations. For example, the Livradois-Forez PNR was behind the creation of an association between LAs, Tourism Offices and itself, on the scale of the whole PNR. This association is currently being transformed into a single large OLT that will include all or part of the existing Tourism Offices.

Organisation of Professionals and the Management of their Competencies

We will only deal here with the management of tourism professionals' competencies, through advisory and training actions. These actions may fall within several frameworks: individual advice and customised training, group actions within thematic networks or group actions within a local framework connected to a collective project (such as action-based training).

Considering all of the needs within a destination, designing responses and engineering and monitoring them constitute a strategic function. Once again, the destination-company analogy leads to considering all local stakeholders, regardless of their status, as belonging to the 'staff' of the destination. In the cases studied, this view is barely touched upon by the stakeholders. A customised training offering is available from chambers of commerce and the CRT. There are thematic networks on scales larger than destinations (hotel networks, Nattitude network in the Auvergne). The respondent stakeholders believed that this function falls within the remit of OLTs, which do not as yet provide it.

PNRs have set up various thematic networks, including the nationwide 'Gîte Panda' holiday residence label (in partnership with the WWF). They are creating a new, more diversified network through the implementation of the European Charter for Sustainable Tourism in Protected Areas (ECSTPA, designed by EUROPARC). In this developing network, willing service providers individually commit to an improvement plan covering the three aspects of sustainable development (economic, environmental and social) and benefit from oversight, advice and training organised by the PNR.

Nevertheless, within the PNRs, as well as outside them, no position has been taken on the organisation capable of fully performing this strategic function for a maximum number of service providers and for every identifiable need (local relationships, local collective actions, networking on various scales and training advice, engineering and monitoring).

Summary and Additions, Conclusion and Discussion

Starting from the assumption that distributed tourism destination management is possible, we analysed the presence of key stakeholders and their role using a typology of strategic functions. First of all, we must point out that the strategic functions that we pre-identified are not yet all performed as such by the stakeholders, particularly the management of non-dedicated resources, competencies or stakeholders.

Regarding the stakeholders, based on our observations, there may be debates, sometimes underlying, sometimes explicit, concerning the respective places of territorial vs. sectoral stakeholders, professional stakeholders and volunteers, elected representatives and technocrats, and entrepreneurs and institutions. Two criteria appear vital for all of these decisions: legitimacy and effectiveness. Although these criteria are not independent of each other, they should not be bunched together. They relate both to each type of stakeholder in a given role and to the organisational forms considered. Our observations and analyses, focused mainly on legitimacy issues, support the pluralist view of management systems. They are largely in keeping with the research by Peters et al. (2011) referred to above.

Strategic marketing is often seen as an inroad for strategic thought. It is a major area of influence for sectoral stakeholders, up to the OLTs, and technical support stakeholders (chambers of commerce and 'département' and regional tourism committees). Territorial stakeholders also have a presence, not only as a last resort for the global tourism strategy, but also sometimes in marketing based on the local offering or identity, or through the overlap between tourism marketing and territorial marketing.

The management of non-dedicated resources has been assessed as important for the destinations studied. Each is developing key projects bringing into play this type of resource and stakeholders who have little to do with tourism: resource operators. This function is often confused with the management of tourism-dedicated resources, the whole being viewed as town planning. Local authorities are at the centre of this function and one of the most important priorities is to ensure effective cooperation between resource operators, both local and external.

The organisation function has been included in our analysis given the multiplicity of legitimate stakeholders within the territorialised tourism system. The analysis is based mainly on the current strengthening in the Auvergne of a unifying player, the OLT, and its upscaling. The OLT is a prototype with an organisational as well as institutional purpose, and which is unifying in the sense that it integrates sector-based and territorial aspects. Other economic sectors, such as farming or forestry, do not have an organisation of this kind. It is the precursor to the central stakeholder in the strategic management of tourism destinations, either as a single manager stakeholder, or the coordinator of a distributed management system. This echoes the article by Haugland et al. (2011).

PNRs have a general competence for supporting development that authorises them to take action on every component of the tourism system. It is a 'task-oriented' type stakeholder that encourages, advises, drives and innovates. It may define a tourism strategy for its territory, formulated within the ECSTPA and the Park Charter. These strategies are not necessarily exhaustive: firstly, parks may decide to focus on certain types of tourism activities; secondly, there may be destinations that remain largely independent. More generally the Parks are very diverse: some are not very touristic while others are faced with mass tourism and the need to protect their heritage. These qualifications aside, we have illustrated some possible characteristics of the PNRs' strategic contribution to tourism: their territorial nature, which brings various forms of legitimacy and concern for stakeholders, their heritage task, which is reflected in the management of non-dedicated resources and the identity-based component of marketing decisions and a possible contribution to development for some sectors.

The principle behind our interpretation framework is to cross-tabulate functions and stakeholders. Other authors have also adopted this type of systematic interpretation, particularly March and Wilkinson (2009) who produced a 'partnership/activities matrix'; however, the functions that they study are less synthetic and strategic. The interpretation framework is only a sketch of a model that gives managerial status to major functions pre-identified by theoretical sources in management. It allows both researchers and stakeholders (tool for reflexivity and self-analysis) to ask questions about 1) the functions not performed within a given territory, 2) the coherence or lack of coherence between functions, 3) the interplay of stakeholders with different rationales. The framework, illustrated by the cross-tabulation of cases, may therefore play an educational role, a heuristic role or a role in helping to formulate priorities and construct shared representations. It may therefore help with the designing of collective actions and public policies.

In terms of discussion, note that this chapter and the study have certain limitations. The chapter focuses on certain functions to look at the crossover between sectoral and territorial aspects and is not intended as a complete model of a management system and its stakeholders. The framework may easily be extended, however, for example by adding the strategic management of production (technological choices, R&D, quality, etc.). The study also concerns an overall model that lacks information about the relationships between components: there is still a lot of work to be done to make progress on the consistencies between strategic functions within a single overall tourism destination strategy, and on the interplay between stakeholders with different rationales. However, this modelling encourages the use of various corpora that are already available, for example those relating to so-called political strategic management approaches (Mintzberg et al. 1998, Martinet 1984).

Regarding the PNRs, the earlier observation concerning one of their paradoxes (they operate in competitive environments while being demonstration territories) illustrates the precautionary efforts needed to adapt company strategy theories to territories. The study of PNRs shows the originality of this institutional construction and its strategic freedoms as partially independent organisations. It should continue to explore the challenges confronting these organisations and to evaluate the solutions implemented, given the scope of their difficult task of embodying sustainable development principles.

References

Barney, J. 1991. Firm resources and sustained competitive advantage. *Journal of Management*, 17(1), 99–120.

Bieger, T., Beritelli, P. and Laesser, C. 2009. Size matters! Increasing DMO effectiveness and extending tourism destination boundaries. *Tourism Review*, 57(3), 309–27.

Candau, J., Deuffic, P. 2012. De la légitimité des usages récréatifs à l'organisation d'un service d'accueil en forêt, in *L'Ouverture des Forêts au Public. Un Service Récréatif*, edited by J. Dehez. Paris: Quae, 67–92.

Cawley, M., Marsat, J.-B. and Gillmor, D.A. 2007. Promoting integrated rural tourism: comparative perspectives on institutional networking in France and Ireland. *Tourism Geographies*, 9(4), 405–20.

David, A. 2002. *Intervention Methodologies in Management Research*. Euram Conference, Stockholm.

Denicolai, S., Cioccarelli, G. and Zucchella, A. 2010. Resource-based local development and networked core-competencies for tourism excellence. *Tourism Management*, 31, 260–66.

Flagestad, A. and Hope, C.A. 2001. Strategic success in winter sports destinations: a sustainable value creation perspective. *Tourism Management*, 22(5), 445–61.

Freeman, R.E. 1984. *Strategic Management: a Stakeholder Approach*. Boston: Pitman.

Haugland, S.A., Ness, H., Gronseth, B.-O. and Aarstad, J. 2011. Developement of tourism destinations – An integrated multilevel perspective. *Annals of Tourism Research*, 38(1), 268–90.

March, R. and Wilkinson, I. 2009. Conceptual tools for evaluating tourism partnerships. *Tourism Management*, 30, 455–62.

Marsat, J.-B. 2008. *Alliance Strategies Environment-Tourism*. Environnement – Management science. Paris, AgroParisTech-Engref PhD (summary): 35. Available at: http://cemadoc.irstea.fr/cemoa/PUB00036795.

Marsat, J.-B., Brault, S., Dazet, B. and Lacroix, C. 2009. Le management territorialisé du tourisme – Des enseignements à partir du programme Porta Natura, in *Destinations et Territoires*, edited by J.-P. Lemasson and P. Violier. Montréal-Québec: UQAM – ESG – TEOROS, 1, 168–77.

Martinet, A.-C. 1984. *Management Stratégique: Organisation et Politique*. Paris: EDISCIENCE.

Mintzberg, H., Ahlstrand, B. and Lampel, J. 1998. *Safari Strategy: a Guided Tour Through the Wilds of Strategic Management*. New York: Free Press.

Mitchell, R.K., Agle, B.R. and Wood, D.J. 1997. Toward a theory of stakeholder identification and salience: defining the principle of who and what really counts. *Academy of Management Review*, 22(4), 853–86.

Oliver, T. and Jenkins, T. 2003. Sustaining rural landscapes: the role of integrated tourism. *Landscape Research*, 28(3): 293–307.

Perdue, R.R. 2004. Sustainable tourism and stakeholder groups: a case study of Colorado ski resort communities. *Consumer Psychology of Tourism, Hospitality and Leisure*, 3, 253–64.

Peters, M., Siller, L. and Matzler, K. 2011. The resource-based and the market-based approaches to cultural tourism in alpine destinations. *Journal of Sustainable Tourism*, 19(7), 877–93.

Porter, M.E. 1980. Industry structure and competitive strategy: keys to profitability. *Financial Analysts Journal*, 36(4): 30–41.

Ritchie, J.R.B. and Crouch, G.I. 2003. *The Competitive Destination: a Sustainable Tourism Perspective*. CABI Publishing.

Sainaghi, R. 2006. From content to processes: versus a dynamic destination management model. *Tourism Management*, 27(5), 1053–63.

Simao, J. 2010. *An Extended VRIO Model as a Framework for Sustainable Tourism Planning*. 4th international conference on sustainable tourism, Ashurst New Forest.

Stokes, R. 2008. Tourism strategy making: insights to the events tourism domain. *Tourism Management*, 29, 252–62.

Suchman, M.C. 1995. Managing legitimacy: strategic and institutional approaches. *Academy of Management Review*, 20, 571–610.

Van der Yeught, C. 2007. *La Resource Based View et le Développement Durable au Service de l'Analyse Stratégique: une Application aux Destinations Touristiques*. XVIème Conférence Internationale de Management Stratégique, AIMS, Montréal.

Wernerfelt, B. 1984. A resource-based view of the firm. *Strategic Management Journal*, 5, 171–80.

Yin, R.K. 2003. *Case Study Research: Design and methods*. Thousand Oaks: Sage.

Chapter 6

Mountain Tourism Development between the Political and Administrative Context and Local Governance: A French-Swiss Comparison

Christophe Clivaz and Emmanuelle George-Marcelpoil

Introduction

The tourism economy, driven by winter ski resorts, is important for Alpine regions. After the Second World War, ski resorts were seen as an economic development opportunity for areas that were often becoming marginalised. After a period of strong expansion, with increasing numbers of resorts and visitors, many factors for change are casting doubt on the future of these ski resorts, and particularly their capacity to innovate and adapt. For instance, in recent years, ski resorts have been directly affected by bullish land and leisure accommodation trends (both in terms of prices and consumption) with, on an economic level, an erosion of commercial tourist beds and, on a social level, housing issues for some more vulnerable populations, both seasonal and local. At the same time, investments in tourism infrastructure, from ski lifts to artificial snow, are differentiating ski resorts according to their financial resources. Mountain resorts have also been called into question as to the sustainability of their development and particularly their ability to adapt to climate change. Finally, they must deal with an increasingly competitive and globalised tourism market characterised by the emergence of new destinations and the widespread use of information and communication technologies in tourism promotion.

Against this backdrop, this chapter first of all looks at the diversity of organisation models of ski resorts in France and Switzerland while putting them in the institutional contexts of the two countries. We have chosen the ideal-typical distinction between the corporate model and the community model proposed by Flagestad and Hope (2001) out of the various possible interpretation frameworks (Svensson et al. 2006, Conti and Perelli 2007, Gill and Williams 2011). Very concisely, the community model is characterised by the presence of many tourism service providers, the lack of a predominant stakeholder and large involvement by the public authorities, while, conversely, the corporate model covers a situation where the public stakeholder has a limited presence and a single private operator dominates, who particularly controls the operation of the ski area and a large share of the commercial accommodation. The chapter then looks at the ability of the existing organisation models to meet the challenges posed by the future of leisure accommodation. The focus on this factor for change is due to the expertise of the two authors in these areas and the impossibility of addressing them all in a single chapter. Finally, we end with a comparison of the French and Swiss situations in terms of ski resort governance and the handling of the accommodation issue, which reveals areas of convergence as well as divergence between the two countries.

Methodologically, the sources and data used come from the publications, studies, contracts and commissions that the two authors have completed over 20 years and from documents published by public authorities.

Similarities in the Organisation Models despite Different Political and Administrative Contexts

Here we retrace the historical evolution of mountain tourism development, highlighting the different institutional arrangements in France and Switzerland and their influence on the governance structure of ski resorts.

In Switzerland: Limited Planning of Mountain Tourism Development and Fragmented Governance

As the favourite playground of the British and then European aristocracy, Switzerland is considered to be the birthplace of Alpine tourism. However, until the start of the twentieth century, mountain regions drew visitors especially during the summer and the idea of also holidaying in the Alps in the winter only gradually took hold. While the summer season still clearly dominated in terms of visitor numbers until the Second World War, the situation changed quickly with the democratisation of skiing. The mountains were then 'stormed' and ski resorts sprang up in the 1960s and 1970s.

Unlike in France with its 'Plan Neige' (Snow Plan, see below), mountain development in Switzerland has not been subject to a global thought process by the central State, or by the relevant cantons. Although planning was significantly absent from the development of winter sports in Switzerland, this does not mean that no thought was given to the issue by the public authorities. For instance, there are various studies relating to the planning of ski areas or better coordination of tourism activities in general, such as, at national level, the Swiss Conception of tourism adopted by the Swiss government in 1981. However, these thought processes are less about looking ahead to future development than a reaction to development considered to be too fast and anarchic. They have also usually not been followed up in the field, except for the federal policy on authorisation for new ski resorts, which became more restrictive as from 1978 (Clivaz 2001). Tourism development therefore largely results from individual private initiatives, supported by the local authorities. This means that winter sports resorts have sprung up as opportunities have arisen and according to the ability of local stakeholders to muster the financing and expertise for the creation and then expansion of ski resorts and accommodation units. These days, to take up the ideal-typical distinction between the corporate model and the community model proposed by Flagestad and Hope (2001), Swiss resorts clearly appear to be in keeping with the community model. Note however, a trend of evolving towards a more corporate model. Firstly, the number of stakeholders in resorts is falling due to the merging of certain private companies or associations active in the same sector. This is what happened, for example, at Crans-Montana at the turn of the millennium, when the resort's three tourism offices merged. The five ski lift companies and the two hotel associations were similarly merged (Clivaz 2006). Secondly, in some resorts we are seeing the institutionalisation of cooperation between some key stakeholders. This is the case at Nendaz, where a public limited company (Nendaz Tourisme SA) groups together the commune, the development company, the ski lift company and the association of craftsmen and merchants. The purpose of this company is to promote tourism, particularly through advertising or promotional initiatives or the organisation of events. At Flims-Laax (Grisons), the Weisse Arena group presents itself as an integrated service company in the tourism field. It combines a ski lift company, hotels and restaurants, sports shops, and a skiing and snowboarding school. These examples remain exceptions, however, and the great majority of resorts are clearly close to the community model.

The division of tourism tasks between public and private stakeholders may, however, vary depending on the commune. There are situations where the municipal authority is very actively involved in the management of tourism affairs and others where it merely ensures basic framework conditions, leaving private and association stakeholders to direct the tourism strategy. Generally speaking, this second case predominates: the commune delegates responsibility for tourism to the tourism office while funding a large share of its budget. The weight of this public financing explains the strong presence of political representatives in the decision-making bodies of tourism offices. We also see the same scenario in the case of ski lift companies. The latter are organised as public limited companies, but a large or even majority share of the share capital is publicly owned. Therefore we are seeing a 'politicisation' of decision-making bodies that are vital for the resort's efficient operation. This politicisation is currently increasingly questioned by private stakeholders, who would like tourism decisions to be less subject to the electoral considerations of elected representatives and focused more on customer and market expectations.

In Switzerland, the modest role played by the national State and even by the cantons in planning mountain tourism development must be placed in the context of federalism. Competences are divided between the three levels (national, cantons and municipal) in accordance with the principle of subsidiarity. In the tourism sector, one can even speak of double subsidiarity (Tobler 1981): 1) competences remain at the level closest to the field (municipal level) as long as this level is able to satisfactorily resolve the collective problem that required public intervention; 2) the Confederation's intervention is also limited in the tourism field because tourism is considered to be an activity essentially within the remit of the private sector.

With the Confederation's hands-off approach to the public management of tourism in general and mountain tourism development in particular, it is the cantons and communes that are more involved, but always in support of private initiative. Almost all the cantons have now adopted laws on tourism with the aim of supporting economic development through tourism activity, particularly with a view to helping 'peripheral' areas. These laws mainly draw on various taxes aimed at releasing financial resources for the promotion, organisation and construction of tourism infrastructure. Canton-level tourism policies are therefore largely financed by the beneficiaries themselves (tourism service providers who pay the taxes) and public authorities commit only relatively modest financial resources compared to the neighbouring Alpine countries. Above all, these policies provide subsidiary assistance to the private sector and are not designed to plan tourism development. As for the communes, these have greater leeway in the management of the tourism sector. However, until now, most of them have not produced reference documents clarifying the targets and resources of a municipal tourism development policy. This almost universal absence of a forward-looking vision has been replaced by ad hoc management as development progresses according to opportunities and the interests of private investors.

In France: Planning of Mountain Tourism Development but Fragmented Governance

Like most Alpine regions, mountain tourism development in France took off at the turn of the twentieth century. Until then, the mountains had been considered as landlocked, dangerous or exclusively reserved for agricultural and pastoral activity. The first tourism initiatives therefore appeared mainly in places where there was summer tourism. The emblematic example is Chamonix, which was the British aristocracy's top spot for Alpine tourism, but saw the introduction of winter activity based on Alpine skiing. This was also the case in other mountain ranges, where initiatives originated with private stakeholders, who provided the capital and/or the property assets, as well as local authorities, which believed in this new form of economic development. For example, Val d'Isère was built in the 1930s at 1800 metres of altitude from private investments (particularly those of J. Mouflier, a Parisian investor) that were later taken up by the Val d'Isère municipality.

However, these first examples of resort-villages remained limited and were part of a political and economic environment where mountain regions in France were still considered to be peripheral. It wasn't until the 1940s and the advent of paid holidays in 1936 that the State, under the leadership of the Vichy government, turned its attention to the mountains and their tourism development, by identifying sites with the potential to become resorts in the mountain ranges. The objective was to create a national tourism sector to compete with other European destinations, such as Austria or Switzerland.

It was in 1946 that the Savoie 'département' took up the pre-war analysis concerning the development of a snow sector and created a resort, Courchevel, on a virgin site in the commune of Saint-Bon-Tarentaise (François and Marcelpoil 2012). The 1960s then saw the devising and implementation of a strong mountain tourism development policy. During the post-war boom years, tourism seemed to be a good route towards development and modernity for the rural world and mountain regions in particular (Chevallier 1996). The State became involved particularly through the order of 1958, which allowed local authorities to reserve land in the name of the general interest and in this case for tourism purposes. This was the period of the 'Plan Neige' (Snow Plan) in France, associated with the emergence of an entire fleet of resorts created from scratch on sites free of any urbanisation. These were integrated resorts close to the corporate model, where the planning of the resort is taken care of by a single developer. Les Arcs and La Plagne were built from this model in the Tarentaise valley, and the image of the large corporation proved to be predominant. Local authorities made a considerable contribution to this tourism development by providing land and financial loans in close collaboration with economic stakeholders. These resorts, built on virgin sites, made it possible to implement the development principles invented and developed in Courchevel, focused on skiing and the most rational spatial organisation possible.

This expansion phase lasted until the 1980s, when the first difficulties appeared for the winter sports economy (slump in property sales, slowdown of visitors, economic problems of the local authorities (Lorit et al. 1990), succession of winters without snow, and so on), which justified the emergence of smaller resorts in terms of ski area and accommodation, at lower altitudes, such as Valmorel. Above all, the local authorities became determined to regain a certain control over their production platform. More generally, note the enactment of the 'Loi Montagne' (Mountain law) in 1985, which established the specific nature of mountain regions, following the Decentralisation laws of 1982–83. It was a real revolution for local authorities and their role in spatial planning. Regarding the resorts, this law, through its founding article 42,[1] enshrined the role of local authorities in the management of the tourism platform, with responsibility for choosing between direct management through public corporations or delegating management to private operators.[2] Today, in the Alps, 57 per cent of ski areas are managed by

---

1 Law No. 85–30 of 9 January 1985 relating to the development and protection of mountains whose article 42 specifies that 'The ski lift service is organised by the communes within the region in which they are located or by groupings of communes or by the département, to which they may entrust, by agreement, within the limits of a defined geographic scope, the organisation and implementation of the service'.

2 This national situation is the result of the legal classification of ski lifts as a public transport service allowing the delegation of their management.

private operators and/or public-private partnerships, confirming the strength of the Public Service Delegation as a management tool (Marcelpoil et al. 2012).

Nevertheless, the other service provider activities, such as accommodation, sports, cultural and promotional activities, are shared between a number of stakeholders, which of course include the tourism office, but also, and above all, a variety of economic stakeholders who often have independent status and are small in size (Gerbaux and Marcelpoil 2006). This means that some French resorts are differentiated both by the historical weight of the ski lift operator and a fragmentation of economic stakeholders. Thus, the two models – community and corporate – are being followed in France, with regions where the corporate model has greater weight, as in the Tarentaise valley, where the 'Plan Neige' and integrated resorts were born, and other mountain ranges, like the Pyrenees, where the local authorities have retained an undeniable role in tourism development.

Currently, we are seeing a dual trend in French resorts. On the one hand, the concentration of the ski lift sector has left few operators, of which the Compagnie des Alpes is the most well-known and the largest. These operators are focusing their efforts on the most promising sites in terms of financial profitability. On the other hand, local authorities are tending to recover the control and management of their production platform, either because of economic problems, such as following the bankruptcy of Groupe Transmontagne (a bankruptcy that has occasionally left ski areas and also tourism residences without a manager, as in Chamrousse or in Praloup in the Alps) or for political reasons. Aside from these two key stakeholders that are the local authority and the ski lift operator, the stakeholder system is complex. On one hand, there are the economic stakeholders who are often reluctant to get involved beyond their strict individual logic, and on the other hand, the civil society that intends to play a real role in the resort and its future. In particular, permanent residents highlight their contribution to the municipal budget and their involvement throughout the year. The mayor's stance is often a balancing act between tourism goals, which are the economic driver of the region, and the expectations in terms of general interest of year-long residents. This management of the destination, which must reconcile different rationales, is based on the relationship between the formal and informal, and between tacit codes and relationships within the local tourism history and culture.

The management of French resorts and their diversity also fits within the more global politico-administrative context, applied to the tourism sector. Thus, it is continuing to implement the Decentralisation of 1982–83, which is now in its 3rd act, enshrining the weight of metropolitan areas as sources of competitiveness. In this context, at national level, the State is mainly focused on the promotion of France abroad, through a 'Groupement d'Intérêt Economique' (GIE, Economic Interest Group), Atout France.

Resort tourism is above all addressed at sub-national, local levels, with an increasing weight given to the regions in the last few decades. Accordingly, mountain tourism assistance policies, mainly targeting mid-mountain resorts, which are considered to be the most vulnerable, fall under project contracts between the State and the region. For instance, the Rhone-Alpine resorts of the Alpine mountain range are covered by a dedicated policy, through medium-sized resort contract schemes over the 2000–2006 period and sustainable resort contract schemes over the 2006–2013 period. These measures were designed to improve the management of resorts, a goal that is driven by a vision of the resort operating as a company. However, they also tried to assist resorts, firstly towards tourism diversification in response to weather events, now known as climate change and, secondly, towards a regional project that goes beyond the resort alone. These goals of the regional schemes dovetail with the positions defended by the State through the 'Schéma de Massif' (mountain range plan) and 'départements', which adopt their own policy. In practice, the local authorities hosting resorts sponsor a contract, with financing provided by the local authorities, mountain range, region and 'département' collectively and the local authority itself. This co-financing principle is intended to promote partnership in a development project sponsored by the resort and its supporting local authority.

The Governance of the Resorts Faced with the Challenge of Leisure Accommodation

Both in France and in Switzerland, the resort governance processes are particularly called into question by the issue of leisure accommodation, which is a real cornerstone of the winter sports economy.

Leisure Accommodation in France: A Factor in the Economic Model's Sustainability

Nowadays resorts are very much up against the challenge of filling accommodation units. Indeed, it may be noted in France, firstly that the inventory of tourist beds is very approximate, and secondly that there are doubts about their commercial occupation (Marcelpoil et al. 2007, Fablet and George-Marcelpoil 2013). This phenomenon is particularly observed for resorts created from the 'Plan Neige', where most of the assets were sold into co-ownership. Given these factors, this type of tourist bed is no longer very suited to tourism demand, as the floor areas are often too small. Many studies are therefore attempting to identify the accommodation capacity of resorts, but the most important issue remains the inventory of so-called individual beds, which are individual because they are not commercial and also because they are scattered throughout the resort. These individual beds need to be put back onto the market and the French legislature has tried to drive a process of rehabilitating this leisure accommodation with the 'Solidarité et Renouvellement Urbains' (SRU, Urban Solidarity and Renewal) law of 2000, through 'Opération de Réhabilitation de l'Immobilier de Loisir'[3] (ORIL, Leisure Accommodation Rehabilitation Operation) schemes. Through the ORILs, rehabilitation tax incentives are given to owners subject to a 9-year lease for the rental of their property through an agency or management structure, often in the 'Société d'Economie Mixte' (SEM, public-private partnerships) category. This laudable initiative has had limited success, however, particularly in terms of accommodation actually renovated and returned to the rental market, but also because of the complexity of the management procedures.

The focus for the past few years has been more to initiate regional approaches designed to enhance the place of co-owners in the creation and operation of resorts. Through clubs, advantages and owners' associations, resorts aim to involve second homeowners and so encourage them to put their property back up for rent.

Recently, in April 2013, Foncière rénovation Montagne was launched sponsored by Compagnie des Alpes and Caisse des Dépôts et Consignations, in conjunction with four local property companies in Les Arcs, La Plagne, Les Menuires and Les Ecrins.

> Within this framework, local property companies will purchase apartments, in blocks or individually, with a view to renovating them and putting them back on the tourism rental market. After a 4–5 year period, these apartments should be sold, the income from the sale being reinvested in new purchases.[4]

The principle is the same as that defended by the ORILs but with an economic stakeholder with large financial resources providing support. The goal of selling within 4–5 years is part of an upscaling of the renovated apartments and therefore of the associated destination, and requires that the destination in question retains its appeal.

Nonetheless, most resorts are now experiencing an unprecedented property programme momentum (Fablet and George-Marcelpoil 2013), despite the 1977 'Directive d'Aménagement de la Montagne' (Mountain Development Directive) that introduced 'Unités Touristiques Nouvelles' (UTN, New Tourism Units), a prerequisite for any new tourism project, and the Mountain law of 1985, intended to govern development in mountain regions. Within the Tarentaise valley alone, which is home to the largest, internationally renowned resorts, 40 per cent of the net floor area was built after 1985, when the Mountain law was introduced (Fablet and George-Marcelpoil 2013). In practice, in recent years tourism residences have seen considerable expansion, regardless of the type of destination. These

---

3   The ORILs were created by Law No. 2000–1208 of 13 December 2000 and are described in article L318–5 of the French urban planning code, the purpose of which is 'the improvement of tourism property assets and the improvement of public spaces, parking, infrastructure facilities and the treatment of the environment'.

4   Press release on the creation of Foncière rénovation Montagne published by Compagnie des Alpes and Caisse des Dépôts et Consignations.

tourism residences, which are often 3-star and synonymous with an upscaling of customers (Marcelpoil et al. 2010), meet tourism demand, with accommodation that is adequate in its floor area and the presence of associated services. They result in 9 to 12 year leases, but after the initial lease period, which is associated with tax breaks in France, tourist beds tend to pass back into the individual sector.

The local authorities, which are responsible for managing their land through 'Plans Locaux d'Urbanisme' (PLU, Local Urban Planning Plans), therefore aim to create leeway in their accommodation assets. In particular, aside from tourism residences, their goal is often to allocate part of their available land with urbanisation potential to the hotel industry, which entails a final use guarantee problem. Indeed, besides the difficulty in finding hotel chains that wish to invest in mountain regions given the strong seasonality constraint, hotels may often be sold on in lots, after a more or less lengthy operating period, contributing to the reduction of the total number of commercial beds.

In addition to the PLUs, land schemes are part of the French legislature's intention to encourage the rollout of SCOTs ('Schéma de Cohérence Territoriale' (Territorial Cohesion Schemes)), introducing planning on a wider scale than the resort alone. The purpose of this tool is to plan developments, particularly tourism-related ones, over a broader scope than one resort, theoretically requiring communes and the associated destinations to carry out at least some collective thought. That said, the SCOT processes are still not very developed in mountain regions and show the difficulty of playing on complementarities in a tourism economy that is still highly competitive.

For mid-mountain resorts, the issue has an additional aspect. Indeed, these sites are admittedly affected by the individual bed phenomenon, but are above all confronted by the process of sub-urbanisation, with new modes of residence. We are therefore seeing a conversion of tourist beds into permanent beds for sites close to dynamic urban centres, as in the 'Sillon Alpin' (Alpine valley) with the towns of Grenoble, Chambéry and Annecy (Marcelpoil et al. 2007). This is combined with the development of day tripping, which results in a reduction in overnight tourism and therefore a change in the customer base and in the business model for ski lift operators.

Swiss Resorts Look for a New Business Model

The fast development of skiing in Switzerland was accompanied by a significant shift in the accommodation structure. The hotel industry, which still largely dominated in the middle of the twentieth century, lost ground in relative terms compared to the commercial operation of apartments and above all second homes, which became the predominant accommodation model in most winter sports resorts. This change proved beneficial in terms of jobs and revenues in the property development and construction sector. However, it threatened the sales of tourism service providers due to the extremely low occupancy rates of second homes. When it comes to leisure accommodation, Swiss resorts are therefore faced with a series of difficulties (Clivaz 2007), such as a reduction in the number of commercial beds (particularly the conversion of hotels into holiday apartments), the ageing of existing hotels, and the difficulty of finding financing for the construction of new commercial beds or the renovation of existing beds. Although it is still considered to have strong tourism potential according to the World Economic Forum's classification (Blanke and Chiesa 2013), Switzerland also suffers from much higher costs for the construction and operation of commercial accommodation structures than its Alpine neighbours, which makes the profitability of investments in commercial resort accommodation very risky.

Given this context, some tourist communes have gradually taken a series of measures (such as setting a contingent of second homes or a quota of primary residences) since the 1980s so as to more or less strictly slow down the increase in the number of second homes and to ensure the provision of housing to the local population at reasonable prices. These measures have mainly been introduced in German-speaking communes, as the French-speaking communes were slower to become aware of the problems associated with an excessively large share of second homes in the accommodation structure. In line with the principle of subsidiarity referred to previously, both the Confederation and the cantons gave communes free latitude over how they intended (or did not intend) to deal with the problem. This bottom-up approach had the following two effects, however (Clivaz and Nahrath 2010: 24):

(1) The putting in place of such instruments, which results from a local decision-making process, depends on the cooperation, respectively the weakening in the position, of property owners and the players in the property sector within the local space planning policy (…);

(2) As these relationships of cooperation and conflict between the different players (…) vary greatly between the different communes, one can thus observe large differences between resorts (including within the same canton) with regard to the use (the ability to use) of these instruments and therefore the ability to regulate problems relating to the proliferation of secondary residences and the urban sprawl of the resorts.

The gradual 'return of the State' from the 2000s, first at the level of some cantons and then at Confederation level, must be understood in this context. One of the aims of the Valais canton in its tourism policy published in 2003 is therefore to limit the number of second homes and promote forms of high added value accommodation (hotels, rented holiday apartments). The Confederation, for its part, publishes various documents designed to help the cantons manage the problem of second homes through their regional development policy.

While both the Confederation and the cantons advocate action by the communes, actual implementation greatly depends on the local power setup. We have already noted the considerable autonomy enjoyed by communes in the

Swiss federal system. The result is a large divergence between the stance of public stakeholders, who favour limiting the number of second homes, and the reality of resorts where, excluding a few exceptions, we are seeing a continuing expansion of second homes. This is one of the factors that may explain the success of the initiative of the ecologist Franz Weber 'To bring an end to the invasive construction of second homes' on 11 March 2012. On this day, the Swiss population narrowly (50.6 per cent of voters) agreed to this initiative, which prohibits the construction of any new second homes in communes where the percentage of these residences exceeds 20 per cent of total accommodation. With the accepting of this initiative, the Confederation now has strong powers in the handling of the second home problem. As for local stakeholders, their business model based on second homes has been brought to a halt.

Given this context of the redistribution of competences between the different levels of Swiss federalism, the fragmentation of local governance complicates the ability of resorts to develop a new business model based on commercial accommodation. The latter, which until now have fiercely defended their autonomy, are now looking for greater support from the canton and the Confederation. In a way, we are seeing a change in the application of the principle of double subsidiarity within the tourism sector, with a weakening of municipal competences compared to canton- and federal-level competences and the increasing weight of the public stakeholder compared to that of the private stakeholder.

Putting the French and Swiss Situations into Perspective

A comparison of the governance models applied to resorts in France and Switzerland and the way in which they have tackled the issue of leisure accommodation provides the following lessons.

Regarding the resort organisation model, the place on the corporate-community continuum varies more in France, while in Switzerland the community model clearly predominates. This is due to the absence in this country, with rare exceptions, of large corporations active in tourist accommodation or ski lifts. However, what more clearly sets France apart from Switzerland is the role played by public stakeholders, and particularly the central State, in the development of mountain regions. While the central State has intervened more widely in France by planning and implementing major ski area development programs, it intervenes more marginally in Switzerland, leaving the initiative for tourism development to the private sector. Moreover, communes in France have less leeway due to higher level regulatory measures, despite the transfer of powers brought by the Decentralisation laws and the Mountain law. By comparison, Swiss communes benefit from greater latitude in the way in which they intend to manage their tourism development, although this has now been reduced by acceptance of the Weber initiative.

Regarding leisure accommodation, Switzerland and France share the same problem of filling second homes, which have formed a large share of the tourist beds in the process of resort creation and development. In Switzerland, as in France, local authorities have historically had strong control over land, which is now being challenged. In France, the recent controversies surrounding both the adoption of a 'Directive Territoriale d'Aménagement' (Regional Planning Directive) covering the Northern Alps and the drawing up of a development charter for the 'Parc National de la Vanoise' (Vanoise National Park) clearly show the wish of the local authorities to retain as much leeway as possible. As for the Weber initiative, its acceptance has radically changed the state of affairs in Switzerland by drastically reducing the prerogatives of communes and requiring local stakeholders to find a new business model based on commercial accommodation. It perfectly illustrates the weight that an institutional rule like the right of initiative can have on the management of resort tourism.

A comparison between France and Switzerland also shows that tourists and owners of second homes (for the latter at least in Switzerland) are kept out of resort decision-making processes. While it is difficult to get the first to participate, and their right to participate in policy decisions may, moreover, be questioned, the integration of the second within the local governance system now seems necessary if the occupancy rate of second homes is to be improved. Both French and Swiss regulations do not make it possible to force owners to put their second home up for rent by tourists. Finally, the issue of leisure accommodation and more generally that of the tourism supply and promotion raise the question, in both France and Switzerland, of what is the 'right' level of governance to manage tourism regions (Clivaz and Nahrath 2010). In an increasingly competitive and globalised tourism market, the municipal level seems ever more inadequate for defining a tourism product that meets the current expectations of customers and so ensuring the sustainability of resorts.

In this respect, it might be assumed that (tourism) globalisation is helping the French and Swiss institutional systems to converge. France, which was originally very centralised, is showing a gradual shift towards the decentralisation of tourism powers, hesitating between several regional levels. The Swiss system, which was initially highly decentralised, is conversely moving towards greater power for national bodies. The question of the 'right' governance level is therefore being answered in both countries as an intermediate level between local and national, as shown in France by contractual tourism policies or SCOTs governing planning, or in Switzerland by the growing trend for cantons to make the granting of financial assistance dependent upon the drawing up of supra-municipal tourism development plans. This trend of convergence between France and Switzerland can also be seen in resort governance models despite the differences highlighted previously. On the one hand, both private operators and local authorities supporting public policies aspire in both countries to economically effective resorts, thus preferring the corporate model. On the other hand, local elected representatives, particularly under pressure from permanent residents, are trying to take back control of tourism development in their commune, compared to private operators who have traditionally been in a stronger position.

This assumption of growing convergence between France and Switzerland, both in terms of resort organisation models (shift towards a more corporate model, return of local elected representatives) and the gradual anchoring of tourism planning power at a 'meso' level (between local and national), have yet to be confirmed by additional research. It would also be worthwhile to analyse the trend in other countries, particularly Alpine ones, to see to what extent this convergence phenomenon exists.

References

Blanke, J. and Chiesa, T. (eds.). 2013. *The Travel & Tourism Competitiveness Report 2013*. Geneva: World Economic Forum.

Chevallier, M. 1996. An expression of modernity: for a new cultural interpretation of the modern winter resort. *Journal of Alpine Research*, 84(3), 29–39.

Clivaz, C. 2001. *Influence des Réseaux d'Action Publique sur le Changement Politique. Le Cas de l'Ecologisation du Tourisme Alpin en Suisse et dans le Canton du Valais*. Bâle: Helbing & Lichtenhahn.

—. 2006. Crans-Montana-Aminona (Switzerland): is there anyone in charge of the resort? *Journal of Alpine Research*, 94(1), 84–94.

—. 2007. L'immobilier en station de sports d'hiver: du laisser-faire au savoir-faire?, in *Les Sports d'Hiver en Mutation. Crise ou Révolution Géoculturelle?*, edited by P. Bourdeau. Paris: Hermes, 111–22.

Clivaz, C. and Nahrath, S. 2010. The return of the property question in the development of Alpine tourist resorts in Switzerland. *Journal of Alpine Research* [Online], 98(2). Available at: http://rga.revues.org/index1198.html [accessed: 14 September 2010].

Conti, G. and Perelli, C. 2007. Governing tourism monoculture: Mediterranean mass tourism destinations and governance networks, in *Tourism and Politics. Global Frameworks and Local Realities*, edited by P. Burns P. and M. Novelli. Amsterdam: Elsevier, 220–35.

Fablet, G. and George-Marcelpoil, E. 2013. Formes et impacts des dynamiques foncières et immobilières en stations de montagne: l'exemple du massif alpin, in *L'Urbanisation de la Montagne*, edited by J.-F. Joye. Université de Savoie.

Falk, M. 2009. Are multi-resort ski conglomerates more efficient? *Managerial and Decision Economics,* 30(8), 529–38.

Flagestad, A. and Hope, C.A. 2001. Strategic success in winter sports destinations: a sustainable value creation perspective. *Tourism Management,* 22(5), 445–61.

François, H. and Marcelpoil, E. 2012. Vallée de la Tarentaise: de l'invention du Plan neige à la constitution d'un milieu innovateur dans le domaine du tourisme d'hiver. *Histoire des Alpes,* 17, 227–42.

Gerbaux, F. and Marcelpoil, E. 2006. Governance of mountain resorts in France: the nature of the public-private partnership. *Journal of Alpine Research,* 94(1), 20–31.

Gill, A.M. and Williams, P.W. 2011. Rethinking resort growth: understanding evolving governance strategies in Whistler, British Columbia. *Journal of Sustainable Tourism,* 19, 629–48.

Lorit, J.-F., Aymeric, M. and Dalmas, D. 1990. *Les Difficultés Financières des Communes Stations de Sports d'Hiver.* Ministère de l'Intérieur, Inspection Générale de l'Administration.

Marcelpoil, E., François, H., Fablet, G., Bray, F., Achin, C., Torre, A. and Barré, J.-B. 2012. *Atlas des Stations du Massif des Alpes.* Grenoble: DATAR, Commissariat de massif des Alpes.

Marcelpoil, E., Bensahel-Perrin, L., and François, H. (eds.). 2010. *Les Stations de Sports d'Hiver face au Développement Durable. Etat des Lieux et Perspectives.* Paris: L'Harmattan.

Marcelpoil, E., François, H., Billet, S., Bonfort, T., Duvillard, S., Herrera, C., Sgard, A. and Devouassoux, A.-S. 2007. *Nouvelles Pratiques Touristiques en Zones de Montagne: vers un Renouvellement des Pratiques de Gestion Foncière?* Paris: Direction du Tourisme.

Svensson, B., Nordin, S. and Flagestad, A. 2006. Destination governance and contemporary development models, in *Tourism Local Systems and Networking,* edited by L. Lazzeretti and C. Petrillo. Oxford: Elsevier, 83–96.

Tobler, C. 1981. *Konzept für die Fremdenverkehrspolitik im Kanton Thurgau unter besonderer Berücksichtigung des schweizerischen Tourismuskonzeptes.* Winterthur: Schellenberg.

Chapter 7

Nature-Based Leisure Activities Put to the Environmental Test: A Pragmatic, Sociological Approach

Ludovic Ginelli

Introduction

Outdoor activities are widely and increasingly pursued in so-called developed countries. In Europe, these activities have increased considerably since the 1960s, and are now widely pursued for the special experience of nature that they provide, i.e. beyond mere relaxation – which was the motivation typically postulated previously (Pröbstl, Elands and Wirth 2009). The French case is entirely in keeping with this European trend, since 80 per cent of those who practice a physical and sporting activity claim to be motivated by 'contact with nature' (Lefevre and Thiery 2011). Activities able to fulfil this 'need for nature' felt by millions of people are actually highly diverse, both in terms of their historical origins and their distribution among the different social groups. Often described as individual and authentic by those who pursue them, these activities refer, however, to norms and values that can be situated both socially and historically (Corbin 1995) and must be clarified.

In the present context of the 'ecologisation of thought' (Kalaora 2001), ecology's cognitive and normative significance is considerably strengthened. It is particularly explicit in the ecological redefinition of areas of practice, a phenomenon that goes straight to the heart of outdoor activities. Here we will look at the relationship between ecologisation – viewed as a cognitive and normative refocusing (see above) – with the nature-based leisure activities that preceded it. When do environmental concerns provoke resistance, and/or are they appropriated and subsequently converted into ecologised practices? Are we witnessing real changes in practices? The revealing of the norms, values and sensitivities expressed in the 'experiences' of nature activity enthusiasts seem to be a prerequisite for understanding their ambiguities in relation to the environment. We will consider them based on two French coastal areas (the Bassin d'Arcachon on the Atlantic coast, and the Calanques de Marseille on the Mediterranean coast) via a sociological approach based on the 'pragmatist' tradition of thought. We have selected activities that are more or less sporting (sea kayaking, underwater fishing, hunting) because they are popular locally (or even nationally in the case of hunting) while being questioned due to individual or regulatory environmental standards.

Literature Review

According to the seminal work by Elias and Dunning (1986), all contemporary forms of sport and leisure are seemingly part of a long-term 'sportisation' process, characterised by a lowering of the violence that is acceptable between humans, and identifiable in the changes made to sporting 'rules of play'. This trend also concerns practices that are not strictly speaking related to sport, such as hunting (Traïni 2004). Furthermore, given that they take place in the natural environment, nature-based leisure activities are profoundly and directly affected by 'ecologisation'. Our hypothesis is that nature-based leisure activities are set apart from other recreational activities through their combining of 'sportisation' and 'ecologisation' concepts. Ecologisation may actually prolong the long-established sportisation concept by extending this process of lowering acceptable levels of violence not only to humans, but also to natural elements. In particular, such concepts as overcrowding, impact and disturbance – inspired by ecology – feature in statutory law (Natura 2000, law on national parks and marine parks) to either regulate or encourage 'softer', 'non-disruptive' practices in keeping with 'respect for the natural environment'. These are underpinned by the idea that 'there are rights of nature that plead in favour of its integrity' (Kalaora 2001).[1] This change brings about a re-evaluation of all outdoor activities in the light of their 'impact' – which is difficult to gauge (Mounet 2007) – on ecosystems. In this regard, the ecologisation process may be viewed as the introduction of new 'rules of play' for nature that may actually prolong the sportisation process, which defines the 'rules of play' between humans.

The sportisation theory would appear to be particularly stimulating for the analysis of nature-based activities, providing that operational questions and hypotheses are deduced from it. In what situations does the ecologisation process provoke resistance, and/or is it appropriated and converted into actual practices? What are the process's ambiguities? How does it relate to the sportisation process, which is performance-oriented? After presenting this theory and its limitations, we will formulate some theoretical and methodological propositions inspired by the 'pragmatic turning point' in sociology. These propositions will be applied to nature-based leisure activities in two study areas in France.

---

1   These standards can be very precisely identified in the management documents in force or under discussions in our two study areas (in French; see http://www.aires-marines. fr/L-Agence/Organisation/Missions-d-etude-de-parc/Bassin-d-Arcachon-et-son-ouvert and http://www.calanques-parcnational.fr/index.php/documents).

The 'Sportisation' Theory: to Be Handled with Care

Elias and Dunning (1986) saw the first signs of a practice on its way to sportisation in the arrival of fox hunting in eighteenth century England, which 'gives free rein to affects and impulses, with a refusal of dangerous violence, self-control and the observance of restrictive prohibitions'. Although since amended, their seminal work on the sociology of sport has allowed us to establish links between the birth and development of modern sport and more global sociological changes, such as the 'process of civilization'.[2] Going beyond sport, the authors extend their theory of 'sportisation' to all leisure activities in which there is a relation of adversity either with other humans or with the natural elements such as the mountains, the sea, animals etc., but one that is always 'controlled' and 'non-violent'. Like sports, these so-called 'mimetic' sports seemingly arouse 'the satisfying excitement of confrontation' while remaining recreational and non-threatening to the social order, unlike confrontations in the non-leisure arena (wars, riots, social unrest, etc.).

Elias's theory, which is based on the very long term, offers an interesting, increased degree of generalisation, however, its extension must be viewed with a critical eye. In particular, its empirical testing should prompt a more qualified, contextualised formulation. The theory's 'sociological consideration of norms and values' also raises questions (Callède 2007: 372–373) since it confers the same level of importance to very different norms, from implicit moral norms that are interiorised and shared by extensive social groups, to sports rules of play, which are explicit instructions, limited to specific spaces and groups, and confined to the duration of the game.

The Theoretical and Methodological Contribution of the Pragmatic Approach

We have advanced the hypothesis that ecologisation could prolong sportisation. Work on the ecologisation concept, for example in the field of the management of nature (Alphandéry and Fortier 2007) or that of agriculture (Deuffic and Candau 2006), systematically emphasizes that this process always involves more than simply putting the issue on the political agenda. Given that it shakes up former categories of thought, ecologisation has a critical and potentially conflictual aspect. We will define it as a cognitive and normative reframing – a change in how we view and consider a form of social behaviour – aimed at a more or less far-reaching environmental reorientation of social norms (legal or implicit) and practices in force in the area considered (agriculture, management of sport and nature-based leisure activities, forest, etc.). Ecologisation may be underpinned by specific environmental standards (such as respect for the biorhythms of wildlife) usually introduced by institutional stakeholders, or it may be conducted more

---

2   The term 'civilization' could be construed as a certain form of evolutionism by Elias. The author defended himself against this criticism, stating that the 'civilization of morals' does not exclude phases of 'decivilisation' of our societies (Elias and Dunning 1986).

informally by more diverse stakeholders (institutions, associations, but also users, citizens, etc.) who refer to multiple registers (environmental ethics, scientific or activist ecology, etc.) that are often inter-related in the field. Clearly, those who push for these normative changes would like to see everyone comply with them. For this reason, ecologisation is usually 'neither straightforward, nor natural' (Mougenot and Roussel 2005) for collectives of users already in place, who are often long-established and do not put ecology or environmental concerns at the centre of their activities in the natural environment. Here we will focus on the specific case of *informal ecologisation* during the course of nature-based activity enthusiasts' ordinary activities.

Our theoretical approach draws on the current sociological revisiting of American Pragmatism by Dewey (2012). In view of this, the starting point of the analysis is 'the experience of an environment', i.e. the transactions that unite individual and collective stakeholders with a physical, social and historical environment (Céfaï and Terzi 2012). This analytical framework is fertile ground for analysing situations perceived as 'problematic' and this is how we will tackle the issue of the environment. By taking the 'experience of the environment' concept as our starting point, we will call upon the pragmatic concepts of 'trouble' and 'inquiry' to question the informal ecologisation of nature-based leisure activities as defined above. The 'trouble' that arises in the experience of an environment is the possible *but not systematic* vector for increased vigilance by stakeholders, for example when users observe an abnormal change in the environment in which they pursue their activities (pollution, disappearance or proliferation of a given species, etc.) and set about trying to understand it and even taking appropriate measures. This is not limited to material elements; it may also designate a 'problematic situation', i.e. an undermining of certain reference points or collective routines, and may foretell inquiry-related activities (Céfaï and Terzi 2012). This inquiry stage may be favourable for forming or consolidating a collective centred on 'common positions', in other words a collective agreement on a certain interpretation of reality. The stakeholders no longer have any reason to continue with their inquiry since common sense has a new anchor point with a view to possible action. For example, when users agree on the causes of a problem such as pollution in the Bassin d'Arcachon, some of them may be tempted to take action to solve this problem.

While the concepts of 'trouble' and 'inquiry' are clearly linked in the pragmatic perspective, their relationships must not be systematised, as we will see in the case of nature-based leisure activities. Firstly, the trouble or problems faced by the stakeholders may remain unchanged and merely arouse passiveness in stakeholders who are weakened or lacking in resources (Céfaï and Terzi 2012). Even if the 'trouble' perceived by a few users prompts an incipient action, the logics of inquiry and proof may be hindered by the specific norms and values inherent in outdoor leisure activities (the utopia of freedom, sporting or predatory performance, hedonism) that are historically and socially established, and that define how the natural environment is experienced.

By underscoring the tangible and perceptual aspects of the outdoor leisure experience, this pragmatic sociology provides a breakthrough compared with radical, constructivist approaches – threatened by extreme relativism since everything is seemingly a 'social construction' – and in relation to traditional forms of sociology according to which 'the social explains the social', to the exclusion, therefore, of tangible, environmental and biological factors. This imperative is guided both by the major importance of the techniques that go hand in hand with any nature-based leisure activity, and the inevitable confrontation with the natural elements, whether living or inert, that these uses entail. It adheres to the underlying premise of today's environmental sociology (Dunlap 2010) of considering tangible elements in these analyses of social phenomena.

Data and Methods

As far as the methodology is concerned, the pragmatic approach implies conducting on-site observations and interviews in order to contextualise the views and interactions observed as accurately as possible. In order for us to express an opinion on the hypothetical ecologisation of these uses, we must therefore start with the situations in which nature-based activities are practised and whose environmental aspect is theoretically not given. This will allow us to avoid overestimating its importance and to question its apparent obviousness. By drawing on the main theoretical and methodological advances of the pragmatic tradition, we will propose an interpretation of the 'informal' ecologisation enacted by users in the context of ordinary sociabilities. Based on a comparison between the two main, competing ecologisation interpretation models, namely 'strategic greening' on the one hand, or the recognised transformation of standards and practices towards more 'eco-centred' conceptions on the other hand, a number of hypotheses may be formulated ranging from voluntary ecologisation to radical protestation, and including strategic, individual appropriation (greenwashing) or collective appropriation.

However, given our focus on actual situations, we must avoid the pitfall of confining ourselves to micro-sociology (Cicourel 1981). To this end, these activities must be considered in relation to elements that form a more 'macro' context, understood in terms of both its institutional and historical components. This objective also means varying the situations in which observations are made and views recorded (environments frequented by our respondents to pursue their leisure activities; public information or consultation meetings; participation in 'eco-citizen' initiatives, etc.). Fifty-six in-depth interviews (30 in the Bassin d'Arcachon, 26 in the Calanques) were conducted in the activity sites, with the help of an interview guide, then correlated with some 20 ethnographic observations made in these different contexts (participation in eco-citizen actions, etc.). The participants were selected to reflect the widest possible range of profiles based on the presence/absence of a protected area, the participants' age, and whether or not they were members of an environmental association. The following subjects were systematically broached: description and justification of the nature-based leisure activities practised, perception of environmental and, if applicable, regulatory changes in relation to the places of activity, networks/associations belonged to and relations with other users of the places concerned.

For the purpose of our research, we selected two French coastal areas, the Bassin d'Arcachon and the Calanques de Marseille, which present the advantage of having a protected area covering only part of their territory. In April 2012, a national park was created in the Calanques de Marseille. For its part, the Bassin d'Arcachon contains a number of protected areas (national nature reserves), and the creation of a marine nature park is under study. Consequently, users on both sites are concerned by environmental standards, which are localised, but are linked to national (federation of nature reserves, National Parks of France, etc.) and international (European Union, IUCN, international conventions, etc.) standards. Some activities were chosen because, in the view of some experts, the implementation of these environmental standards appeared to pose problems (hunting birds using bird lime[3] and underwater fishing in the Calanques de Marseille; waterfowl hunting in the Bassin d'Arcachon), and were compared against other seemingly less problematic activities (sea kayaking, bow hunting). A comparison of these otherwise very different activities is made possible since they are pursued on the same site. This means that we can characterise the opinions of different stakeholders concerning the same area, subject to the same environmental standards.

Results

In this section, we put forward the idea that, despite very different historical and social origins, the nature-based leisure activities in question, which the 'advent of leisure' in the 1960s had already gone some way to reconciling, actually converge in their relationship with nature and, more precisely, their 'experience of the natural environment'. For hunting, Traïni (2004: 42) clearly shows how the justification registers for this leisure activity, which are often multiple for the same person, 'have to be viewed in the context of distinct phases in the history of this practice'. We have chosen to extend this approach to all of the nature activities considered in order to establish a genealogy of reasons that often appear to be mixed and multiple for the same person.

---

3 A 'traditional' form of hunting that consists in attracting certain species of bird (thrushes and blackbirds) by spreading adhesive birdlime on branches to capture them alive.

'Sportised' Nature-Based Leisure Activities?

In both the Bassin d'Arcachon and the Calanques coastal areas, the activities considered have all been inherited from the 'leisure civilization', and are part of a sportisation trend that is the oldest justification register for these activities. All have been transformed by the advent of leisure (Corbin 1995), in other words, by the invention of leisure time (paid leave, reduced weekly working hours). All have been gradually regulated on a national and European scale, including activities inherited from local usage rights. Indeed, according to Elias and Dunning (1986), the harmonisation of regulations is clearly a trait that distinguishes modern sports and leisure from earlier forms of activities, the rules of which were often local and unstable.

For example, while hunting is an ancestral practice, the strengthening and harmonisation of the associated regulations intensified markedly in the 1970s, when the practice became widespread. In France, the introduction of paid hunting permits in 1975, including a theory exam, marked both the entry of this usage right into the commercial sphere, and the integration of 'theoretical' naturalist knowledge into the informal training that previously prevailed. Above all, from the 1990s onwards, the chaotic and highly conflictual transposition of the European Birds and Habitats Directives played a key role with regards to the ecologisation of hunting regulations (Alphandéry and Fortier 2007). In particular, it concerned the hunting of migratory birds, two forms of which we consider: hunting using bird lime, and waterfowl hunting (ducks and geese). The ecologisation tendencies also concerned underwater fishing. These only came about later, but intensified from the early 2000s with the introduction of France's maritime policy ('Grenelle de la Mer') and as a result of the ethical controversy surrounding this practice.

Objections and Ambiguities in Relation to Sportisation

Irrespective of the activity concerned, sportisation is neither linear nor consensual. For example, in the early twentieth century, French canoe/kayak pioneers used the tourist vocation of their activity as grounds for objecting to the sporting inclinations of some members (Marsac 2008). Even today, these tensions endure within two kayak clubs covered by our study in the Bassin d'Arcachon. The sportisation of hunting and underwater fishing has met with opposition on account of the 'traditional' aspect of these pursuits. Politicised in France in the 1990s and 2000s by the 'Chasse, Pêche, Nature et Traditions' political party, this traditionalist register has been largely taken up by waterfowl hunters and thrush trappers (using bird lime) to justify their practices. For all that, the 'tradition' they refer to also conceals their own many technical innovations (use of new materials and new weapons, improvement of decoys and hunting techniques). It is clearly out of step with the transformation of practices, but remains a powerful cognitive brake on the appropriation of environmental standards, perceived as 'restrictions' and exogenous 'change':

It's one restriction after another. And ecologists seem to have more power than hunters. They carry more weight. (Waterfowl hunter, retired office employee, aged 60, who practices in a non-protected area).

The sportisation of hunting bears testimony to an 'intellectualization of the violence of the cynegetic act, and a sublimation of the animal's killing' (Traïni 2004: 43). This consists in distancing the activity's food-related aspect in favour of its recreational aspect, underscoring fair play and disqualifying those who go against this norm by giving in to over-easy predation:

We don't hunt to fill up the freezer, we do it for the pleasure of hunting (…). There's a lot of preparation and in the end, you don't have to fire your arrow to say that you've won. Last year, I had a roe deer in my sights, and knew that he'd lost, so that was that … (Bow hunter, cook, aged 42).

However, the ambiguity of the sportisation process is rarely emphasized. And yet, it brings about two opposing norms: fair play on the one hand, where an over-easy kill is frowned upon, and competition between peers on the other hand, which is a driver of performance, whether sporting or predatory. Nowadays, it seems that the fair play norm is violated less for food purposes (which harks back to practices prior to the sportisation process) than in the name of performance which, after all, is encouraged by sportisation:

Young hunters go for the kill not so much for the meat, but for the score. There's this idea of competition and what counts for them is getting the highest score. (Waterfowl hunter, retired teacher, aged 65).

Similarly, the quest for sporting performance overshadows, or even conflicts with environmental concerns when, for example, the organisers of a sea kayak sporting event in the Bassin d'Arcachon decide to ignore the procedures imposed by the Natura 2000 European Directive. These two observations are proof that the links between sportisation and ecologisation are highly ambiguous. An institutional approach might see ecologisation – defined as the defining of rules of play that are more respectful of nature – as an extension of sportisation, however, the pragmatic approach, which is focused on ordinary, in-field activities, reveals that the performance norm inherent to sportisation may lead to violations of ecologised fair play, i.e. moderation in the utilization of natural resources.

Activities That Free Users from Restricted Space-Times

Despite territorialities that often differ considerably as a result of these different uses of nature,[4] it is the 'naturalization' of hitherto rural practice areas that is apparent in our two fields of study. The Calanques and the Bassin d'Arcachon are increasingly protected (Calanques national park, planned marine park in the Bassin d'Arcachon) and users visit them as focal points of nature that are far removed from their daily lives:

> I find that it's really important, especially during very intense periods of work. Underwater fishing while holding your breath, the part that involves yoga, breathing and relaxation, is an excellent way of relieving stress. (…). Blending in with the environment, thinking like a fish, it's really important to get into that mind-set! (Underwater fisherman in a protected area, aged 35, teacher-researcher in marine ecology).

In the case of nature-based leisure activities, the opposition with limited time which, by definition, is valid for all forms of leisure, is further heightened by a particularly marked spatial frontier. In fact, there is a term-for-term opposition and a 'double frontier' between restricted, artificialised, urban space-times on the one hand, and 'nature-based leisure activities', which provide a release and are carried out in naturalised places away from the city, on the other (Cronon 1996). Although often described and experienced on an individual, authentic basis, 'the experience of nature' is, in reality, defined by specific social norms (reaffirmation of specific sociabilities, performance, deployment of techniques, etc.) that contribute to further eclipsing environmental concerns. When individuals resist environmental standards perceived as falling outside their playing area, they are not merely opposing a specific rule or standard, they are also defending a space-time that they see as representing a form of release and that is the opposite of their daily lives.

Convergent 'Experiences of Nature'?

Most of the respondents lay great stress on how important it is for them to experience nature in a solitary way, or within a small group, and ideally without the burdens of a club. This trend is common to many leisure activities associated with nature (Rech and Mounet 2011). The so-called traditional forms of hunting considered here that seem to represent a laborious, often collective attempt at domesticating nature (hunting cabins, work completed in natural areas, use of decoys) are less suited to this utopia. Moreover, they are struggling to appeal to a

---

4 We can establish a continuum in the ways of apprehending the places of practice, from territorialities inherited from the rural world and confined within a delimited territory (hunting societies, fixed hunting cabins) to those, more mobile and usually more urban, of sea kayakers or underwater fishermen.

new audience (declining and ageing population of hunters in France). However, all the other practices considered (bow hunting, sea kayaking and underwater fishing), in which participant levels are stable or even increasing, are suited to the utopia of self-immersion in the wilderness. By representing a place of refuge preserved from the ills of our societies, this form of utopia has been seen in a favourable light since the end of the nineteenth Century (unlike in earlier periods). Even though this idea is highly debatable (Cronon 1996), it still has great resonance:

> There's nothing better for getting out and seeing birds and animals! That's how I got into kayaking ... It allowed me to get a bit closer to nature, to have the feeling that I was part of something, part of nature, and not just an add-on. (...) I have rarely had moments of plenitude like it. (Kayaker, bow hunter and fly fisherman, aged 54).

This often quite radical search for 'nature' seeks to reverse – point by point – the dominant values of consumer society (consumerism, obtaining power and recognition through wealth) that go hand in hand with urban life. It is by no means insignificant that most respondents refer to their preferred leisure activities as 'passions'. Generally speaking, these passions fill the lives of their followers during their free time and vacations, however, they may – exceptionally – lead them to adopt radical positions, as in the case of the following person whose 'real life' is centred on his underwater experiences:

> It's a sporting passion. (...) It's more than that in fact. What I'm about to say might be a bit mad, but it's been more important for me to live underwater than on land. There you have it. (...) We divers, we like it when we're underwater; we like to meet up in the evening for a drink together and talk about what we did, and about what we're going to do, because that's what we live for! (Underwater fisherman, aged approx. 50, Marseilles port employee).

From 'Trouble' to 'Inquiry': The Environment Faced with the Experience of the Natural Environment

Knowledge of the natural environment, which is always necessary for going about the given activity and even controlling certain risks (sea kayaking, underwater fishing), is a key factor in terms of recognition among peers. It distinguishes the experienced hunter, able to draw on his knowledge to overcome a prized game animal, from the amateur. Similarly, in the eyes of fellow enthusiasts, expert knowledge of the natural environment is what sets the experienced kayaker, capable of organising a sea expedition while considering conditions such as the weather, tidal schedules and coefficients, direction and strength of the wind, apart from his or her less seasoned counterpart. Following on from Roux et al. (2009), we will talk about 'cognitive passions' to designate activities in which knowledge of the natural environment is derived from a passion for something (an animal, a natural element such as the sea) to produce in situ knowledge. As with all cognitive passions, the nature-based leisure activities studied here are part of a perceptual, long-term relationship with a natural environment, and gain meaning within a 'community' of enthusiasts. By considering them as such, we can account for the knowledge and local investments that they produce beyond mere usage (wildlife numeration, maintenance and vigilance practices, etc.), and the possible 'inquiry' activities concerning the environment in which they are pursued. This knowledge circulates on specific exchange networks where individuals discuss and prolong the defining of the frameworks for their experience of nature which, consequently, is not only individual and sensitive, but also collective and cognitive. Organised communities (hunting clubs and associations) or informal groups (based on relations of affinity) form the most frequent and numerous exchange networks in which every aspect of nature-related leisure (specific sociabilities, sporting or predatory performance, knowledge of the environment) is regularly discussed, at the risk of occasionally creating certain tensions. Given that some individuals are members of multiple groups, the ideas shared by these 'communities of enthusiasts' may come into contact with those formulated in other networks. By belonging to environmental networks, notably France's 'Ligue de Protection des Oiseaux' (Bird Protection League – a significant French environmental protection association), or institutional networks (wildlife observation networks, exchanges with protected area managers), some kayakers, hunters and underwater fishermen effectively become the 'entrepreneurs' of an informal form of ecologisation. These 'entrepreneurs' integrate various environmental registers (ethical, scientific) that they attempt to encourage others within their community to share. In their view, the environment, and even ecology itself, is just as important as sporting performance or mastery of the environment in which the activity is practised.

If we adopt a pragmatic interpretation, the 'informal ecologisation' of some nature-based leisure enthusiasts may be the result of some form of 'trouble' in their experience of these activities. This is the case, for example, with a kayaker who was previously convinced that his activity was entirely 'eco-compatible', but who now questions the disturbance caused to migratory birds: is it negligible, or does the energy burnt by these disturbed birds when flying away risk compromising their chances of survival (when wintering) or that of their brood (when nesting)? However, the 'trouble' may designate something other than difficulty in interpreting the natural environment; it may also allude to a certain malaise caused by the breaking of an established routine. For nature-based leisure enthusiasts, this may be a situation in which one or more users hesitate over the practice, or the official line to adopt, since the standards that guide them have lost their inevitability. Note the example of a hunter who questions his predatory act:

> Right now, I'm thinking about stopping hunting. I don't know if I'll carry on with it next year. […] Not that that will stop me from coming to the marshes and enjoying nature. I would really miss it if somebody said to me 'You can't

go to the Bassin any more, stay at home'. (Waterfowl hunter in a protected area,
aged approximately 55, retired office employee).

Our survey data have allowed us to identify these forms of 'trouble' among
certain hunters and kayakers. However, they are always a minority of their activity's
community, and this malaise does not always bring about a collective 'inquiry'
in the pragmatic sense of the word. Based on our observations, any 'trouble'
experienced will usually lead to a 'personal' form of ecologisation initially, where
the individual concerned will search for and cross-check information, or even take
part in information networks outside the activity's community. Some users will
then attempt to create or join collectives in which the environmental aspect is
given greater importance, even if it is not central. For example, in the Calanques,
an underwater fishing association, 'Chasse Sous-Marine Passion', was formed to
break away from certain practices (in particular underwater fishing competitions)
and to militate in favour of 'integrated management' of the activity's area. In
rare cases, the ecologisation may be 'activist', i.e. sponsored by one or more
stakeholders as entrepreneurs of a cause who seek to raise the awareness of their
peers, and who investigate and militate to put ecological concerns among the
'motives' of nature-based leisure enthusiasts.

Conclusion and Policy Recommendations

From an institutional perspective, ecologisation, identified by the increasing
prevalence of environmental standards in the policies and regulations applicable
to nature-based leisure activities, would indeed seem to prolong the sportisation
of these activities, since written, fixed and largely homogeneous rules of play
affect not only the relationships between stakeholders (sportisation), but also
their relationship with nature. The pragmatic approach adopted here, which is
attentive to experiences of the natural environment understood in their perceptible,
cognitive, collective aspects and resituated in their historical formation, presents a
number of advances in the analysis of the cognitive and normative appropriation
of the environment by outdoor leisure enthusiasts. It serves to qualify the
continuity between ecologisation and sportisation by showing that both always
provoke objections and infringements. Regardless of the nature-based leisure
activities considered in both coastal areas, it also reveals the fragility of the
'ecological experience' (Kalaora 2001) implied by the acknowledgement of
nature's intrinsic value that would appear to have replaced the former model,
according to which it was 'consumed' like any other cultural asset. Despite
their considerable publicising and even their widespread approval in the light of
recent statistical surveys conducted by the French Ministry of the Environment
(Commissioner-General for Sustainable Development 2011), environmental
concerns have not brought about an ecological revolution in the experience of the
natural environment. Our hypothesis concerning the ambiguities of ecologisation

is thus validated; it confirms work conducted on the same process in other areas of activity (Deuffic and Candau 2006). This research has allowed us to specify the nature of these ambiguities. They are attributable to the values sought by users who pursue these activities – sporting or predatory performance, hedonism and the search for activities that offer a release from daily life – and that come into conflict with ecologisation impulses. Consequently, the implementation of this process is not facilitated or complicated according to more or less 'eco-compatible' uses; this is another important result of this research. While ecologisation may indeed come about as a result of some 'trouble' in the perceptual and cognitive experience of the natural environment, the shift towards activism and a successful inquiry (usually collective) contributing to the ecologisation of a given practice must be considered with great caution, whatever the activity. To understand the different possible paths, it would appear necessary to identify the stakeholders and networks that shoulder the environmental cognitive and normative framework, taking into account the prevailing norms within these communities that may be opposed to it. Indeed, the inquiry activities driven by an ecologisation undertaking have to confront social norms already in place (tradition, the utopia of freedom, performance, sociability, etc.) as well as the 'counter-inquiries' of other collectives on the same issues intended to define other common positions to uphold their own cause.

The nature-based leisure activities examined here are the source of historically formed norms and collectives and their associated usage rights; reinterpreting them in the light of environmental logics, often passed down from other decision-making levels (especially international), is not self-evident. Highlighting these ambiguities should make it possible to better match the objectives of nature policies with the expectations of users, thereby conferring greater legitimacy on these policies in the eyes of users. These results should encourage public decision-makers to consider the different aspects of users' 'experience of the natural environment' when implementing environmental, incentive or regulatory standards. They tend to support the new, more concerted nature protection and management policies, such as they are taking shape, for example, with France's latest generation of national parks, provided that attention is paid to the risk of unequal participation by users in these schemes (Deldrève and Deboudt 2012).

Acknowledgements

I would like to thank Jacqueline Candau and Vincent Marquet for their review. This text is the result of work conducted in France in the Bassin d'Arcachon (Osquar project, funded by the Aquitaine Region) and in Marseilles (Un Parc national pour les calanques)? (A national park for the calanques?), funded by the French Ministry of the Environment).

References

Alphandéry, P. and Fortier, A. 2007. A new approach to wildlife management in France: regional guidelines as tools for the conservation of biodiversity. *Sociologia Ruralis*, 47(1), 42–62.

Bell, S., Simpson, M., Tyrväinen, L., Sievänen, T., and Pröbstl, U. (eds.). 2009. *European Forest Recreation and Tourism: a Handbook*. Abingdon: Taylor and Francis.

Callède, J.-P. 2007. *La Sociologie Française et la Pratique Sportive (1875–2005). Essai sur le Sport. Forme et Raison de l'Echange Sportif dans les Sociétés Modernes*. Bordeaux: MSHA.

Céfaï, D. and Terzi, C. (eds.). 2012. *L'Expérience des Problèmes Publics*. Paris: Editions de l'EHESS.

Cicourel, A.V. 1981. Notes on the integration of micro- and macro-levels of analysis, in *Advances in Social Theory and Methodology: toward an Integration of Micro- and Macro-Sociologies,* edited by K.D. Knorr-Cetina and A.V. Cicourel. Boston, London and Henley: Routledge and Kegan Paul, 51–80.

Commissariat Général au Développement Durable. 2011. Les perceptions sociales et pratiques environnementales des Français de 1995 à 2011. *La revue du CGDD*, October 2011.

Corbin, A. (ed.). 1995. *L'Avènement des Loisirs: 1850–1960*. Paris: Flammarion.

Cronon, W. 1996. The trouble with wilderness; or, getting back to the wrong nature. *Environmental History*, 1(1), 7–28.

Deldrève, V. and Deboudt, P. (eds.). 2012. *Le Parc National des Calanques: Construction Territoriale, Concertation et Usages*. Versailles: Quae.

Deuffic, P. and Candau, J. 2006. Farming and landscape management: how French farmers are coping with the ecologization of their activities. *Journal of Agricultural and Environmental Ethics*, 19(6), 563–85.

Dewey, J. 2012 (1927). *The Public and its Problems*. Edited and introduced by M.L. Rogers. Penn State University Press.

Dunlap, R.E. 2010. The maturation and diversification of environmental sociology: from constructivism and realism to agnosticism and pragmatism, in *International Handbook of Environmental Sociology*, 2nd Edition, edited by M.R. Redclift and G. Woodgate. Cheltenham, UK: Edward Elgar, 15–32.

Elias, N. and Dunning, E. 1986. *Quest for Excitement: Sport and Leisure in Civilizing Process*. Oxford: Basil Blackwell.

Kalaora, B. 2001. A la conquête de la pleine nature. *Ethnologie française*, 31(4), 591–97.

Lefèvre, B. and Thiery, P. 2011. Les principales activités physiques et sportives pratiquées en France en 2010. *Stat-Info, Bulletin de Statistiques et d'Etudes*, 11(02) 1–6.

Marsac, A. 2008. *Canoë-Kayak, des Torrents au Stade d'Eau Vive. Sociologie des Pratiques et Ethnographie des Apprentissages*. Doctoral dissertation in sociology, University Nanterre La Défense.

Mougenot, C. and Roussel, L. 2005. To poison or to trap? The ecologisation of 'pest' control. *Sociologia Ruralis,* 45(1/2), 115–29.

Mounet, J.-P. 2007. Sports de nature, développement durable et controverse environnementale. *Natures Sciences Sociétés*, 15, 162–66.

Rech, Y. and Mounet, J.-P. 2011. Les sports de nature en débat: réceptions différenciées de la gestion participative dans le Parc naturel régional de la Chartreuse. *Développement Durable et Territoires* [Online], 2(3). Available at: http://developpementdurable.revues.org/9085 [accessed: 8 April 2013].

Roux, J., Charvolin, F. and Dumain, A. 2009. Les 'passions cognitives' ou la dimension rebelle du connaître en régime de passion: premiers résultats d'un programme en cours. *Revue d'Anthropologie des Connaissances*, 3(3), 369–85.

Traini, C. 2004. Territoires de chasse. *Ethnologie Française*, 34(1), 41–48.

Chapter 8

Consumer Co-Construction and Auto-Construction Mechanisms in the Tourist Experience: Applications to the Resort Model at a Destination Scale

Isabelle Frochot

Introduction

The tourist experience imagined by tourists as they embark on their holiday is a complex mixture of tranquillity and excitement and diverse expectations as regards the tourist service offering. Tourism is a complex domain, an experience that takes place over several days and weeks and that includes multiple encounters with various providers, both public and private. Within these encounters, recent literature on marketing services shows the relationship between consumers and providers as a co-construction process: consumers contribute to the service provided by choosing services that will allow them to develop their own holiday and define the use and value of the service consumed. Whilst most experiences often take place within a service provider realm, consumers will also seek to develop their own service experiences independently from the service provider (auto-construction). Hence the holiday can be seen as a succession of multiple encounters where the relationship between the consumer and the provider varies. This chapter aims to investigate these relationships within the tourist resort context. It will analyse how the service is managed within an integrated resort where the offering is totally managed and controlled by the provider but where consumers are free to compose what they personally expect from their holiday. The chapter will then look at French mountain resorts to understand how this integrated model can be transposed to a situation where the resort is set in a public place, with disjointed public and private service providers.

The Specific Context of Services

Characteristics of Services

A widely accepted definition of services has been provided by Kotler et al. (1996: 588) who defined a service as 'any activity or benefit that one party can offer to another which is essentially intangible and does not result in the ownership of anything. Its production may or may not be tied to a physical product'. Originally, the intangible aspect of a service was commonly seen as its most distinctive feature. However, other characteristics now also appear to define its specific characteristics, which can be summarised into four key traits:

- *Intangibility*: this trait has traditionally been recognised as the fundamental distinguishing characteristic between services and products from which all other differences would emerge. However, services display different proportions of tangible and intangible elements. The rule of thumb is that the more a service is composed of tangible elements, the easier it is to standardise.
- *Inseparability of production consumption*: this means that services are sold, produced and consumed simultaneously. Since the consumer is involved in the consumption and production processes, potential dissatisfaction has to be dealt with on the spot.
- *Heterogeneity* relates to the high variability in the performance of services and the difficulty to standardise them. Hence, the quality of a service is difficult since it can vary due to elements outside the provider's control and is heavily dependent on the provision of human services.
- *Perishability* means that services cannot be stored to be sold at a later date, implying that a service unsold is a service lost. This characteristic has led to very interesting strategies in terms of yield management.

Those four traits have several implications for service marketing. Compared with products, services need to be considered more broadly, by conceptualising their consumption process as a whole experience. This experience is customarily described as all the interpersonal and human-environment interactions that take place during the service. This notion is at the heart of the servuction model (Eiglier and Langear 1987), which views the service experience as an interaction between a client, the visible part of the service provider, the service environment and other customers.

The concept of service encounter refers to the interaction between the consumer and the firm (Surprenant and Solomon 1987) and is commonly defined as 'a period of time during which a consumer directly interacts with a service' (Shostack 1985: 244). The service encounter therefore includes all the customers' interactions with a service firm such as the personnel, physical facilities, tangible elements and other customers. The understanding of service encounters and their influence on the service experience is an aspect that has been intensively researched. This interactive process is seen as an important step in shaping customers' perceptions of the service received and is often referred to as the firm 'moment of truth'.

When studying services, researchers have traditionally looked at categories of services that can be qualified as functional services (banks, insurance services, etc.). These services involve situations in which consumers buy a service for rational and functional purposes. The service delivery usually encompasses a short service encounter principally monitored by an employee and the delivery takes place in a limited environment. However, when studying leisure and tourism services, their inherent characteristics challenge those assumptions: they involve long encounters, of a non-functional nature, involve multiple encounters and take place in wide settings (indoors and outdoors). The next section will investigate further those characteristics and debate the necessity to review the notion of service delivery in those specific contexts.

Is Service Delivery Different in a Tourism and Leisure Context?

Whilst this chapter cannot review all the specific characteristics of leisure and tourism services, it will analyse the specificities of their delivery. One aspect that needs to be addressed is the dimensions of the servuction, which may or may not be different in these contexts. Several studies on this subject have provided interesting results.

First of all, in 1983, Lovelock argued that the best way to understand services was to differentiate their nature based on two dimensions: the level of staff and the level of facility interactions. Many other studies have been conducted on this aspect, and most of the service classifications available usually include at least two of the following criteria: degree of interaction, customisation, and level of the facilities accompanying service delivery. Other studies in the tourism/leisure fields have also done a lot to develop this issue. For instance, Crompton and Mackay (1989) studied service perceptions in the context of recreation centres: painting class, senior trips, gentlemen's hockey and fitness class. Their study indicated that: 'In a high facility-low staff intensive activity the ambience of the facility and equipment are likely to be of central importance to a satisfying outcome, whereas in painting classes, which are high staff-low facility intensive, the physical ambience is not likely to be crucial to a satisfying outcome' (Crompton and Mackay 1989: 371). These findings were confirmed by Hamilton et al. (1991) in a study on State Park visitors who followed a similar reasoning and demonstrated that according to the type of services delivered in each park, the service quality dimensions did not display similar importance ratings. Hamilton et al. (1991) suggested that because of the reliance of the parks' service on settings and facilities (rather than on staff services), aspects such as tangibles and reliability were of most importance to visitors.

In this line of thought, Frochot and Hugues (2000) conducted a study that indicated that in the context of historic houses, services display specific features. First of all, the interaction with staff is comparatively not as direct as in functional services. A functional service is mainly handled by staff: a customer approaches the service firm with a request which will be dealt with by staff who will generally handle most of the service delivery. On the contrary, in the context of some tourism services such as historic houses, staff do have a role in providing some services but the consumption of the whole attraction is mainly done by the customer on his own (unless in the case of a guided tour). Visitors tour the property (park, garden and/or house) in large part on their own. The enjoyment of the visit is facilitated by the guidance provided (informative leaflets, signs, guides' advice) and the appreciation of the whole property is also centred on the quality of the tangible aspects (property upkeep, restoration, etc.). Both the guidance and tangibles quality are a service provided by the staff although this service is not direct. Therefore, in the case of visitor attractions, staff contributions also tend to be indirect through maintaining or improving the quality of the resource, rather than through direct involvement with visitors (Frochot and Batat 2013, Swarbrooke 1995). This part of the service remains invisible but has an important impact on the visitor experience and consequently needs to be included in a service quality appraisal. This aspect is often not recognised in functional services, which concentrate primarily on the human and direct aspects of the service delivery. Although the importance of staff is not denied, it is argued that this role might be more limited in the case of historic houses. Hence, although staff will welcome, serve or inform visitors, the consumption of the main service (the visit of the house or the park) will be done mainly on their own. This reasoning can be applied to other types of tourism services. For instance, national parks, museums, town/destination visiting, are central tourist activities that are mostly spent on their own.

This notion of indirect service is particularly interesting since it engages researchers and practitioners to consider that their provision involves a delivery even when they are not present. This notion has been developed throughout the 2000s with the notion of the consumer being active rather than passive in the service delivery (co-construction). This aspect will be addressed in the following section.

Notions of Co-Construction and Auto-Construction

The joint production of goods and services between the company and the customer is not a new idea: fast food or supermarkets have gained some of their success through customer participation in order to reduce production costs. Historically, consumer participation in service production was first studied as a strategy to improve productivity by using the client as a free labour, thereby achieving a lower price.

The Service Dominant Logic (SDL)

The Service Dominant Logic was set in 2004 by Vargo and Lusch who aimed to establish a new vision of consumers in service contexts. In this original article, Vargo and Lusch (2004) indicated that all economies are service based where knowledge and specialised skills are the fundamental source of competitive advantage and unit of exchange. Those authors viewed societies as composed of two elements: operand and operant resources. Operand resources are the basic resources available at a destination and that are acted upon to market them to potential customers. They should include for instance physical resources such as forests, mountains or beaches. Operant resources are the physical and mental skills and knowledge used to transform those operand resources. These could include for instance the skills of a lift operator to manage a mountain, the relational competencies of the staff in a tourist office, etc. In Vargo and Lusch (2004) vision, the key to a competitive business lies with those operant resources.

The most important finding of the SDL is the notion that consumers are co-producers. Traditionally, the notion of value is conceived as the difference between the prospective customer's evaluation of all the benefits and costs of an offer, in comparison to the perceived alternatives. Vargo and Lusch (2004: 6) indicated that resources do not have value as such but that their value is co-created with customers when they are used: 'value is defined and co-created with the consumer rather than embedded in output'. The general idea in co-production is that a service only develops value (interactive value) when it is used by consumers and that this use necessitates active participation from consumers (Cova and Carù 2004, Grönroos 2000). The firm and the customer cooperate in order to create unique offers, and value can be seen as a flow of experiences co-created by the customer. Value co-creation takes place in the context of a service system and is the result of resource integration and the involved stakeholders' use of their knowledge and skills. The knowledge, skills, and motivation of the employees are the primary determinants of a service system's ability to co-create value with customers (Lusch et al. 2007).

The Situation of Auto-Construction in Service Delivery

In 2010, Grönroos published a very interesting article revisiting the extent of the concept of co-creation with a vision that 'the unique contribution of a service perspective on business (Service logic) is not that customers always are co-creators of value, but rather that under certain circumstances the service provider gets opportunities to co-create value together with its customers' (Grönroos 2010: 279). Grönroos (2010) rightly questions the notion of value and co-creation. His article first states that customers in all service situations do not always actively seek to create value; it is preferable to state that value emerges from the use of the service. His vision is that 'it is the customers as users who are in charge of their value creation and the service provider could be invited to join in this process as co-creators' (Grönroos 2010: 288). Grönroos aims to draw attention to the fact that it is customers who create value by using resources made available within the firm environment. Among those resources, some are brought by the customer and others are part of the firm's environment. In tourism, we can confidently ascertain that a vast amount of resources are naturally there (the landscape, the sea, the weather, the flora and fauna, etc.). The role of the firm is therefore to facilitate access to those resources through designing, delivering, manufacturing them, etc.

Finally, the latest advances that need to be taken into consideration are the acknowledgement that all services include simultaneous situations of co-construction on one hand and auto-construction on the other hand. In other words, services can be classified along a continuum that represents those different situations.

The Service Continuum

The service continuum integrates the idea that services can be understood in regard to their relative proportion of indirect service (Cova and Carù 2006). This continuum emerged from the notion of indirect services which, in the context of tourism, brings particularly useful information. It indicates that consumers vary in their reliance on a service provider to co-construct their product. In a study on ski resorts Durrande-Moreau et al. (2012) also produced a continuum ranging from self-organised activities to business-organised activities. Their premise was that customers define, understand and operate on resources in service systems in different ways depending on what they want to achieve, their own resources and their capabilities as well as their financial situation. Indeed, their study shows that tourists build their value by referring to the various activities they engage into and depict themselves as active organisers of their holiday.

The objective of this chapter is to understand the extent to which this continuum can be applied to the context of mountain resorts and the implications that it brings in terms of resort management.

Methodology and Results of Field Work

Methodology

An in-depth qualitative study was conducted in winter 2009 with 80 customers in four different ski resorts in the French Alps. The objective of this study was to assess the satisfaction of customers currently staying in a given resort, to relate it to specific services at the resort and to identify their relative reliance or autonomy with the service provision. The choice of a qualitative approach was justified by the fact that it was relevant in this context to let customers evoke spontaneously their impressions about their stay and their satisfaction. It was also essential to understand which words consumers used to express the experience they were currently living, instead of asking them to evaluate each part of the service on a formatted quantitative questionnaire. The interviews lasted 15 to 20 minutes on average. The tourists were first asked to talk to the researchers about their holiday at the resort and then about the resort itself and their use of the services offered on site. No direct questions were asked about co-construction or auto-construction, the visitors just described the activities they undertook during their stay and then detailed them. The objective here was for the researchers to direct the discussion so that they could identify the dimensions in the service experience that were linked to the consumers and/or providers. All the interviews were recorded by the interviewers.

The interviews took place at the resorts on Wednesdays to Fridays, to make sure that the interviewed tourists were fully immersed in their consumption experience (all tourists had arrived the previous Saturday). It was indeed important that tourists already knew about the services offered at the resort, had already used them or formed intentions whether or not to use them, and had an opinion about the whole service quality.

Four different ski resorts were investigated to assess whether natural as well as architectural surroundings could have an impact on the visitor experience. There was one traditional village with typical alpine architecture and chalet (La Clusaz), a modern high-altitude high-standard integrated resort with a restricted access to motor vehicles (Avoriaz), a lower altitude modern village made of small concrete buildings (La Toussuire) and a modern but traditional looking high-altitude resort favoured by British customers (Méribel).

The saturation criterion was used to assess the quality of the collected data in each resort: information saturation is reached when new interviews do not provide any further information. On average 20 interviews were conducted in each resort. The study was funded by a local Destination Marketing Organisation (Savoie Mont Blanc Tourisme) in charge of the marketing and promotional activities for the Savoie and Haute-Savoie departments and by the IRSTEA research centre (a national research institute on agriculture and the environment). All the data collected during the interviews were transcribed then analysed using a statistical software application (Sphinx Lexica).

Results

The results obtained from this study provided very interesting information regarding consumers' perceptions and use of the various services provided. The results clearly indicate that visitors had paid services ranging between direct and indirect services in the resort.

First of all, the results showed that tourists seek periods where they can be 'away' from the resort, or at least with a level of privacy away from the vicinity of the provider. One of their objectives, during their holiday, is to spend quality time together, often with their family or at least with friends, and these times require access to quiet moments during which they will have quality time together. This intuitively implies that visitors do not expect to live extraordinary moments at all times of their holiday. Their choices can be quite simple in fact, not expecting extraordinary or adrenaline-based experiences but simply the opportunity to enjoy their time together. These experiences can involve times when the family will play cards inside their rental, prepare a meal together or simply watch the sun set at the end of the day. In those instances, qualified as indirect service, the role of the provider is moderate since consumers seek to experience intense personal moments without any direct intervention from the provider. These services can be summarised as intense periods of auto-construction: the consumers get their satisfaction from the outcome (the quality of the experience) and do not seek intervention from the provider. The auto-construction dimension of those experiences is not merely a way to use a service, the fact that consumers produce such moments by themselves also creates intense satisfaction (self-reliance).

At the other end of the spectrum, consumers can seek experiences that are entirely under the provider's supervision and control. This is the case with some specific activities that require special skills (physical skills or knowledge) that consumers do not feel they have. Elements of safety might also influence that choice. In those instances, consumers feel that relying on a provider will provide them with a superior service and an enhanced experience. Those experiences cover most sport activities (hang gliding, beginner mountain biker, mountain climbing, swimming lessons, etc.). It can also cover services where consumers feel that they do not have the necessary knowledge to fully experience an element. For instance, guided tours to heritage sites or flora and fauna guiding all require direct service from a service provider. In those instances, the level of auto-construction is minimised and consumers are willingly more reliant on the provider's skills and knowledge. These experiences involve qualified and trained providers and are usually charged for a fee. The level of auto-construction is very low. The consumer is mostly reliant on the provider although some elements of cohesion (bonding) between the participants might occur.

In between the above experiences can be found experiences that require an indirect service provision. For instance, hiking will provide enjoyment if the trail is secure (paths have been well restored and maintained), if its difficulty levels have been well assessed and if the directions have been correctly indicated (signage is correctly managed). All those elements require some services from the provider but of an indirect nature. This experience is very much one of co-construction: the provider has set up facilities that will allow visitors to enjoy the experience by themselves. However, auto-construction is also present as consumers will develop their own experience (sharing with others, bringing their own knowledge and skills to enhance the enjoyment of the experience).

The idea of a continuum stems from the recognition that tourist services have very different facets and can either be totally, partially or very marginally co-created. The continuum underneath details those various dimensions (Figure 8.1).

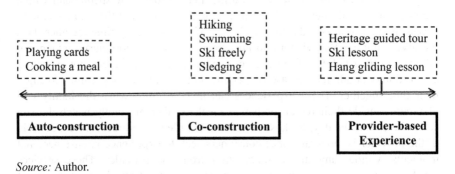

Source: Author.

Figure 8.1   The service continuum

Extension of the Study of the Consumer Co-Construction at the Resort Level

So far, the chapter has addressed the characteristics of services and the specificities of service delivery in a tourism and leisure context. The role of the tourism industry has been to cultivate professionally operant resources, in other words skills that allow professionals to make the most out of a destination tourism resource to commercialise them efficiently to their customers. Two tourism contexts can be encountered: the packaging of the tourism resource within the setting of a resort or the provision of service delivery within a destination.

The Integrated Resort Model

The first instance, the situation of a resort, is the easiest context for managing the consumer experience. Resorts have been designed to package the tourism offering within a closed environment where the service provider can manage and deliver the service more efficiently. Usually the resort belongs to one entity (often a large multinational or hotel group) which simplifies its unity in terms of architecture, service delivery, staff training, decors, etc. The physical proximity of the different components of the service delivery facilitates the use of the service. For instance, the different activities, catering and accommodation facilities will all be close and consumers will easily access any of them when necessary. The services might be provided on an all-inclusive basis which implies that even the decisions, especially regarding budget, will have been dealt in advance when purchasing the product. The consumer therefore knows that all facilities (food and drinks, accommodation, activities, entertainment) are included in the price paid and do not require extra expense. In this type of offering, the flexibility of the service offered is essential. The rationale behind the all-inclusive offer is to remove the stress associated with having to organise and plan activities. The holiday can then take place in 'total freedom' regarding any imposed timing. For instance, resorts offer late breakfasts, all-day snacks and activities, etc. A range of excursions outside the resort are also provided (at a cost) but save the burden, and often the anxiety, that this category of tourists might feel about venturing outside the resort.

In this context, the notions of auto-construction and co-construction are present. The idea behind the integrated resort is to provide a wide range of offerings from which consumers can choose freely. As stated previously, the rationale is not to impose any pace or obligations upon tourists since this freedom to choose is part of the tourists' enjoyment. Whilst this experience is totally managed by the provider, the role of the consumer is still present. Co-construction is actually very present in this offer in the sense that the enterprise proposes a range of offerings from which tourists make their choice to co-construct. However, is there place for auto-construction? Probably in this context auto-construction is less present than in other types of holidays (especially if organised independently). Nonetheless, within this form of holiday, tourists will also want to spend time 'on their own'. For instance, they might simply want to spend time gazing at a landscape, reading a book or practising an activity. Auto-construction also refers to moments of privacy when tourists will want to spend time with their family in occurrences that can be described as fairly normal. Resort managers have fully understood this demand and make sure that auto-construction remains possible by not imposing any choice.

Whilst the resort model is a very effective context created to manage the consumer experience efficiently, it is a model which is more difficult to adapt to a destination-based tourist resort. The following section will illustrate how this can be conceptualised in the context of mountain resorts.

The Destination-Resort

France has a long history in terms of mountain resort development. After the Second World War, local authorities decided to invest heavily into the ski industry and requisitioned land to make way for an extensive and coordinated development of high altitude mountain resorts. While each of those resorts was designed by various developers and architects, they had in mind to develop a service offering that was structured around convenience. The heart of the resort concentrated the buildings, and ski-access right from the buildings was seen as a key selling advantage. In other words from the heart of the resort, consumers could access by ski the entire skiing domain without needing to rely on their car or public transport. Vast parking areas were organised to park the cars on the outskirts of the resort and a few resorts were designed to be totally car free. All shops and services were to be located at the centre of the resort. They included ski pass resale points, ski rental shops, restaurants, supermarkets and tourist office centres. At the time, the developers wanted to make sure that they could achieve maximum convenience through the proximity of services and the direct access to skiing slopes.

This model was most certainly ahead of its time when created and has remained a very successful concept. The only difficulty however appeared with the extension of the resorts over the years. Indeed, when resorts expanded, they built more buildings on the outskirts of the original centre. This evolution means that for the consumers located outside the main centre, the original aim of convenience has been diminished (longer walking distances to the heart of the resort or even the need to rely on public transport/private cars). Problems of congestion, parking difficulties have also been experienced. Whilst the original resorts were built with a unified style in mind, successive years saw the construction of buildings impregnated by the architectural styles of their era. Even though resorts are still mostly wooden covered and have kept an 'alpine style', successive years have witnessed different forms of buildings and different taints of wood.

In comparison with integrated resorts, the experience in those destination-based mountain resorts is very different for the various consumers. Because the experience is mostly organised independently (we will not discuss here the few examples of integrated hotels within those resorts, they are far from being the norm), the concept of co-construction is still very present but more difficult to organise.

The lack of links between the different stakeholders inside the resort means that consumers have to purchase and pay independently each of those services. For every service, consumers have to choose a service supplier, experience a different service encounter and a different service provider and spend a length of time in each of those services. The whole challenge, therefore, is now to rethink those resorts and envisage how they improve their service.

To What Extent Can the Integrated Resort Concept Be Integrated in a Destination Resort Context?

Destination resorts whilst developing an organisational framework similar to integrated resorts, have encountered difficulties in providing similar service provision to those resorts. Indeed, unlike integrated resorts, they have a multitude of owners who are both public and private. Most of the public, or semi-public, service provision (such as chair lifts, information centre, accommodation, etc.) is managed separately and independently from each other. The problem as such is not so much linked to the convenient location and physical layout of the resort but rather to the multiple ownership that challenges the possibility to have a common managerial vision. A single owner cannot manage collectively all those stakeholders which creates a complex difficulty to be able to provide a cohesive and convenient service.

The biggest problem tackled so far by mountain resorts has been to develop strategies to close the gap between the different services provided in order to provide an offer similar to that of an integrated-resort provision. These initiatives have in mind to ease the co-construction of the holiday. The resorts aim to ease the use of services to send the message to consumers that they are putting in place various systems that will allow them to use their services more efficiently.

In winter, most services are still provided separately. For instance, ski passes, ski rental, child care or ski lessons are all supported by different providers who market their services in different offices. The main improvement with respect to those services has been to remove the inconvenience of queues by providing direct sales on Internet and advance-booking options. Hence consumers can book in advance their ski passes, ski lessons or rent their ski equipment. Whilst this improves waiting times while at the resort, this still implies that the consumer has to organise all these elements by himself.

For several decades, tourist offices evolved from a role of information provision to that of designing communication and positioning strategies and event planning within the resort. In the last decade, those tourist information centres have developed online central reservation services (*'centrales de réservation'*). These represent the best approach to providing a combined services' offer to tourists. These reservation centres offer accommodation booking (rented apartments, hotels, etc.) often combined with ski passes and sometimes ski rental, ski lessons and child care facilities. Most large-scale resorts now have developed this online tool and have encountered some success by finally offering to visitors the possibility to book, in one go, the main services that they will require during their holiday. Most booking centres will base their service on a services offering from which visitors can choose those necessary for their holiday (http://www.lesmenuires.com/hiver/ for instance). Recently, the products on offer have increased to include a wider range of options such as spa treatments, water park, ski insurance, private transfers and even a night out dining in a mountain chalet (see for example: http://www.valthorens.com/hiver).

Most of those initiatives come from the tourist information centres although accommodation providers (such as Pierre & Vacances) and some ski lift operators (La Belle Montagne for instance) also provide similar packages.

Another element that eases the tourist's convenience upon arrival is the possibility of booking via Internet a package of basic food and domestic products that are delivered to the rental. Because most visitors will stay in rented flats, they need to shop for food during the skiing holiday. Kreziak and Frochot (2011) showed that in the case of ski resorts, the supermarket is indeed listed as the most important side-service expected in a resort.

The question of marketing a packaged offer is more challenging in the summer. Indeed, when tourists visit those same resorts in the summer their activities will be different. For instance, they will rely less on ski lifts, go hiking, swimming at the local pool, and will engage in leisure activities (football, mountain biking, etc.). Most visitors in high-altitude resorts will not engage into strenuous physical activities (hiking) but will rather tend to favour activities organised at the resort level. In this case, fewer providers are involved in the service provision and for those involved, they are mostly marketing sports/leisure activities. In this context, tourist information centres have developed an offering that combines several leisure provisions into a pass with a daily cost. One of those most successful passes has been provided by the *Portes du Soleil* domain (which groups together Chatel, Avoriaz, etc.). This multi-pass is available across 12 resorts/villages and offers unlimited access to 50 activities ranging from ski lifts, to water parks, swimming pools, museums, public transport, etc. The pass is sold for 1 euro per person and per day. Again, this pass is ideal for holidays where most tourists will be staying in self-catering rentals but will be looking for ease of access and convenience when using the different services/activities offered by the resort. In this respect, the pass provides a good initiative towards an all-inclusive offer (at least for activities), giving ample scope for tourists to co-construct their holidays with the resort. Necessarily, the auto-construction dimension of the holiday is still present and is even more prominent than in winter. Indeed, summer visitors tend to seek a more tranquil holiday than in winter: the pace of the holiday is more relaxed and tourists clearly want to indulge themselves with leisurely and relaxing attitude towards their time spent at the resort. They require fewer child services as their objective is also to spend quality family time together.

Conclusion

This chapter has presented the complexity of the services provided in a tourism context and analysed the extent to which the experience is co-constructed with the provider. It proposed a fairly extensive analysis of the complexities encountered by resorts, destination-based, at replicating the convenience and efficiency services that characterise integrated-resorts. In that regard, one of the main challenges is that the destination encounter is linked with the diversity and independence of their tourism stakeholders. Moving towards a service that provides similar convenience to integrated-resorts is essential as it matches current trends in tourists' expectations in the twenty-first century.

The advent of the Internet has improved the capacity of those resorts to provide a packaged commercialisation of their services. Indeed, Internet has provided a platform from which destinations can finally coordinate the resale of their services and package them into a single offering. This, however, does not mean that on a day-to-day basis the different services are physically and commonly managed but it has certainly increased the coordination between those stakeholders since they can commonly advertise themselves on a single website. As was also indicated, other providers (supermarkets, ski rentals) have attempted to organise in-house delivery to avoid going physically to different providers to obtain their services, but there is still scope for improvement in that domain.

The general idea behind these various actions is to improve the co-construction process between consumers and tourism stakeholders with the ultimate objective to increase and facilitate co-construction mechanisms by easing and increasing the convenience in use of the services on offer. This does not imply that all services have to be co-constructed; one of the pleasures of a holiday is to have access, autonomously, to various services on consumers' own choices. Therefore, mountain resorts are aiming to provide a setting where co-construction is as efficient as can be achieved, removing the stress and burden from consumers and freeing their time for auto-construction. The ideal service is one that offers opportunities for co-construction, auto-construction as well as provider-based activities.

References

Cova, B. and Carù, A. 2004. How service elements wrap the consumer's experience. The case of music consumption at the auditorium of Milan. *Finanza Marketing e Produzione*, 22(2), 5–28.

Crompton, J.L. and Mackay, K.J. 1989. User's perceptions of the relative importance of service quality dimensions in selected public recreation programs. *Leisure Sciences*, 11, 367–75.

Durrande-Moreau, A., Edvardsson, B., Frochot, I. and Kreziak, D. 2012. *Value Creation in a Composed Service System*. AMA SERVSIG International Service Research Conference, Helsinki, Finland, 7–9 June 2012.

Eiglier, P. and Langeard, E. 1987. *Servuction: le Marketing des Services.* McGraw-Hill.

Frochot, I. and Batat, W. 2013. *Marketing and Designing the Tourist Experience.* London: Goodfellow Publishers.

Frochot, I. and Hughes, H. 2000. HISTOQUAL: an adaptation of SERVQUAL to historic houses. *Tourism Management,* 21(2), 157–67.

Grönroos, C. 2000. *Service Management and Marketing: a Customer Relationship Management Approach.* West Sussex, UK: John Wiley and Sons.

—. 2010. Value co-creation in service logic: a critical analysis. *Marketing Theory,* 11(3), 279–301.

Hamilton, J.A., Crompton, J.L. and More, T.A. 1991. Identifying the dimensions of service quality in a park context. *Journal of Environmental Management,* 32, 211–20.

Kotler, P., Armstrong, G., Saunders, J. and Wong, V. 1996. *Principles of Marketing.* European Edition. London: Prentice Hall.

Kreziak, D. and Frochot, I. 2011. Co-construction de l'expérience touristique: les stratégies des touristes en stations de sport d'hiver. *Décisions Marketing,* 64, 23–33.

Lovelock, C.H. 1983. Classifying services to gain strategic marketing insights. *Journal of Marketing,* 47(summer), 9–20.

Lusch, R.F., Vargo, S.L. and O'Brien, M. 2007. Competing through service: insights from service-dominant logic. *Journal of Retailing,* 83(1), 5–18.

Shostack, G.L. 1985. Planning the service encounter, in *The Service Encounter,* edited by J.A. Czepiel et al. New-York: Lexington Books, 243–54.

Surprenant, C.F. and Solomon, M.R. 1987. Predictability and personalization in the service encounter. *Journal of Marketing,* 54 (January), 85–101.

Swarbrooke, J. 1995. *The Development and Management of Visitor Attractions.* Oxford: Butterworth-Heinemann.

Vargo, S.L. and Lusch, R.F. 2004. Evolving to a new dominant logic for marketing. *Journal of Marketing,* 68, 1–17.

PART III
Tourism and Recreation: Opportunities for Places?

PART III

Chapter 9

Tourist Contribution to the Financing of Natural Areas: The Significance of Non-Economic Motivations

Jeoffrey Dehez, Asma Ben Othmen and Tina Rambonilaza

Introduction

In France, access to protected natural areas (such as national parks or public forests) is mostly free, even today. Financing the management of these sites usually calls on public funding. Whenever any contribution by users (notably tourists) is envisaged, it relies on direct and indirect redistribution mechanisms such as taxes. The best known mechanism is no doubt that of visitors' tax ('taxe de séjour' in France), paid by tourists to their hosts, and subsequently transferred to the municipality (or groups of municipalities). However, this does not mean that entrance fees to natural areas are entirely excluded. And so, in France, a number of pilot experiments have been introduced in recent years at highly popular, emblematic sites (Pointe du Raz in Brittany, Dune du Pilat in Aquitaine). The justifications for entrances fees to these sites cite the need to regulate uses that have reached a level considered excessive and that could otherwise speed up the deterioration of the natural environment, but especially the need to generate new financial revenue to cover maintenance costs. This has led to the re-examination of the issue of visitors' potential contribution once again, including via a financial contribution. However, pricing the access to natural sites is still a subject of controversy. For reasons of fairness, it brings out opposition. Moreover, there is no guarantee that the revenue collected will cover the costs incurred. In other words, the introduction of any price system must answer at least two fundamental questions: who pays, and through which mechanism? In this context, nature-based tourism is often considered as being somewhat disposed to contributing to the preservation of the natural environment (Bell et al. 2009). However, this segment of demand is still difficult to grasp, and the motivations that underpin the decision to make a financial contribution to a site's protection and facilities appear to be highly diverse.

Generally speaking, recreational services are associated with 'use value', i.e. a value resulting from the direct use of the service by individuals (Hanley et al. 2003), which fits in fairly well with the act of visiting a place (i.e. going to a site to enjoy its attributes). For all that, since the ground-breaking research by Krutilla (1967), standard microeconomic theory recognises other sources of individual utility that are not necessarily related to any one form of consumption. We thus talk of 'non-use value' (Freeman 1993) which implicitly refers to a broader range of motivations. Bequest value, for example, reflects a form of intergenerational solidarity via the value that individuals allocate to the transmission of certain components of the natural heritage to future generations. In this respect, we can also refer to a form of altruism, even more present in 'existence value' which is supposed to measure the importance granted by individuals to the preservation of endangered species (or the environment in general), without them ever coming into contact with these species (Freeman 1993). However, the difference between use and non-use values is nowhere near as clear. Some authors argue, for example, that non-use value is derived independently of any present or future tangible contact, whereby the benefits of non-use can be generated simply by knowing that these species exist and that their existence is safeguarded (Crowards 2009). Meanwhile, other authors claim that use is the very foundation of non-use value (Aldred 1994). Here, non-use value is seen as representing an intrinsic value inherent to the asset; it must therefore be dealt with alongside use value.

In this context, certain studies have sought to extend the foundations of the economic value of recreational services and, consequently, related motivations. Willis et al. (2000) thus add an 'availability value' for contemporaries, reflecting a form of altruism or solidarity, even if this value risks being limited to 'normal' sites devoid of any emblematic character. More recently, Rulleau (2008) highlighted motivations specific to non-use values in the adherence to the introduction of an entrance fee to certain beaches in the south west of France. First among the arguments are responses such as 'I want to maintain the state of the site for future generations', 'I'm concerned about the environment' or even 'everyone must be able to benefit from the site'. Other authors have gone further by tackling the problem directly from the perspective of motivations. That is what we propose to do in this chapter, by looking at the motivations behind the decision made by tourists to make a financial contribution to the management of natural sites.

The chapter is structured as follows. Firstly, we will recall the main economic principles which, until now, have governed entrance fees to natural areas, drawing attention to the issue of demand analysis in the process. Next, we will look back at a series of studies that have sought to establish new foundations (which we will collectively refer to here as 'non-economic motivations') to explain tourists' willingness to contribute. We will then give an illustration based on a survey conducted in the area of the Gironde estuary in the south west of France. We will go on to present the empirical protocols and the theoretical models used, followed by a series of results. We will conclude by looking at the various opportunities offered by the consideration of non-economic motivations in the analysis of tourists' behaviour.

Literature Review

Pricing of Access to Natural Areas and Economic Optimum

In economic literature, the pricing of access to natural areas has generally been broached as the regulation of a recreational service provided by natural areas. Thus, when Fisher and Krutilla (1972) ponder the definition of an economic optimal level of use, they soon raise the question of the tools needed to reach that optimum. Consequently, the entrance fee would have to be calculated based on a set of social (and environmental) costs on the one hand, and on the characteristics of demand on the other. Since then, the entrance fee has always been presented as an unavoidable management tool (Loomis and Walsh 1997), and the resulting analyses have been gradually redefined. At one point, for example, it was to minimise congestion phenomena (McConnel 1985). Later it was to cover production costs and avoid operating loss (Wilman 1988), and later still to discriminate against users, treating those who visit at peak periods differently from those who visit off-season (Silby 2001). All these analyses lead to price systems of varying complexity, depending on the given context. They all aim to achieve an economic optimum based on attaining equal marginal costs and marginal utilities, a condition that, in theory, maximises the social surplus. These approaches were invariably based on detailed knowledge of the structure of the demand for outdoor recreation.

Economic Evaluation of the Demand for a Non-Market Service and Motivations

Tourism literature oriented primarily towards the analysis of actual stays (a composite good that incorporates recreation and other market goods and services) has seldom addressed the specific demand of access to natural sites. We must thus turn to the environmental economics literature to find benchmarks for analysing and evaluating demand for these recreational services, which often have a non-market character. The consumer surplus approach, by directly evaluating their Willingness To Pay (WTP), provides a monetary measure of marginal benefits.[1] This subsequently involves identifying the factors that explain the variation in these WTP values within the target population in order to understand the heterogeneity of demand. Among the factors to include in the analysis of demand functions, variables that effectively represent consumers' motivations are far from obvious. In their textbook on the economics of outdoor recreation, Loomis and Walsh (1997) evoked the need to integrate visitors' tastes and preferences by referring to the basic characteristics of individual personality, while recalling the

---

1 There is a wealth of literature on this subject. Indeed, recreational services are undoubtedly one of the best documented fields of application. For an overview of the most recent approaches, we refer to work by Hanley et al. (2003), for example.

genuine difficulties faced in measuring this kind of variable[2] (which explains why we often seek to approximate them – inaccurately – with other socio-demographic variables such as age or income). Among other things, the authors suggest drawing on the list of motivations established by Driver (1977) for outdoor activities. This list identifies 20 or so motivations, including the quest for personal achievement, nostalgia, creative inspiration and escape from social pressure. By way of illustration, Loomis and Walsh (1997) cite the study by Miller et al. (1977), one of the first on this subject, in which eight of the motivations listed in Driver's typology alone account for 15 per cent of the variations in WTP. For all that, this typology remains focused on the satisfaction of individual needs related to the use of natural areas. And yet, there is growing evidence that the palette of motivations is in fact much broader.

Environmental Preferences via the Application of the New Ecological Paradigm

The creators of the 'New Ecological Paradigm' (NEP), Dunlap et al. (2000) proposed a typology of individuals' representations of the problems raised by the relationship between humans and the environment, or by the behaviours to adopt to limit the impact of human activities on nature. A number of concepts, such as responsibility, moral satisfaction or 'green concerns' are specified. The items proposed by the 'New Ecological Paradigm' have been used in social science studies, including in economics. Nunes and Schokkaert (2003) thus relied on methods developed in social psychology to quantify the attitudes, and even to establish psychological profiles, based on responses to a series of preselected statements. These attitudinal variables subsequently served to establish 'ethical profiles', which were introduced as an explanatory variable of WTP values. While Nunes and Schokkaert (2003) turned their attention to the attitudes of individuals faced with various items connected to environmental conservation, they also examined the motivations for the act of donating in general. They thus distinguished several profiles, some of which are clearly rooted in environmental concerns, while others are more oriented toward broader social concerns. This kind of empirical approach could also serve to address the separability of economic and non-economic components of the WTP. A similar approach – more specific to leisure and tourism – was adopted by Godard (2010) through a study of the economic value associated with the quality of bathing water along several French beaches. The author sought to establish the 'psycho-environmental profiles' of individuals before testing their possible effect on WTP. The results are less decisive since ultimately, individual choices on the recreational attributes (and the related WTP) remain highly contingent on the direct utility to be had, which reflects the use value. 'Psycho-environmental profiles' play an indirect role via their effect

---

2   It should be noted that, at about the same time, the authors of the report on the NOAA Panel on Contingent Valuation also recommended introducing 'attitudes' in contingent valuations (Arrow et al. 1993).

on whether or not a person consents to the 'principle to pay', defined beforehand, with the prospect of contributing to environmental protection in general, which will itself subsequently have an impact on the definition of WTP values for the quality of bathing waters. In any case, these attempts to associate new motivations for leisure activities remain highly stimulating, and prompt us to go beyond the framework of strictly environmental concerns, by testing other non-economic considerations. We propose to maintain this CAP-based approach to highlight the weight of tourists' non-economic motivations in view of a funding contribution to a program for the conservation of natural areas for recreation purposes.

Data and Methods

Presentation of the Study Area and the Collection of Data

In this chapter we will present the results of an analysis based on an on-site survey conducted with tourists (individuals who stayed for leisure in and around the Gironde estuary in France) during the 2010 summer season. The survey was conducted on 17 sites along both banks of the Gironde estuary. Several sites were selected in each municipality with a view to conducting the questionnaire close to tourist information offices, natural sites and coastal resorts. The survey places and dates were chosen to ensure the sample's best representativeness. A stopping off place for migrating birds and a habitat for diverse and abundant fish, the Gironde estuary is part of the marshlands along the Atlantic coast. It is often presented as the best preserved of Europe's large estuaries given the number of species of migrating fish (11 in all) that can still be found there. In particular, the estuary is still the only natural habitat for a wild population of European sturgeon. Moreover, the cultural and historical heritage of the areas bordering the estuary remains remarkable: world-renowned vineyards and wine-making châteaux eagerly sought out by tourists, the Blaye citadel, and the locks designed by Vauban, to name but a few. Given the estuary's diversity of landscapes and natural sites (such as its islands), the development of nature-based tourism is a serious issue. The financing of infrastructures to gain access to these sites and to oversee their maintenance remains an open question.

Our questionnaire sought to gather information on tourists' characteristics, the nature of their stay, their affinities and their preferences in terms of recreation. By way of information, Table 9.1 compiles the main variables used. The survey also included a section on non-economic motivations. In this respect, a series of statements were put to the individuals polled. In response, they had to say whether or not they agreed ('agree' / 'don't agree'). The way an individual responds to a statement is assumed to reveal the presence (or absence) of their motivation. It is coded in the form of a binary variable (Table 9.1) that is subsequently referred back to in the modelling of choices (see below). Several non-economic motivations were broached, based on questions used in other studies found in the literature.

Table 9.1   Definition of the variables used in econometric models

Category	Label	Definition	Type
Nature of the contribution	*VM*	Willingness to accept to contribute voluntarily to conservation funding programmes	0/1 (no / yes)
	VMBid	Willingness to accept a voluntary contribution of €5	0/1 (no / yes)
	PSM	Willingness to accept to make a payment to access a service provided	0/1 (no / yes)
Characteristics of the individual	*LnHous*	Natural logarithm of the number of persons in the household	Continuous and positive
	LnInc	Natural logarithm of household income per consumption unit	Continuous and positive
	Car	The tourists came to the Gironde estuary by car	0/1 (no / yes)
Characteristics of the stay	*WatTour*	The tourists have already carried out at least one activity associated with river tourism since their arrival	0/1 (no / yes)
	NaturVisit	The tourists have already visited at least one natural site since their arrival at the Gironde estuary	0/1 (no / yes)
	NaturInterest	Tourist motivated by visiting natural sites along the Gironde estuary	0/1 (no / yes)
NEP motivations	*FinanceBiod*	Motivation: 'Receipts go to the funding of programmes for biodiversity conservation'	0/1 (disagree / agree)
	RegulPark	Motivation: 'Improved parking services also help to limit unauthorised visits which deteriorate the sites'	0/1 (disagree / agree)
Bequest value motivations	*ExcepSite*	Motivation: 'It is an exceptional site that belongs to everyone'	0/1 (disagree / agree)
	FutGen	Motivation: 'It is an exceptional site whose conservation is essential for future generations'	0/1 (disagree / agree)

Category	Label	Definition	Type
Altruism motivations	*Habit*	Motivation: 'It is our custom to participate in the collective effort'	0/1 (disagree / agree)
	StateFail	Motivation: 'The State does not give sufficient money to finance biodiversity conservation, so it's up to us to do so'	0/1 (disagree / agree)
Usage motivations	*FinanceProtect*	Justification: 'Receipts will genuinely be allocated to conservation funding programmes'	0/1 (disagree / agree)
	NoStateFail	Justification: 'The State does not give sufficient money, so it's not up to us to do so'	0/1 (disagree / agree)

The motivations relating to environmental preferences (variables *FinanceBiod* and *RegulPark)* are inspired by the NEP. Concerns that tie in with the notion of non-use value distinguished the bequest value (variables *ExcepSite* and *FutGen*) and altruism (variables *Habit* and *StateFail*). Lastly, two additional questions were reserved for situations where, even though non-economic motivations seemed absent, the respondents could adopt unusual behaviour. A first question targeted the impact of the information provided on the nature of the response (variable *FinanceProtect*). A second question focused on the 'crowding-out effect' (variable *NoStateFail*) as identified by Roberts (1984), in other words, when private expenditure opposes public funds to acquire collective goods and services.

The section of the questionnaire focused on the evaluation of tourists' willingness to contribute financially ties in with the type of motivations. As shown in Figure 9.1, the contingent scenario takes place in two steps. Firstly, we asked tourists if they adhered to the actual principle of making a voluntary contribution ('To finance the conservation of natural sites in the Gironde area, the municipalities plan to request a financial contribution. Would you be willing to participate in this approach?'). Secondly, to those who responded positively, we proposed making a single contribution of €5 (via a parking fee). To the others, the parking fee (still €5) was presented as payment for a service provided. In this last case, we assume that the decision is mainly guided by the use value, and that the questions about motivations have not been asked; instead, the two questions on the information available and the crowding-out effect (see above) were asked. It must be remembered that the objective of this research is to test the role of non-economic motivations with regard to directly adhering to the principle of a financial contribution, not to evaluate the individual WTP for accessing and maintaining natural sites along the Gironde estuary. As a result, we can dispense with certain auction protocols habitually used in WTP estimates (Hanemann and Kanninen 1998). In this context, the second step in the procedure (with the

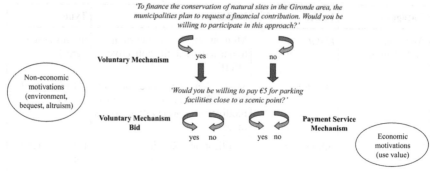

Source: Authors.

Figure 9.1   The various contribution mechanisms

€5 fee) is presented as a step for validating the answers given in the previous step. In short, we are looking at three dichotomous choices: the first on the willingness to participate in a voluntary contribution (identified by variable *VM* below), the second on the amount of the contribution (*VMBid*) and the third on the adherence to the principle of payment for a service provided (*PSM*).

Econometric Models

The choices that we are looking at here are binary choices represented by dichotomous variables. For example, if the tourist accepts the principle of a voluntary contribution, and this decision is represented by variable *VM,* then this variable takes the value 1 in the sample, and 0 otherwise. Applied to all the respondents, the results obtained on variable *VM* define the probability for any individual *i* of accepting the financial contribution for the conservation programme. To explain such choices, we drew on models with latent variables in which the variable observed, for example *VM,* actually reflects the behaviour of another unobserved variable, the latent variable, here noted *VM**. This latent variable can take continuous values and, more importantly, can be explained by a set of exogenous variables x_i. In economics, these models have undergone many developments (Greene 2003) since the pioneering work of McFadden (1974). Consequently, the discrete choice process can be represented as follows

$$VM_i^* = \beta_i x_i + \mu_i$$

$$VM_i = \begin{cases} 1 & if\ VM_i^* > 0 \\ 0 & else \end{cases}$$

(1)

The β_i parameters are associated with variables x_i and μ_i are random error parameters that reflect the fact that part of the information escapes the observer (Greene 2003).

However, users may also make a second simultaneous decision in addition to the one concerning their willingness to pay (Brookshire et al. 1986). This decision may regard the number of sites to visit, the frequency of trips or quite simply the possibility of making at least one visit during the stay (as measured by variable *NaturVisit* in our case). As a result, variables that are more or less related to these actions cannot be considered completely exogenous; we could thus attempt to model their variation using a process similar to the one described by equation (1) above. In fact, this is the option we selected in this study, effectively prompting us to adopt bivariate probit models. These involve the regression of two equations at the same time:

- a selection equation that models the probability of accepting the first question in the evaluation; and
- a *NaturVisit* equation, which only concerns the probability of visiting at least one natural site by the tourist since his or her arrival on the site.

Finally, the use of bivariate probits also means considering the variables' potential endogeneity, in other words, testing the possibility that the two decision-making processes may be related to one another, at least partially. Again, this hypothesis is highly conceivable with a variable such as the number of visits (*NaturVisit*). In fact, just as the number of visits to a site is an unavoidable indicator of the use value attributed to it by individuals and, as a result, affects their willingness to pay for its maintenance, this variable is often impacted by several factors of the structural equation (such as loyalty to the place, proximity to the site, free time available, etc.). To get around this kind of bias, other econometric models have been developed, notably the 'seemingly unrelated probit model' taking account of endogeneity (Maddala 1983). This model follows the simultaneous equations models defined by Maddala (1983):

$$\begin{cases} VM_i^* = \delta_{1i}NaturVisit_i + \delta_{2i}x_i + \mu_{1i} \\ NaturVisit_i^* = \gamma_i z_i + \mu_{2i} \end{cases} \tag{2}$$

As in the simple probits, VM_i^* and $NaturVisit_i^*$ are observable latent variables, x_i and z_i are exogenous variables, δ_{1i}, δ_{2i} and γ_i are the function's behaviour parameters, and μ_{1i} and μ_{2i} are the error terms of the two equations.

All these models are estimated using the maximum likelihood method. Hereinafter, the potential endogeneity is tested on each of the three types of willingness to pay.

Results and Discussion

Data

The sample consists of 391 individuals. A few trends emerge after the first reading of the data. Most of the tourists polled (64 per cent of the total) state that they would agree to contribute voluntarily to programmes for financing the conservation of natural sites along the Gironde estuary. The main non-economic motivation behind their choice is ensuring that the receipts from their contribution are genuinely allocated to conservation programmes (51 per cent of the sample), which could reflect the desire for some form of involvement in concrete environmental protection actions. A second set of motivations refers to the expression of the non-use value (12 per cent refer to 'future generations' and a further 3 per cent to the 'outstanding' character of the sites). Next, 58.8 per cent of tourists who previously agreed to participate financially in the programme accept the proposed level of contribution. Moreover, these respondents represent 37.5 per cent of the total sample of tourists polled. By comparison, 24.5 per cent of individuals who refused the voluntary contribution would agree to pay in return for a service provided. These respondents represent 8.9 per cent of the total sample. A relatively limited fraction of the tourists have actually visited the estuary's protected sites (28 per cent) or carried out activities related to the river (20 per cent). By contrast, more than half of the sample (56 per cent) claim to be interested by such practices. The car remains the respondents' most widely-used means of travel (88 per cent), a result confirmed by many other surveys. This would tend to confirm the significance of the reference to a parking fee as a means of payment and which, at the same time, avoids certain forms of bias related to the credibility of the scenarios.

Table 9.2 offers a simplified summary of several components of the econometric estimates obtained for each of the three models.[3] It includes the coefficients of the variables and the value of the *Rho* which indicates (or not) the relevance of using bivariate models. In each of the three models, we note that *Rho* values are significantly different from zero. The bivariate probit models are therefore suitable. However, they take different forms, depending on how endogeneity is addressed.

Willingness to Accept the Principle of Voluntary Contribution

The socio-demographic variables are all significant and show coefficients with signs that are consistent with standard theoretical assumptions. Income in particular has a positive impact on the choice of accepting the contribution. The size of households acts positively. This could reveal the effect of lowering the cost per visit, or the expression of some form of intergenerational solidarity. Variables

---

3   For easier reading, we chose not to present all the models tested, nor all the parameters of the econometric estimates.

Table 9.2   Tourists' willingness to accept different financing systems

Variables	Financing mechanism		
	Willingness to accept the voluntary contribution	Willingness to accept the voluntary contribution amount	Willingness to accept payment in return for a service provided
	VM	*VMBid*	*PSM*
LnHous	*4.02	-0.06	0.03
LnInc	*0.70	0.11	*0.32
Car	***3.60	0.18	N/A
WatTour	*1.74	0.06	0.05
NaturVisit	***4.65	N/A	0.21
NaturInterest	0.25	0.12	***0.76
FinanceBiod	***21.58	***1.74	N/A
RegulPark	***18.35	**1.08	N/A
ExcepSite	**15.21	***1.46	N/A
FutGen	***16.90	***1.43	N/A
Habit	**17.49	**1.85	N/A
StateFail	***13.54	**2.25	N/A
FinanceProtect	N/A		***6.05
NoStateFail	N/A		***6.27
Constant	-3.59	-0.96	-5.37
Wald Test (Rho=0)	**5.04	***6.61	**0.02
Wald Test	**194.14	**111.09	***182.40

Note: * significant at the 10% threshold, ** significant at the 5% threshold, *** significant at the 1% threshold.

related to the number of visits to the sites (*WatTour* and *NaturVisit*) have a positive effect, thereby confirming the link between use value and financial contribution. Finally, all the non-economic motivations expressed are found to have a significant and positive impact. However, a gradient in the responses could be seen, since motivations associated with the environmental paradigm (*FinanceBiod* and *RegulPark*) are those with the highest coefficients, ahead of habit *(Habit)* and the two motivations associated with bequest value (*ExcepSite* and *FutGen*). The motivation linked to the altruistic nature of the responses (*StateFail*) comes in last.

Willingness to Accept the Level of the Voluntary Contribution

In this equation, the variables representative of socio-demographic characteristics (including income), and those relating to use (*WatTour*, *NaturInterest*) all show statistically insignificant coefficients. The effect of these variables would thus seem to mainly come about during the phase prior to the decision. As with the first equation, the variables on motivations all show positive and significant coefficients. By contrast, the comparison between these variables does not reflect the same hierarchy: here therefore, motivations related to altruism (*Habit* and *StateFail*) are the ones with the highest coefficients. The weight of environmental preferences is not quite as obvious: while the first variable chosen in this respect (*FinanceBiod*) clearly shows a high coefficient, the second one (*RegulPark*) exhibits the lowest coefficient. Lastly, non-use values (variables *ExcepSite* and *FutGen*) lie between the two.

Willingness to Accept the Payment Mechanism in Return for a Service Provided

In this third equation, we again find the usual positive sign of the coefficient on income. In addition, although 'use' is central to the decision (since the user is invited to pay in return for a service provided), variables *WatTour* and *NaturVisit* have insignificant coefficients, unlike *NaturInterest*. It would therefore seem that the willingness to accept does not depend so much on the activities already carried out up until that time during the stay (a boat trip on the river or a visit to a natural site) as on those activities that individuals intend to carry out, one way or another, during the stay (reminder: variable *NaturInterest* reflects the tourists' interest in this type of activity that they seek to practice at some time or other during the stay). Similarly, we could imagine that the 'service' is not defined in relation to highly specific activities, but rather as a composite, more general 'nature service'. From this perspective, it would be better represented by variable *NaturInterest* which does not focus on either a given activity (such as *WatTour*) or a given site (such as *NaturVisit*). The coefficients of the other two variables, *FinanceProtect* and *NoStateFail*, are both positive, which would tend to validate the importance of the information provided on the one hand, and the presence of a crowding-out effect on the other. However, these results should be further explored via specific studies.

Conclusion

Generally speaking, when dealing with the pricing of access, there is a tendency to focus on demand characteristics such as the price elasticity or the income elasticity of consumption (Loomis and Walsh 1997). This type of information serves not only to anticipate the amount of expected revenue, but also the effects of future pricing on visiting numbers. However, by focusing exclusively on these variables, there is a risk of overlooking the importance of many environmental and social motivations which, while clearly not economic in nature, are equally based on the users' propensity to become involved in the protection of natural areas, including via a financial contribution. For our purposes, the role of motivations in tourists' decision appears at two levels: their acceptance of the very principle of paying on the one hand, and their willingness to accept a certain price level on the other hand. Motivations play a part in these two steps (e.g. the equations on *VM* and *VMBid*) and, contrary to what we could have imagined, are a dominant factor in the second step. For all that, in no way do they cancel out the influence of economic factors (income in this case) or uses (effect of activities practised). This brings us towards a combination between use and non-use on the one hand, and between economic and non-economic considerations on the other hand. In this context, breaking down the payment mechanism into two steps (questioning of the very principle of contributing, and the level of this contribution), as demonstrated by Godard (2010), would appear to be particularly appropriate. However, measuring and introducing these attitudinal variables remains a problem and, beyond identifying a 'non-economic component', the precise characterisation of this component is far from being achieved. Indeed, in our study, we could have expected a greater level of discrimination between the variables on motivations (which, we may recall, are all significant in all the models; only their hierarchy changes). Be that as it may, these results clearly show that recreation is not 'just another' economic service, and that economists have everything to gain by integrating this specificity as best they can.

References

Aldred, J. 1994. Existence value, welfare and altruism. *Environmental Values*, 3(4), 381–402.

Arrow, K., Solow, R., Portney, P.R., Leamer, E., Radner, R. and Schuman, H. 1993. *Report of the NOAA Panel on Contingent Valuation*. Federal Register, USA.

Bell, S., Simpson, M., Tyrväinen, L., Sievänen, T. and Pröbstl, U. (eds.) 2009. *European Forest Recreation and Tourism: a Handbook*. Abingdon, Oxon: Taylor & Francis.

Brookshire, D.S., Eubanks, L.S. and Sorg, C.F. 1986. Existence values and normative economics: implications for valuing water resources. *Water Resources Research*, 22(11), 1508–18.

Crowards, T. 2009. *Non-Use Values and Economic Valuation of the Environment – A Review*. CSERGE Working Paper. University College London.

Driver, B. 1977. *Item Pool for Scales Designed to Quantify the Psychological Outcomes Desired and Expected from Recreation Participation*. Rocky

Mountain Forest and Range Experiment Station, Fort Collins, CO: USDA Forest Service.

Dunlap, R.E., Van Liere, K.D., Mertig, A.G. and Jones, R.E. 2000. Measuring endorsement of the new ecological paradigm: a revised NEP scale. *Journal of Social Issues*, 74, 1121–25.

Fisher, A. and Krutilla, J.V. 1972. Determination of optimal capacity of resource-based recreation facilities. *Natural Resources Journal*, 12(July), 417–44.

Freeman, A.M. 1993. *The Measurement of Environmental and Resource Values – Theory and Methods*. Washington, DC: Resources for the Future.

Godard, J.-Y. 2010. *Recherche Empirique sur les Déterminants du Consentement à Payer pour une Amélioration de la Qualité de l'Environnement – Cas d'Application à la Qualité des Eaux de Baignade du Littoral Aquitain*. PhD dissertation, University Montesquieu Bordeaux 4, Bordeaux.

Greene, W.H. 2003. *Econometric Analysis*. 5th Edition. Upper Saddle River, NJ: Prentice Hall, Pearson Education International.

Hanemann, W.M. and Kanninen, B. 1998. *The Statistical Analysis of Discrete-Response CV Data*. Working Paper n. 798. Department of Agricultural and Resource Economics and Policy, University of California at Berkeley.

Hanley, N., Shaw, W.D. and Wright, R.E. 2003. *The New Economics of Outdoor Recreation*. Cheltenham, UK and Northampton, MA, USA: Edward Elgar.

Krutilla, J.V. 1967. Conservation reconsidered. *American Economic Review*, 57, 787–96.

Loomis, J.B. and Walsh, R.G. 1997. *Recreation Economic Decisions: Comparing Benefits and Costs*. 2nd Edition. State College, PA: Venture Publishing.

McConnell, K.E. 1985. The economics of outdoor recreation, in *Handbook of Natural Resources and Energy Economics, Vol. II*, edited by A.V. Kneese and J.L. Sweeney. London: Elsevier, 677–722.

McFadden, D. 1974. Conditional logit analysis of qualitative choice behaviour, in *Frontiers in Econometrics*, edited by P. Zarembka. New York: Academic Press, 105–42.

Maddala, G.S. 1983. *Limited-Dependent and Qualitative Variables in Econometrics*. Cambridge, UK: Cambridge University Press.

Miller, R., Prato, A. and Young, R. 1977. *Congestion, Success and the Value of Colorado Deer Hunting Experience*. Paper to the 42nd North American Wildlife and Natural Resources Conference, Wildlife Management Institute, Washington, DC.

Nunes, P. and Schokkaert, E. 2003. Identifying the warm glow effect in contingent valuation. *Journal of Environmental Economics and Management*, 45, 231–45.

Roberts, R.D. 1984. A positive model of private charity and public transfers. *Journal of Political Economy*, 92, 136–48.

Rulleau, B. 2008. *Services Récréatifs en Milieu Naturel Littoral et Evaluation Economique Multi-Attributs de la Demande*. PhD dissertation, University Montesquieu Bordeaux 4, Bordeaux.

Silby, H. 2001. Pricing and management of recreational activities which use natural resources. *Environmental and Resource Economics*, 18(3), 339–54.

Willis, K., Garrod, G., Scarpa, R., Macmillan, D. and Bateman, I. 2000. *Non-Market Benefits of Forestry*. Report to the Forestry Commission, Centre for Research in Environmental Appraisal and Management, University of Newcastle upon Tyne.

Wilman, E.A. 1988. Pricing policies for outdoor recreation. *Land Economics*, 64(3), 234–41.

Chapter 10

Resorts, Hinterlands, and Local Development

Dominik Cremer-Schulte and Jean-Christophe Dissart

Introduction

Coastal areas are among the fastest growing regions in the world. About two thirds of the world population live there, and surveys forecast that in 25 years, the three quarters of the world population will live in or close by coastal areas (Bouyer 2004).

The French coastline totals 5,500 km along three seaboards (the North Sea – the Channel, the Atlantic Ocean – Brittany, and the Mediterranean Sea) and experiences growth and in-migration, especially on its western and southern coasts. Today, residential attractiveness adds to the long-known success of coastal tourism, which results in an on-going movement of people and firms towards the coast (a phenomenon labelled *littoralisation* in France). From an economic viewpoint, sea-related traditional activities (shipbuilding, fishing, etc.) are on the decline and most of the new jobs are created in the service sector, as well as in the tourism and recreation sector. In 2001, coastal tourism represented 44 per cent of the maritime added value, with over 150,000 jobs and a turnover that was 12 times as big as that of fisheries (Bouyer 2004). In 2011, coastal tourism (both in urban and rural areas) accounted for 31 per cent of overnight stays in France (DGCIS 2012).

This intense context of tourism is deemed as being a significant challenge to sustainable development (EC 2008). Issues include impacts on the local economy, e.g. employment opportunities, increase of income and more generally the emergence of resort towns and cities as mass tourism destinations (Smith 1991); on the environment (land development, transportation, pollution, erosion, threats to land and marine ecosystems and to biodiversity) (Hall 2001); and on local populations with cultural changes, in-migration and resident displacement issues (Gormsen 1997).

Though the impact of tourism has been largely explored, the economic impact of resort tourism on regional development remains unclear. As far as we know, no quantitative analysis of the links between tourism resorts, neighbouring areas and local development has been carried out in France. Therefore, the purpose of this chapter is to investigate the situation of coastal municipalities (French *communes*) and districts[1] (French *cantons*) as compared with their hinterlands, by exploring associations between resort designation, tourism activity and local development variables. As resorts and concentrated tourism also exist, for instance, in mountain areas, we also compare winter sports and coastal resorts and their neighbouring territories in terms of socio-economic situations. Differences do exist in tourism resources, in the functioning of the tourism economy and spatial spill-over effects. In our analysis, we put into perspective tourist areas in contrasted situations (coastal tourism vs. winter sports tourism; and resorts as concentrated tourist destinations vs. their hinterland), and since the issue of local impacts and spill-overs is complex, the aim is to start bridging that gap in an exploratory manner.

The next section provides key references on the definition of resorts and their socio-economic impact. Then, we give an explanation on the data and methods used for the analysis. The results are laid out for municipalities and districts according to three different methods: mapping, descriptive statistics and regression analysis. In the conclusion, we sum up the main points of the analysis and we outline issues for further research.

Literature Review

Coastal tourism in France impacts many places and resorts, with potentially significant socio-economic benefits. However, the resort concept is somewhat fuzzy, and empirical analyses of the links between tourism resorts and local economic development are scarce and often case-study oriented.

Resorts and Existing Classifications

A resort corresponds to a location of any size, where tourists can find accommodation and the services they require during their stay (Vlès 1996). From pre-tourist villages to resort cities reaching into the hinterland, resorts are a produce of tourism development, characterised by a concentration of tourist accommodation and a local economy relying largely on tourism and visitor demand (Smith 1991).

In France, some statutory definitions classify municipalities as 'tourist municipality' (*commune touristique*) or 'classified tourism resort' (*station classée de tourisme*). They apply to the municipal level and are based on legal texts that have changed over the years. In particular, the application decree of Law n°2006–437 (14 April 2006) lists the requirements for a municipality to be firstly labelled as tourist municipality and secondly as classified tourism resort.

Accordingly, first of all municipalities should: 1) have a classified tourist office; 2) organise tourist activities; and 3) provide a minimum tourist accommodation capacity as a function of its population. For example, if the municipality counts

---

1   A local level 1 administrative unit in the United Kingdom, according to EU classification.

less than 2,000 inhabitants, the minimum share of accommodation capacity is 15 per cent; but if the population exceeds 10,000 inhabitants, then the minimum share of accommodation capacity is 4.5 per cent.

Then, secondly, only a subset of legally designated tourist municipalities may get the 'classified tourism resort' recognition. The 2006 reform regrouped various categories of tourism (for example, spa therapy stays, winter sports or seaside) in a single one ('classified tourism resort'), which is validated by decree for 12 years and is based on the following criteria (DGCIS 2008): 1) it should provide various types and quality of tourist accommodation; 2) it should offer various cultural, sporting and physical leisure pursuits in phase with the local heritage, with natural and built resources and using local professional know-how; 3) it should avail of local stores and adequate health services; 4) it should have a local urban plan and be committed to protecting heritage and enhancing the living environment; 5) it should supply information in several languages on tourist activities and sites; and 6) it should facilitate access to the destination for all types of people. In addition to boosting its tourism destination image, a classified tourism resort can get various benefits, such as more government transfer funds due to tourist influx, the right to levy the property transfer tax directly or in some cases the possibility to set up a casino (DGCIS 2008). In February 2009, 537 (1.5 per cent) municipalities benefited from the 'classified tourism resort' recognition.

Other definitions of 'resort' exist in France. For example, Ambiaud et al. (2004) identified tourist-oriented functional economic areas as areas providing for example a tourist accommodation capacity exceeding 1.5 beds per permanent resident. Also, IFEN (2005) created a typology of seafront municipalities by taking into account the accommodation type and capacity (e.g. campgrounds vs. second homes), and identified six different types of seaside resorts on municipality level.

To conclude, the resort concept tends to vary in classifications and time, from a more inclusive meaning (a destination with tourist accommodation and corresponding services) to a more exclusive legal definition ('classified tourism resort' municipalities). Moreover, tourism development may vary significantly in terms of facilities and services, with hard to define spatial boundaries, as in mountain resorts where skiing areas may be spread over several municipalities.

Resort Impact

There is evidence of coastal tourism impacts on national economies (e.g., Dritsakis 2012), but regional and local effects are much less known. A major reason lies with the difficulty of delineating the 'tourism sector' and its economic impacts (Smith 1988): tourism affects an array of economic dimensions, starting with direct impacts on specific industries and branches, the generation of income for administrations and residents, to more indirect impacts on the population and employment through inter-sector spill-over effects. Moreover, the identification of causal relations shows difficulties: impacts of tourism on economic development imply a causal direction, but resorts and tourism have also been means of economic development policies. Consequently, the results of research on local economic spill-over effects of the resort and tourist activity remain inconclusive (Song et al. 2012).

In terms of literature, different techniques are used to explore the impacts and to estimate tourism multipliers (Van Leeuwen et al. 2006); others focus on the creation of local income and use expenditure data in case-specific contexts, e.g. Mayer et al. (2010) on the impacts of tourism in German National Parks or Johnson and Moore (1993) on the impact of white-water recreation in Oregon (USA). Qualitative local and regional case studies (e.g., Violier 2008) in the French context complete this strand of literature.

Addressing the economic spill-overs of resort planning, Vlès (1996) wrote that accommodations accounted for 60 per cent of the total investment, reinforcing the construction sector; he further mentioned direct employment in hotels, restaurants, travel agencies and tour operators as well as induced employment in sectors where the revenue came for over 50 per cent from tourism. The multiplier effects of the tourist economy were described as high in resorts (due to high visitor numbers), making it an important tool for regional planning. However, in addition to several figures on the national scale and a few selected examples (especially in the Pyrenees mountain range), there was no quantitative analysis of the impact of resorts.

On the basis of the accommodation capacity and an estimation of tourism-related employment, Dissart et al. (2009) identified some functional economic areas (i.e. small areas in which inhabitants have access to both employment and facilities) relying on tourist activity (i.e. accommodation capacity and tourism-related employment are more than twice the national average). In these rural areas, which numbered 102 in metropolitan France, tourism specialisation was associated with lower population, employment and income levels, thereby casting doubt on tourism-based local development. These results, however, could also mean that tourism cannot fully address particularly lagging situations. Investigating spatial spill-overs of employment dynamics within the Italian local tourist systems, Lazzeretti and Capone (2009) showed that the long-term growth of tourism-related employment in functional economic areas (local labour systems) was spatially interdependent. Through regression analysis, they provided evidence that systems of tourism located close to localities having a high economic growth rate tended to show a higher development level, thereby confirming the hypothesis of spatial spill-overs between local tourist systems. These two studies, however, did not focus on resorts, so their results cannot be extended to estimate the effects of resorts on local development.

To evaluate the impact of tourism on the socio-economic indicators of hosting communities, Urtasun and Gutiérrez (2006) suggested a method based on descriptors of tourism activities (in terms of importance and concentration level) and the regional quality of life (social welfare measured by 12 partial descriptors). The analysis, which was carried out in Spanish provinces, showed that the impact of tourism on the residents' quality of life is very much dependent on the considered dimension. For example, tourism activity was positively associated with health services and employment, but negatively associated with environmental quality (e.g. a large share of dwellings with little green area). From their analysis the authors inferred thresholds that tourism destinations could reach without adversely affecting the host regions.

To conclude, to our knowledge there is neither an analysis of the links between seaside resorts, their hinterlands and local economic development nor an exploratory comparison with winter sport resorts as another type of concentrated tourism activity.

Data and Methods

We use mapping, descriptive statistics and regression analysis to assess the extent to which the variation of key indicators of socio-economic development (dependent variables) is linked to the variation of various development factors (independent variables), including geographic location, tourism development, and economic structure.

Scope

The scope of the analysis includes coastal resorts and their hinterlands, as well as winter sport resorts and their hinterlands. We assume that they share common features such as a concentrated tourism activity and a natural resource base (the sea or slope and snow). As resort definitions vary, we choose to define them in terms of access to resources and activities. The analysis is carried out on two geographic levels, municipalities and districts, because 1) the preliminary mapping analysis revealed a sharp contrast in accommodation capacity between seafront vs. hinterland municipalities, and 2) limited data on income distribution is available at municipality level for confidentiality reasons.

Therefore, we define a 'seaside resort' as any municipality or district providing access to the seafront, regardless of the importance of tourism activity. Winter sport resorts do differ from coastal resorts in terms of tourism resources and they are more difficult to allocate to distinct host communes. Indeed, skiing areas may be spread over various municipalities or resorts. Due to a lack of data on ski areas and their host municipalities, we used the Gouvstat (Cemagref-DEATM 1989) database which links ski resorts to municipalities (and by extension, to districts) on the basis of accommodation locations.

Hinterlands are identified using buffer zones surrounding the resorts. Research on spatial economics increasingly uses geographic information systems and buffer zones to account for differentiated economic impacts across space. For example, that approach was used to estimate the regional economic impact of military base closings in Germany (Paloyo et al. 2010), or household location choice as a function of air quality in the United States (Banzhaf and Walsh 2008). We use three spatial zones to account for neighbourhood effects in the analysis:

1) a 'resort' zone for a municipality or a district hosting a seafront resort or a winter sports resort, further differentiated into legally recognised 'classified tourism resorts' vs. resorts with no statutory classification; 2) a 'resort neighbour' zone for a municipality or district being adjacent to a seafront resort or a winter sports resort; and 3) a 'hinterland' zone for a municipality or a district located between the resort-neighbour municipality or district and a 30-km strip starting at the resort (the threshold value was decided on the basis of the average daily travel-to-work distance in France, which is about 30 km (Baccaïni et al. 2007)). Other statutory resort municipalities (i.e. neither seaside nor winter sports), located in the 30 km radius, are also included in the analysis.

Dependent Variables

Local development encompasses many dimensions so it is usually assessed using an array of indicators. Here, we measure local development using dependent variables on population, employment, income, and facilities. Calculated at municipality and district levels, the main data sources are the population census (2007), the INSEE (National Institute of Statistics and Economic Studies) income tax dataset (RFLM 2007), the facility database (BPE 2010) and geographic data from the National Geographic Institute (IGN) (see Table 10.1).

Table 10.1   Study variables and data sources

Variable	Description and unit	Source (Year)
Dependent variables		
POP	Population	INSEE RP (2007)
JOB_W	Number of jobs at place of work / 1,000 inhabitants	As above
JOB_R	Number of people employed at place of residence / 1,000 inhabitants	As above
MEDINC	Median income per consumption unit (€)	INSEE RFLM (2007)
INTERD	Income interdecile ratio per consumption unit	As above
FACLT	Number of facilities / 1,000 inhabitants	BPE (2009), INSEE census (2007)
Independent variables		
SEA_R	Dummy: a seafront district comprising a classified tourism resort	IGN geofla (2007), DGCIS (2010)
SEA_NR	Dummy: a seafront district without any classified tourism resort	As above

Variable	Description and unit	Source (Year)
SEA_NB	Dummy: a neighbour district of a seafront district	As above
SEA_30	Dummy: a district located between SEA_NB and a 30-km strip from the shore	As above
WS_R	Dummy: a winter sports resort district comprising a classified winter sports resort	As above
WS_NR	Dummy: a winter sports resort district without any classified winter sports resort	As above
WS_NB	Dummy: a neighbour district of a winter sports resort district	As above
WS_30	Dummy: a district located between WS_NB and a 30-km strip from a winter sports resort municipality	As above
R_OTHER	Dummy: a district including a classified tourism resort (neither seafront nor winter sports)	As above
POP_DEN	Population density (people/km²)	INSEE RP (2007), CLC (2006)
BEDS	Number of tourism beds / 1,000 inhabitants	INSEE tourism division, INSEE census (2007)
SEC_HOM	Share of second home beds in the tourism bed total (per cent)	As above
JOB_2	Share of employment in the secondary sector (per cent)	INSEE RP (2007)
JOB_3	Share of employment in the tertiary sector (per cent)	As above
D_CENT	Distance to the closest urban centre (minutes)	IGN ROUTE120 (2007), IGN GEOFLA (2007), INSEE ZAUER code (1999)
D_MOT	Distance to the closest motorway access (minutes)	As above

Notes: BPE: 'Base Permanente des Equipements'; CLC: Corine Land Cover; DGCIS: 'Direction Générale de la Compétitivité, de l'Industrie et des Services'; INSEE: 'Institut National de la Statistique et des Etudes Economiques'; RFLM: 'Revenus Fiscaux Localisés des Ménages'; RP: 'Recensement de la Population'.

Variables on employment and facilities are calculated as density values per 1,000 inhabitants. A distinction is made between employment density at place of work vs. place of residence. The first one is important to be able to assess the capacity of territories to provide jobs (regardless of the workers' residence place), whereas the second one measures the employment of the residents in a territory.

Income is assessed using two variables. Firstly, the median income is the level of income corresponding to half of the population being studied earning less and the other half earning more than that level; it reflects the distribution of income better than the mean of the income. To compare the living standards of households with different composition, the median income is adjusted for Consumption Units (CU) by a weight system. Secondly, the D9/D1 interdecile ratio, where D9 is the salary below which lie 90 per cent of all incomes, is a measure of income inequality that shows the gap between the top and the bottom of the income distribution.

Finally, an index is created to reflect access to facilities and services (be they public or private). The index uses data on four facility classes: market facilities (e.g., supermarket, bank, clothing store), non-market facilities (e.g., police station, child care centre, post office), health facilities (e.g., physician, maternity ward, emergency services), and education facilities (e.g., secondary school, high school). The index is created by a summation of facilities at district scale, in relation to its population

Independent Variables

Independent variables reflect the factors that are thought to influence local economic development. Here we are taking into account their access to tourism resources, the resort status, the accommodation capacity and type, the local economic structure and accessibility (Table 10.1).

Access to tourism resources is described using nine dummy variables depending on their classification as a seaside, winter sports or other resort, and their location in the three buffer zones. Accommodation capacity relates to both tourist accommodation density (accounting for beds in hotels, campgrounds and second homes) and its type. For the latter, we use the proportion of non-market beds, i.e. in second homes, which is important from an economic perspective because of generally low occupancy rates. Finally, distance variables reflect ease of access to or conversely, remoteness of, a territory. It is calculated (in minutes of car travel) for every municipality to 1) the closest urban centre, and 2) the closest access to the motorway.

Mapping and Descriptive Statistics

Mapping and descriptive statistics are used to assess the distribution of key variables at the municipality and district scales, especially with respect to the context of tourism, i.e. seafront vs. neighbour vs. hinterland situations. In addition to mapping the variables shown in Table 10.1, we use the LISA indicator (Local

Indicators of Spatial Association) to investigate spatial clusters of tourism. LISA is a local measure of spatial association (Anselin et al. 2006) that helps identify the locations where high (or low) values of a given variable are adjacent to high (or low) values of that variable in the surrounding municipalities. It thereby allows for the investigation of inter-municipal clusters.

Regression Analysis

Regression analysis is used to assess the relative contribution of explanatory variables to the variation of selected development indicators. As data are explicitly spatial, it is likely that the location of a given district has an effect on the value of the dependent variable, in other words spatial autocorrelation exists. In this case, Ordinary Least Squares (OLS) estimators are unbiased but inefficient, and the estimates of the variance of the estimators are biased, which negatively impacts the accuracy of the estimates and the reliability of hypothesis testing (Dubin 1998). To assess global spatial autocorrelation of all dependent variables, Moran's *I* test is used. Depending on test results, two models are estimated. If Moran's *I* test is not significant, then a classic OLS estimation is performed. If Moran's *I* test is statistically significant, then a spatial error model is estimated using maximum likelihood (Dubin 1998):

$$Y = X\beta + u$$

$$u = \lambda W u + \varepsilon$$

Where Y is a vector of observations on the dependent variable; X is a matrix of observations on the independent variables; β is a vector of regression coefficients to estimate; u is a vector of spatially auto-correlated error terms; λ is the spatial autoregressive parameter for error u; ε is a vector of identically and independently distributed (iid) error terms with mean zero and finite variance σ^2; W is a spatial weights matrix. We choose a 'Queen' contiguity matrix of rank 1, which means the municipalities included in the analysis are those directly adjacent to the municipality of interest. Estimations are done using GeoDa™ (Anselin et al. 2006).

Results

Mapping and Descriptive Statistics

As expected, descriptive analysis shows a stark difference in the spatial distribution of classic indicators of the local economy (population, jobs, and income) and tourism indicators (accommodation). Indeed, tourism activity is distinctly located in seafront municipalities; whereas other indicator values (such as employment) are more scattered between seafront and hinterland. This observation applies to any region under consideration, including the Channel – North Sea area.

As an example, Figure 10.1 shows the distribution of tourist accommodation density at municipal level as opposed to job density (by place of work) along the Mediterranean coast. Tourist accommodation density is clearly concentrated in seafront municipalities, except in the Côte d'Azur hinterland where high density values are observed both on the seafront and in the hinterland. A map displaying values for the other seaboards would reveal a South effect as density values are generally higher in the southern half of the Atlantic seaboard and on the Mediterranean coast. These higher density values are due to links between several types of attractiveness: a warmer climate that attracts tourists and amenity migrants; more accommodation capacity found in hotels, campgrounds, resort cities, and second homes. Job density is less concentrated on the seafront, and some of the highest values are actually found inland.

Cluster maps of LISA produced for the same indicators show local spatial autocorrelation for tourism activity and less spatial association for other indicators. Figure 10.2 shows LISA indicator values for job density vs. tourist accommodation density along the Mediterranean coast. Again, accommodation density values tend to oppose seafront to hinterland locations, e.g. close to Montpellier and Perpignan, where high value clusters are found on the seafront and low value clusters in the hinterland. However it is worth noting that the Côte d'Azur hinterland (the area inland of Nice) also displays clusters of high tourist accommodation values. These are probably associated with rather low population densities, high (winter and summer) tourism attractiveness, and second home development. On the contrary, there are few clusters of employment, which means job density values are more scattered across the Mediterranean region. Globally, the cluster maps indicate functional specialization of territories along the Mediterranean coast, linked to urban agglomeration effects and the presence of tourism resources. Places of mass tourism and urban agglomerations tend to not coincide.

To compare seaside resorts with mountain resorts, descriptive statistics were calculated at district level. To obtain a finer perspective, mean values were calculated within a context of spatial tourism (Table 10.2), i.e. on the one hand, legally classified vs. non classified seaside resorts, and on the other hand, seaside vs. winter sport resorts (differentiating resort vs. resort neighbour vs. hinterland situations).

Generally speaking, 'seaside' and 'mountain' follow the same trend from 'resort' to 'hinterland' situations, i.e. generally decreasing variable values, except for population variables. Contrasted patterns (i.e. decreasing from seashore to hinterland vs. increasing from mountain resort to hinterland) are probably due to increasing urban development on the seaside whereas in mountain areas most of the population still resides in the valleys and their urban centres. Employment density at place of work shows a unique pattern because it is higher in the 'resort' situation (seaside 343, mountain 371), decreases in the 'resort neighbour' situation (seaside 304, mountain 319), but increases in the 'hinterland' situation (seaside 329,

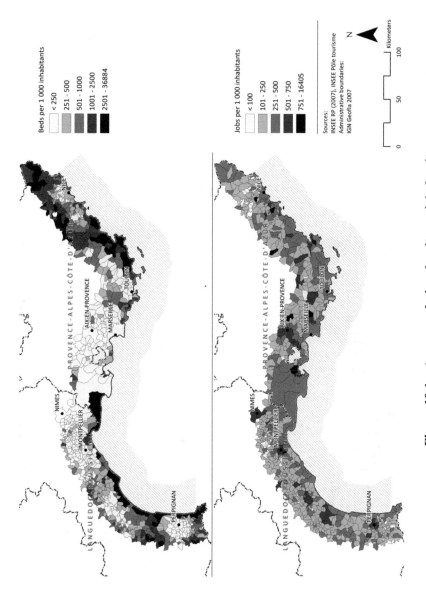

Beds per 1 000 inhabitants
- < 250
- 251 - 500
- 501 - 1000
- 1001 - 2500
- 2501 - 36884

Jobs per 1 000 inhabitants
- < 100
- 101 - 250
- 251 - 500
- 501 - 750
- 751 - 16405

Sources:
INSEE RP (2007), INSEE Pôle tourisme
Administrative boundaries:
IGN Geofla 2007

N

0   50   100
Kilometers

Figure 10.1   Accommodation density vs. job density

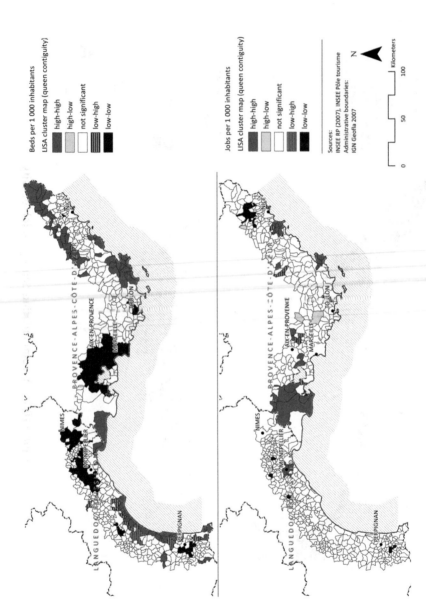

Figure 10.2   Accommodation density vs. job density (LISA)

Table 10.2 Mean values for each spatial context (selected variables)

Situation	'Resort' seaside district	'Non-resort' seaside district	Seaside district	Neighbour district of seaside district	Hinterland district of seaside district	'Mountain resort' district	Neighbour district of mountain resort district	Hinterland district of mountain resort district	All
N	138	150	288	230	187	165	268	407	1,501
	'Legally classified vs. non-legally classified' seaside				'Seaside vs. mountain'				
Population	35,387.93	16,846.73	25,731.06	16,449.58	16,739.47	9,479.63	11,378.77	15,425.62	15,967.57
Population density	687.31	301.46	486.35	270.36	231.44	62.68	237.24	322.42	277.83
Employment (place of work)	354.48	333.01	343.29	304.03	329.32	371.10	318.81	334.86	332.59
Employment (place of residence)	373.55	392.18	383.25	405.20	410.23	447.30	409.97	408.15	408.03
Median income (€)	17,465.75	16,516.64	16,971.42	16,583.20	16,374.63	17,183.02	16,598.26	16,595.70	16,671.90
Income interdecile ratio	5.29	4.54	4.90	4.49	4.44	4.13	4.34	4.59	4.51
Accommodation density	2,320.88	1,135.28	1,703.38	368.95	367.41	3,038.58	985.50	635.63	1,077.15
Share of second homes (per cent)	35.80	21.06	28.12	9.97	9.73	37.73	19.65	13.79	18.78

mountain 335). This result suggests that territories adjacent to tourism resorts are more residential and offer less employment, with their inhabitants commuting to either resort or hinterland locations.

Regression Analysis

Table 10.3 shows the results of the regression analysis in the 1,501 surveyed districts. For easier readability only the sign and level of significance of independent variables are presented. All models are statistically significant (*F* test results). Except for the population model (POP), all models are spatial error models estimated by maximum likelihood. As indicated by condition index values of less than 30, the level of multicollinearity is moderate. Finally, coefficient of determination (R^2) values range from 0.27 (INTERD) to 0.65 (MEDINC). The reference category that has been omitted from the model specification is the dummy for 'hinterland' seaside districts.

Table 10.3   Regression analysis results (N=1501)

Variable	Population POP	Employment (work) JOB_W	Employment (residence) JOB_R	Income (median) MEDINC	Income (ratio) INTERD	Facilities FACLT
Constant	NS	+(***)	+(***)	+(***)	+(***)	+(***)
Seaside, classified resort	+(***)	-(***)	-(***)	+(*)	+(***)	+(***)
Seaside, no classified resort	NS	-(***)	-(***)	NS	NS	NS
Seaside district neighbour	NS	-(***)	NS	NS	NS	NS
WS resort, classified resort	NS	+(***)	+(***)	NS	+(**)	+(***)
WS resort, no classified resort	NS	NS	+(**)	NS	NS	NS
WS resort neighbour	-(*)	-(**)	NS	NS	-(**)	NS
Hinterland of WS resort	NS	NS	NS	NS	NS	NS
Classified resort, not seaside nor WS	NS	+(***)	-(**)	NS	+(***)	+(***)

Variable	Population POP	Employment (work) JOB_W	Employment (residence) JOB_R	Income (median) MEDINC	Income (ratio) INTERD	Facilities FACLT
Population density	+(***)	+(***)	-(***)	-(***)	+(***)	+(***)
Accommodation density	-(***)	+(***)	+(***)	-(***)	-(***)	+(***)
% beds in second homes	NS	-(***)	+(***)	+(***)	-(**)	-(***)
% jobs in secondary sector	NS	+(**)	+(***)	+(***)	-(***)	-(***)
% jobs in tertiary sector	+(***)	+(***)	NS	+(***)	+(***)	+(***)
Distance to urban centre	NS	-(***)	NS	-(***)	NS	NS
Distance to motorway	NS	+(***)	-(***)	-(**)	-(***)	+(***)
Lambda		+(***)	+(***)	+(***)	+(***)	+(***)
F	***44.80	***39.01	***33.67	***55.11	***29.80	***66.10
R²	0.31	0.29	0.59	0.65	0.27	0.41
Condition index	28.25	28.25	28.25	28.25	28.25	28.25
Log-likelihood		-9,280.74	-7,260.82	-13,120.02	-2,937.65	-3,754.54
Moran's I	NS	***2.99	***26.09	***21.99	***8.42	***3.06

Notes: *** p<0.01; ** p<0.05; * p<0.10; NS: Non Significant; WS: Winter Sports.

The signs and statistical significance levels of the estimated parameters show a strong association between local development dimensions and the tourism resort statutory classification. Indeed, when the district of interest does not host a classified municipality, dummy variables are largely non-significant, both in seaside and winter sports contexts. Hosting a classified tourism resort is generally associated with higher levels of socio-economic development. More specifically, seaside classified resorts are positively associated with population, median income and facilities, but negatively with employment density (either by place of residence or place of work) and equality (higher interdecile ratio). These findings may be related to the urbanisation process (including resort destinations) taking place on the French seaside, with an increase in population, income and service facilities, but also higher inequality. Winter sports classified resorts are positively associated with employment density (by place of residence and place of work) and facilities, but negatively with income equality. No statistically significant relation is found with respect to the population and the median income variables. Winter sports resorts seem to represent more concentrated tourism entities offering employment in generally lower density areas.

If other independent variables are considered, tourist accommodation density presents a negative association with the population and the median income variables, but a positive one with employment density, income equality (a negative sign for interdecile ratio) and facility density. However, the share of tourism beds in second homes is associated with a negative impact on jobs counted by place of work and on facility density, but positively related to employment counted by place of residence, median income and income equality; there is no statistically significant effect on the population.

Variables that describe spatial structure are differently associated with dependent variables. For example, distance to the closest urban centre is not significant in 4 of 6 models (the closer to urban areas, the higher the employment density and the income level) whereas distance to the motorway is significant in 5 of 6 models: positively associated with employment (place of work) density, income equality, facility density, but negatively associated with employment at place of residence and with median income. Population density, capturing an urban effect, is positively associated with the population level, the employment and facility density, but negatively associated with employment at place of residence, median income and income equality. Thus, denser areas such as cities tend to provide more jobs and facilities, but are associated with more inequality.

Finally, the local economic structure shows relatively similar associations with dependent variables. Both the secondary and tertiary sectors are positively associated with population, employment, and median income. However they display opposite signs for income distribution (more inequality associated with the tertiary sector) and facility density (lower levels associated with the secondary sector).

Results in terms of local development dimension may be summed up as follows:

- Population: all binary variables of the context are non-significant, except for seaside classified tourism resort (positive); the 'winter sports resort neighbour' dummy variable is weakly negative (10 per cent significance). All other independent variables are not statistically significant, except for population density and the share of employment in the tertiary sector (both positive), and tourism bed density (negative).
- Employment: results vary depending on whether employment is considered at place of work or at place of residence. For the two variables, winter sports classified resorts, accommodation capacity and employment in the secondary sector are positively associated with the level of employment. In contrast, seaside contexts are negatively associated with the level of employment. Variables showing opposite signs are classified resorts

(neither seaside nor winter sports), population density, share of beds in second homes, and distance to the motorway.

- Income: median income and income interdecile ratio are generally weakly associated with indicators of geographic situation, except for classified tourism resorts (positive). Finding a common pattern across other indicators is more difficult. For example, tourism beds are associated with a reduced income inequality, but also with a lower median income. The employment share in the secondary sector is the only independent variable with a sign that meets expectations in terms of a balanced development (higher median income, lower interdecile ratio).

- Facilities: the density of facilities (market, non-market, health, education) is positively associated with all independent variables, except for the share of second homes in tourism beds and the share of employment in the secondary sector. The resort contexts that are not classified are statistically not significant. A positive association with the distance to the motorway access seems to reflect the specific situation of resorts, i.e. a major tourism development that is not necessarily close to major routes. This finding runs counter to the belief that accessibility is paramount for tourism and local development.

Conclusion

The analysis of coastal resorts and their neighbour territories showed the importance of the municipal scale for tourism indicators: a concentration of tourism activities seems to occur close to tourism resources at the smallest scale. It revealed the presence of tourism clusters – spatial agglomerations of high values – on the seafront vs. tourism 'holes' in the hinterland. Descriptive statistics showed similar patterns for seaside and winter sports resorts with respect to socio-economic indicators, especially from resort hosting districts to the hinterland. Regression analysis showed, *ceteris paribus*, the clear association between resort statutory designation and local economic development. Moreover, higher tourist accommodation density is associated with more employment and more facilities for the local population, though second homes seem related to more residential patterns (i.e. more jobs counted by place of residence). Finally, the analysis showed differences depending on the spatial context, between tourism destinations and hinterland places, thus pointing at the role played by tourism and resources in development dynamics.

There are several limits to this exploratory analysis. First, the applied methods do not allow for identification of both resort and larger tourism effects on the local economy. Specifically, regression analysis indicates links with socio-economic development, but causality is debatable. For instance, it is not clear whether resorts impact or are impacted by local development. Second, a cross-section analysis cannot adequately capture on-going regional dynamics. Because indicator levels are compared at a given point in time, convergence phenomena cannot be observed in this research design, for example between resorts, resort neighbours and hinterland contexts. Also, descriptive and regression analysis were not carried out in each major geographic area, which means that no distinction was made between the Channel – North Sea, Atlantic and Mediterranean seaboards. Thus, the design of the analysis did not take account of the specificity of development paths, for example the Côte d'Azur vs. Brittany contexts. Therefore, the links that have been highlighted by the results are rather general, and the contextual diversity may lead to varying interpretations of the significance of tourism in local economies, pointing to the relevance of context-adjusted public policies.

However, these limits do not overshadow the contributions of our analysis. As underlined in the introduction, the economic importance of tourism is known at the national level but less so at the local scale for reasons of data availability and difficulties to estimate the share of 'tourism' in the local economy (vs. meeting the permanent resident demand). This study provides a finer analysis of the significance of tourism at the municipal and district levels and its links with several local development dimensions. The results also raise questions about the comparability of situations between mountain and seaside resorts. Indeed, whereas both designations relate to concentrated tourism activity, mountain resorts are built in more remote and less populated areas, where land development is more difficult. This reinforces the distinction between territories where tourism is produced vs territories where people employed in the tourism sector live. Thus, the impact of tourism is to be evaluated against the specificity of the development context: on the seaside, tourism complements existing coastal assets, whereas in mountain areas the primary objective of tourism development tends to be employment creation and the prevention of population loss. In this sense, it is potentially easier to identify the effect of mountain tourism on employment, since both the resident population and other employment sectors are smaller, and overlapping urbanisation processes are less significant.

To conclude, a dynamic analysis of tourism destinations over several decades would constitute a way for research to move forward by identifying potential catching up or convergence processes. In other words, since the analysis showed several statistical associations between resort hosting territories and socio-economic development indicators, the hypothesis of a latency period between resort development and impact on the host and surrounding regions may be made. Due to data availability issues, however, a more dynamic analysis, though useful, is not necessarily easy to carry out over a longer period of time.

Acknowledgements

We gratefully acknowledge the financial support of DREAL Bretagne.

References

Ambiaud, A., Blanc, M. and Schmitt, B. 2004. Les bassins de vie des bourgs et petites villes: une économie résidentielle et souvent industrielle. *INSEE Première*, 954.

Anselin, L., Syabri, I. and Kho, Y. 2006. GeoDa: an introduction to spatial data analysis. *Geographical Analysis*, 38(1), 5–22.

Baccaïni, B., Sémécurbe, F. and Thomas, G. 2007. Les déplacements domicile-travail amplifiés par la périurbanisation. *INSEE Première*, 1129.

Banzhaf, H.S. and Walsh, R.P. 2008. Do people vote with their feet? An empirical test of Tiebout. *American Economic Review*, 98(3), 843–63.

Bouyer, C. (ed.). 2004. *Construire Ensemble un Développement Equilibré du Littoral*. Paris: La Documentation Française.

DGCIS (Direction Générale de la Compétitivité, de l'Industrie et des Services). 2008. *Un Nouveau Régime Juridique pour les Communes Touristiques et Stations Classées de Tourisme*. [Online]. Available at: http://www.dgcis. redressement-productif.gouv.fr/files/files/guides/brochure-def200209.pdf [accessed: 24 April 2013].

DGCIS. 2012. *Mémento du Tourisme: Edition 2012*. DGCIS.

Dissart, J.-C., Aubert, F. and Truchet, S. 2009. An estimation of tourism dependence in French rural areas, in *Advances in Tourism Economics: New Developments*, edited by Á. Matias et al. Heidelberg: Physica-Verlag/Springer, 273–94.

Dritsakis, N. 2012. Tourism development and economic growth in seven Mediterranean countries: a panel data approach. *Tourism Economics*, 18(4), 801–16.

Dubin, R.A. 1998. Spatial autocorrelation: a primer. *Journal of Housing Economics*, 7(4), 304–27.

European Commission. 2008. *The Impact of Tourism on Coastal Areas: Regional Development Aspects*. Brussels: European Parliament.

Gormsen, E. 1997. The impact of tourism on coastal areas. *GeoJournal*, 42(1), 39–54.

Hall, C.M. 2001. Trends in ocean and coastal tourism: the end of the last frontier? *Ocean & Coastal Management*, 44(9–10), 601–18.

IFEN (Institut Français de l'Environnement). 2005. *Offre Touristique des Communes Littorales Métropolitaines: Capacité d'Hébergement et Types d'Accueil*. [Online]. Available at: http://www.onml.fr/onml_f/fiches/Offre_touristique_ des_communes_littorales_metropolitaines_capacite_dhebergement_et_types_ daccueil/types_accueil.pdf [accessed: 24 April 2013].

Johnson, R.L. and Moore, E. 1993. Tourism impact estimation. *Annals of Tourism Research*, 20(2), 279–88.

Lazzeretti, L. and Capone, F. 2009. Spatial spillovers and employment dynamics in local tourist systems in Italy (1991–2001). *European Planning Studies*, 17(11), 1665–83.

Mayer, M., Müller, M., Woltering, M., Arnegger, J. and Job, H. 2010. The economic impact of tourism in six German national parks. *Landscape and Urban Planning*, 97(2), 73–82.

Paloyo, A.R., Vance, C. and Vorell, M. 2010. The regional economic effects of military base realignments and closures in Germany. *Defence and Peace Economics*, 21(5–6), 567–79.

Smith, R.A. 1991. Beach resorts: a model of development evolution. *Landscape and Urban Planning*, 21(3), 189–210.

Smith, S. 1988. Defining tourism – A supply-side view. *Annals of Tourism Research*, 15, 179–90.

Song, H., Dwyer, L. and Zheng Cao, G. 2012. Tourism economics research: a review and assessment. *Annals of Tourism Research*, 39(3), 1653–82.

Urtasun, A. and Guttiérrez, I. 2006. Tourism agglomeration and its impact on social welfare: an empirical approach to the Spanish case. *Tourism Management*, 27(5), 901–12.

Van Leeuwen, E.S., Nijkamp, P. and Rietveld, P. 2006. Economic impacts of tourism: A meta-analytic comparison of regional output multipliers, in *Tourism and Regional Development: New Pathways*, edited by M. Giaoutzi and P. Nijkamp. Aldershot: Ashgate, 115–34.

Violier, P. 2008. *Tourisme et Développement Local*. Paris: Belin.

Vlès, V. 1996. *Les Stations Touristiques*. Paris: Economica.

Chapter 11

Tourism as a Catalyst for Development Projects

France Loubet and Liliane Perrin-Bensahel

Introduction

Rural areas have been steadily developing over the last 40 years. With such phenomena as peri-urbanisation, neo-rurality and amenity migration, there is today a wealth of research that provides us with a broad panel of analysis tools. At the same time, tourist practices have also undergone several transformations: development of local tourism, search for authenticity or a need to get close to nature (Bensahel and Donsimoni 1999). Almost naturally, public policies have tried to exploit this link. However, after more than one decade of these tourist practices, it seems legitimate to examine the actual role played by tourism in rural development strategies and how this role is measured.

In this perspective, we propose the development of an original analysis framework that combines the capability approach with the territorial economy approach. The objective is to use multi-dimensional analysis tools while keeping a 'territorial perspective' on the tourism phenomenon. This brings up two aspects of tourism activity (link with the territory and multidimensional character) that are often mentioned in the literature on the subject. This is because tourism is, by definition, an activity that draws on local resources for its development (environment, culture, heritage). As a result, it is inherently difficult to relocate. Tourism also impacts several aspects of the local environment: economic, cultural or even social characteristics.

In the first part of this chapter, we will present the original theoretical framework. Next, we will set out the elements of empirical methodology. The related literature contains many methodological proposals for applying the capability approach. The approach presented here combines a quantitative and a qualitative analysis. The field study was conducted comparatively on rural territories of the Rhône-Alpes region. The results show that tourism facilitates the emergence of development projects.

The Capability Approach Applied to the Region

Regardless of the research undertaken, the use of the capabilities theoretical framework requires a certain number of specifications. This is because the research conducted under this approach is rich and encompasses many scientific disciplines. Furthermore, the capability approach has given rise to many developments in terms of both its methodological and empirical aspects. Designed as a tool for measuring individual freedom, it is today revisited by researchers who address the collective aspect of freedoms (Dubois et al. 2008).

Collective Capabilities: Empowerment and Structures of Living Together

The capability approach proposes a framework for analysing development processes. It serves as a normative framework for the evaluation and assessment of individual well-being and social arrangements, the design of public policies and proposals about social change in society (Robeyns 2005). Although the approach is often considered as belonging to social justice theories, defined by Arnsperger and Van Parijs (2003: 10) as 'all the principles that govern the definition and equitable distribution of rights and duties between members of a society', it can also be used as a theory of development. This is the proposal that we are making, using the capability approach as a tool for measuring development at the territorial level.

The central concept of the approach developed by Amartya Sen is that of capability. Capabilities constitute the first information base about issues of well-being and development (Sen 1993). They are defined as all the real freedoms that individuals enjoy. The concept of capabilities makes it possible to focus on what people are effectively able to do and to be, and not on their consumption or income (Robeyns 2003). Therefore they correspond to the freedom that an individual or group has to promote or to achieve functionings that it considers important. These are all the opportunities that can be seized by an individual (Alkire 2005).

For Sen, the individual must be placed at the centre of the analysis. However, many critics contend that it is essential to take the collective dimension of capabilities into account for evaluation purposes (Alkire 2005). By focusing on the evaluation of well-being at the individual level, the capability approach does not make it possible to make recommendations since it does not take the role of collective action, institutions and other social structures into account (Alkire 2008). Reflections on the collective dimension of capabilities make it possible to evaluate the influence of the collective in the improvement of well-being and living conditions.

According to Ibrahim (2006), collective capabilities are linked to individual, social, institutional, political and economic characteristics. Collective capabilities are capabilities that are present only through the collective action process, and it is the community as a whole that benefits from the new capabilities generated. These are capabilities that a single individual would not be able to obtain without a commitment to the community. They are specific to a group and cannot be dissociated from it (Dubois et al. 2008).

Two concepts of the collective aspects of capabilities co-exist in the literature. The first one is based on the notion of empowerment, i.e. the capability of individuals to act (power to, power with, inner power): individual capabilities fall under collective capabilities acquired through the collective action of a group of individuals. The interaction between individuals produces social capital, which will itself generate the collective action by establishing standards and trust. It is therefore the relationships between individuals that will generate these social links and contribute to placing the action within the society. Empowerment is therefore the capability of a group of individuals to take control of their destiny, create their own capabilities and use the opportunities provided by public policies if they are useful to their projects.

The second concept takes into account the role of the context in which individuals find themselves in the construction of individual freedoms by proposing to address the issue of 'structures of living together'. The capabilities to which individuals have access are linked to their 'endowments', i.e. to their economic, cultural and social resources, as well as to their personal characteristics. These depend on the economic, social and political institutions that make up the society in which these persons live: these are the 'structures of living together' (Deneulin 2008), which are defined as structures that belong to a specific historic community and cannot be reduced to interpersonal relationships. Structures of living together must also constitute a space for evaluating living conditions. In this framework, collective capabilities are defined as capabilities linked to the individual being part of the territory. For example, these capabilities may relate to mobility (existence of public transport networks in the area) or to policies implemented by the local communities (role of community centres, presence of public services, etc.).

Collective agency is born of these two aspects of collective capabilities. It is the capability of a group of persons to act with the objective of achieving goals that go beyond personal interest alone. Engaging in this collective agency will generate collective capabilities which in turn will enable them to achieve collective functionings and thus contribute to the improvement of well-being, at the individual as well as the collective level.

The capability approach challenges the 'traditional' measurement of wealth through Gross Domestic Product (GDP). The application of this theoretical framework to the territory is also a criticism of the measurement of the 'wealth of territories'. This is because the territorial economy proposes an assessment based on the territory's level of production, its level of specification and the anchoring of activities. However, a high GDP cannot be systematically linked to a high quality of life, especially in today's environment where living, leisure and production areas are highly dissociated (Davezies 2008).

The notion of the 'wealth of territories' is defined in relation to that of 'marginal territories', i.e., those that do not have access to the same level of wealth or services (whether public or private). For the elected representatives of these regions, tourism often appears as an opportunity to overcome this marginality. The fact that tourists visit the region is proof of its attractiveness and therefore a way out of marginality and a means of increasing wealth. This activity is perceived as a relatively undemanding solution to implement that increases the collective and individual capabilities of the territory. A tourism development strategy is therefore not directly aimed at individuals, as is the case with other public policies such as welfare benefits. The objective of this type of policy is to draw on the specific characteristics of a region to improve the territorial dynamics and consequently, the quality of life of its inhabitants. Recent developments in the capability approach highlight the collective dimension of these specific characteristics. This brings us to question their territorial dimension. Here, the question raised is that of the existence of a dimension of individual opportunities related to the living space of individuals.

The Notion of Territorial Capabilities

Structures of living together, as defined in the literature on collective capabilities, constitute a set of economic, political, environmental and social characteristics that influence capabilities at the individual level. On the other hand, as we have seen, there are two co-existing approaches and definitions of collective capabilities: the approach concerning collective action, and the one that analyses the context in which the individual lives. These two approaches are linked and constitute the tools for analysing the territory.

The territory is not only a source of endowments for individuals (geographical location, culture), but also enables them to access opportunities. The notion of 'territorial capabilities' thus makes it possible to conceptualise the territorial dimension of individual capabilities (Loubet et al. 2011). They form a scale of evaluation of the territory's level of development. Development is defined here as an increase in the real freedoms of individuals. Policies and development strategies decided at the territorial level can also have an impact on these freedoms. The notion of territorial capabilities therefore makes it possible to conceptualise the specific role of structures, institutions, social groups and territorial dynamics on these freedoms. Furthermore, the territory comprises not only stakeholders involved in development and production issues, but also a set of resources, physical factors and policies. Consequently, it can be considered as an institution according to the definition by Perret (2002), i.e. capable of structuring the collective area and organising social life. Territorial capabilities are defined broadly as encompassing the various characteristics that can have an impact on individual opportunities. They tie in with both the capacity for collective action by the stakeholders and the institutions established within the territory.

Territorial capabilities also comprise the territorial resources available. These resources result from a stakeholder construct and enable the territory's development. Indeed, the link created between stakeholders during the identification, construction or even the enhancement of the resources may constitute a capability for the individuals within the territory.

Territorial capabilities are therefore defined as all the opportunities enjoyed by individuals to live the life that they desire: these capabilities may be included in the scope of the territory.

The definition and assessment of territorial development against the yardstick of capabilities requires the ability to establish comparisons between territories. Kanbur and Venables (2005) define spatial inequalities as inequalities between social and well-being indicators, and between geographical units within a country. The definition of 'territorial capabilities' therefore makes it possible to measure these inequalities and to compare the level of development of the various territories.

This last point is essential. Our research examines the impact of tourism development strategies on rural territories. Reasoning in terms of capabilities thus provides a basis for making these comparisons. Inequalities between territories have been assessed in the light of capabilities.

Empirical Approach: Comparative Study

The objective of the methodology proposed is to measure the impact of tourism on the development of marginal rural areas, where this development is defined as an increase in capabilities at the territorial level. To do this, we have chosen the Rhône-Alpes region as our field of study. It is the second richest region in France after the Paris region in terms of GDP. It presents a broad diversity of territories, comprising a mixture of rural areas, mountainous and very urbanised areas, with three large urban areas: Lyon, Saint-Etienne and Grenoble. In terms of tourism, Rhône-Alps is positioned as the second largest tourist area in France, thanks mainly to its ski areas, but also to 'green' tourism. Through the diversity of its territories and the strong tourism activity observed in this region, Rhône-Alpes is particularly suited for this research.

Defining the Significant Territorial Capabilities of Rural Areas in the Rhône-Alpes Region

The first stage in creating a methodology for applying the capability approach consists in examining a list of 'valid' capabilities that are 'valued' within the context of the research. Capabilities form a particularly rich space for evaluation because they provide information about the various possible options. The capabilities-based analysis does not impose a vision of society, of what constitutes a good or a bad life (Robeyns 2006). For Sen, the approach must enable users to evaluate the possibilities that people have of choosing the life that they want to live, without imposing a vision of what this life is expected to be. The use of capabilities makes it possible to eliminate all moral judgement from the evaluation. It is in this sense that the list must contain valid and valued capabilities. However, the data available for evaluating capabilities are factual and are therefore not based on elements that could or might have materialised. Therefore, from a very pragmatic viewpoint, the evaluation of capabilities is limited by the databases available.

In this respect, there are two possible options: make the evaluation based on the potential functioning that is most important in the individual's eyes (which requires a lot of information), or based on the functioning effectively chosen by the individual. This is what Sen suggests (1993) when he speaks of 'elementary evaluation': evaluate capabilities based on the functioning achieved and not on all functionings. Aside from taking freedom into account for the analysis, there is another aspect that is central to the capability approach: multi-dimensionality. Indeed, the construction of Sen's approach ties in with two objectives: on the one hand, taking into account the actual freedoms of individuals, rather than the individual-level utility; on the other hand, Sen also questions the focus of development theories on income and growth. And yet, evaluation based on functionings makes it possible to preserve the fundamental nature of the capability approach. Doing evaluations based on functionings does not rule out taking into account the various dimensions of development in the analysis.

However, 'measurable' functionings must be associated with each of these capabilities. For the purposes of this research, the list of capabilities proposed must respond to several challenges.

First of all, we must determine the significant development dimensions at the rural territory level, in a broader context than the Rhône-Alpes region. To do this, we must ask ourselves what defines development in these territories. This element represents a key issue insofar as the capability approach has mainly been applied to developing countries. Consequently, existing literature mainly refers to 'basic capabilities' such as illiteracy. In developed countries, the use of these capabilities is not relevant since there are very few variations between individuals in terms of this capability.

The second problem is linked to the scale of analysis. This is because the functionings related to these capabilities will be measured at the sub-national level, and therefore on a very small scale with respect to the Human Development Index, which is calculated at the national level by the United Nations Development Programme (UNDP). This raises the issue of the data available at this scale. The choice of relevant capabilities will therefore also depend on the accessible data.

We therefore propose a list of functionings valued within the rural territories. The indicators chosen are those that make it possible to measure the levels attained by these functionings at the territorial level. Table 11.1 proposes a summary of capabilities, their related functionings and the indicators chosen to measure them. We have drawn up this list of functionings based on the related literature. The list contains seven capabilities: income, human capital, social capital, local economic fabric, infrastructure, housing and employment.

Research Methodology: A Quantitative and Qualitative Approach

For the field study, we chose a combined approach (quantitative and qualitative based on semi-structured interviews) to enable an in-depth investigation. This approach is in keeping with all the traditional methodological proposals drawn from the literature on the capability approach.

Table 11.1 Territorial capabilities, functionings and indicators

Capability	Functioning	Indicators
Local economic fabric	Living in an economically dynamic territory	Change in the number of companies
		Number of companies per inhabitant
Access to employment	Having access to employment at the territorial level	Share of persons with stable employment in the total employed active population
		Share of households in which two persons are actively employed in relation to all households
Human capital	Having access to skills at the territorial level	Share of managerial staff and senior intellectual workers in all the socio-professional categories
		Available labour
		Share of persons with a higher education diploma in the entire population considered
Access to services	Living in a territory that provides a high level of access to services	Share of competitive facilities per inhabitant
		Share of non-competitive facilities per inhabitant
		Share of health facilities per inhabitant
		Share of educational facilities per inhabitant
Income	Having access to a satisfactory level of income	Share of the number of income tax households taxed
Access to housing	Living in a territory that provides easy access to housing, both as a tenant and as an owner	Share of principal residences in relation to second homes

First of all, descriptive statistics are used to build knowledge of the dynamics of the Rhône-Alpes rural area and the different aspects of capabilities. For example, we can compare the functioning levels reached in the entire Rhône-Alpes region and in its rural area, and also describe the disparities that exist between the region's rural territories. It is therefore relevant to come back to the 'marginality' issue. It is these difficulties of territories in relation to the larger whole of which they are part that we want to highlight.

Correlation analysis (Pearson correlation coefficient and Principal Components Analysis, PCA) is the second component of our methodological approach. It is used to attain three objectives: evaluate the association between dimensions of capacities; establish typologies of territories within the Rhône-Alpes rural space in terms of capabilities; highlight the position of tourism in these typologies.

This analysis was conducted on the region's 114 rural 'cantons', taking into account the six chosen development dimensions (in the absence of secondary data on social capital) and tourism. The 'canton' is the smallest institutional division of France for which we have statistics. A canton usually comprises several municipalities. These cantons were selected on the basis of INSEE's ZAUER (Zonage en Aires Urbaines et en aires d'emploi de l'Espace Rural – zoning of rural space into urban areas and employment areas) classification established in 2007, which divides metropolitan France into rural-dominant or urban-dominant categories. The cantons selected are those which have at least half of their municipalities in the predominantly rural area. The objective is therefore to see whether it is possible, across all cantons, to identify a statistical association between the level of overall development (measured against the yardstick of capabilities, by calculating a global indicator that encompasses all the capabilities identified as significant for Rhône-Alpes rural areas) and the level of tourism development (measured by the number of tourist beds per inhabitant).

In the analysis, variables were associated with each development dimension: level of tourism development, local economic fabric, access to services, human capital, income, access to housing and lastly, access to employment. Overall, the usefulness of descriptive methods lies in structuring a set of data. This is particularly true for PCA which, by grouping all the variables and observations, enables their categorisation. Here, the advantage of this method is that it establishes categories of territories in terms of capabilities. This also enabled us to measure the sensitivity of our analysis to a change in the weighting of capabilities.

Next, a comparative qualitative approach was carried out on three territories selected from quantitative research: a touristic and well developed canton, the canton of Bourg d'Oisans (Oisans community of municipalities); a moderately developed industrial and farming canton, the canton of Saint-Symphorien-de-Lay (CoPLER – Communauté de Communes du Pays entre Loire Et Rhône – community of municipalities); and an industrial canton in difficulty – the cantons of Cheylard and Saint-Martin-de-Valamas ('site de proximité des Boutières' – Les Boutières local development agency).

Each territory represents a facet of the characteristics of the region and its rural areas, which makes it possible to compare the territory's form of development with its capability level.

This phase was conducted using semi-structured questionnaires to evaluate the level of capabilities by the territory's stakeholders (about 30 stakeholders per territory, namely local elected representatives, tourist offices, tourism private stakeholders, chamber of agriculture's union representatives and technicians, works councils and trade union representatives, company directors and artisans, heads of educational institutions). The questionnaire addressed their perception of their territory, the role of tourism in their territory, the standard of living, access to employment, training, the assessment of social capital (number of associations, presence of links and networks), access to services, housing and the quality of life. The objective of this qualitative approach was to provide a more in-depth analysis and to highlight differences that are not otherwise revealed by quantitative analysis. In particular, we were unable to include social capital in the correlation analysis because of the difficulties inherent in its measurement. However, we were able to study this component through the interviews conducted.

Lastly, the tourism aspect was addressed in the following manner: we chose to talk about tourism in rural areas and not rural tourism. This is because the objective of the research is to propose an analysis of the impact of tourism on rural development in general. This involves taking into account the influence of all forms of tourism, not merely rural tourism. This is particularly true in the Rhône-Alpes region, where the influence of the economy generated by ski resorts cannot be ignored.

Tourism areas were identified empirically based on the number of tourist beds available per inhabitant (the threshold defined by INSEE in 2003 is 1.5).

Results

Our research identified several types of results. The first one was the determination of a typology of Rhône-Alpes territories, and the second one was related to the role of tourism in rural area dynamics.

Typologies of Territories in Terms of Capabilities

There are different types of territories within Rhône-Alpes rural areas, based on various criteria: place of agriculture, tourism, industry, economic dynamism and proximity to urban areas.

Our study enabled us to determine four types of rural territories using the various indicators presented above: touristic and developed territories, touristic and marginal territories, non-touristic and marginal territories and lastly non-touristic and non-marginal territories.

The analysis of the level of each development dimension produced results concerning development disparities. First of all, it is interesting to compare result differences between the rankings of cantons in terms of income vs. development. We do not systematically find the same territories in the two rankings, nor do we find the territories in the same place.

The descriptive analysis enabled us to compare rural areas of different regions in France. Of all the development dimensions, the ones in which Rhône-Alpes rural areas stand out the most are local economic fabric, human capital, access to employment and access to housing. There is a substantial difference with respect to local economic fabric, which means that Rhône-Alpes rural areas are particularly dynamic when it comes to entrepreneurship and business creation compared with other French regions.

Furthermore, in the marginal cantons, we also find a relatively higher proportion of farmers and pensioners than in the developed territories, and much lower demographic dynamics. In the developed cantons, farming is replaced by industry and the service sector. This means that in territories where farming continues to be important and where demographics are lower, access to certain capabilities is more difficult.

Role of Tourism in the Dynamics of Rural Territories

We compared the level of capabilities between the region's touristic and non-touristic cantons. First of all, it is interesting to observe that access to employment is not difficult for either of these categories. This is because, in the non-touristic cantons, employment is the most developed dimension, with an index[1] of 0.70 (Table 11.2). This means that the absence of tourism development in rural areas does not make it more difficult to find a job. Employment is the second most developed dimension in touristic cantons. Thus, despite the propensity of tourism to create precarious employment, access to employment is nevertheless a capability that is well developed in tourist areas. Furthermore, it does not represent an element that differentiates tourist and non-tourist territories.

The second most developed dimension in non-touristic cantons is income, which is practically at the same level as for touristic cantons. The lowest dimension in the region's non-touristic cantons is access to services with an index of 0.22. Access to services therefore seems more difficult in non-touristic cantons than in touristic cantons, where the index is 0.31.

In touristic cantons, the most developed dimension is income, while the least developed is housing. Lastly, another development dimension where we observe a significant difference between touristic and non-touristic rural territories is

Table 11.2   Level of development of capabilities in the rural territories of the Rhône-Alpes region

	Touristic cantons	Non-touristic cantons
Income	0.55	0.59
Human capital	0.39	0.38
Housing	0.03	0.25
Services	0.31	0.22
Employment	0.50	0.70
Local economic fabric	0.39	0.28
Overall development	0.38	0.40

---

1   This index has been calculated according to the model of the Human Development Indicator (IDH): Index = (value observed – minimum value) / (maximum value – minimum value) for all individuals.

that of local economic fabric. Touristic territories have a higher ranking for this dimension than non-touristic territories. This shows that economic dynamism is greater in touristic territories, in particular with respect to business creation.

Several points must be emphasised with respect to the role played by tourism in territorial development. First of all, tourism structures one of the axes of the PCA, which clearly shows the importance of this economic sector in the structuring of Rhône-Alpes rural areas. Secondly, there are no significant differences in terms of the level of tourism development between marginal cantons and developed cantons. Furthermore, we did not find any significant correlation between tourism and the overall level of development.

However, tourism is related to a high level of certain capabilities: local economic fabric, income and access to services. Conversely, there is less correlation between the level of tourism development and access to employment and housing. This observation confirms our intuition about the links between tourism and these two aspects of capabilities. Indeed, when tourism activity goes beyond day tripping, it leads to the consumption of land as a result of hosting permanent and temporary populations. This pushes up the price of housing, making it less accessible for local populations. With respect to the link between tourism and access to employment, it appears relevant to further analyse the global indicator used. This is because tourism and precarious employment are strongly correlated. However, the unemployment rate is lower in territories where tourism has developed significantly.

From the viewpoint of the quantitative analysis, there is therefore no formal link between tourism and the overall development level. However, the qualitative analysis served to highlight specific aspects that are overlooked by statistics.

The semi-structured interviews conducted with the stakeholders of the three selected territories first enabled us to further refine descriptive analysis results. The tourist territory's stakeholders effectively observe difficulties in terms of access to housing. As far as employment is concerned, observations made by the stakeholders are consistent with the quantitative data. In other words, jobs created by the tourism activity are primarily precarious. However, the territory's inhabitants find work easily. And yet, the stakeholders stress the population's strong attachment to its territory and, therefore, a need to find local employment. This need is fulfilled by the tourism sector. In the other two territories, the stakeholders focus largely on the difficulties in finding work. However, for the territory of Saint-Symphorien-de-Lay, proximity to the urban centres of Roanne, Lyon and Saint-Etienne is an advantage.

With respect to human capital, only one of the three territories, Les Boutières, has developed specific skills. With its production of jewellery, the territory's local workforce has effectively improved its skills through meticulous jobs. In the tourism-dominant canton, an analysis of the observations made by the stakeholders does not reveal any development of specific skills. However, the stakeholders emphasise a high ability to adapt, in particular from one season to another. Furthermore, even if the level of qualifications is low, there are still skills that are developed simply by the fact that the territory is highly tourism-oriented: hospitality, languages or in another context, rope access work, for example.

The qualitative interviews also highlighted aspects that were not revealed by the statistics, in particular the strong link between tourism, territory and social capital. Tourism is anchored in the territory, which makes it a business sector that is particularly interesting for developing capabilities at this level. Indeed, in order for tourism to be developed, consideration must be given to enhancing all aspects of the territory: heritage, economic and cultural. Implementing this consideration will create ties between all the territory stakeholders, which will in turn constitute a resource for creating other territorial projects.

Furthermore, tourism is multi-dimensional and will influence every aspect of a destination, in particular its identity, for two reasons. First of all, the consideration of tourism development will push stakeholders to question what differentiates the territory, and thus create a common identity and culture. Next, the outside view of tourists on the territory will help to reveal resources which the local stakeholders may not necessarily be aware of.

Tourism thus has an impact on the two facets of territorial capabilities. On one hand, on 'structures of living together': access to services, to a certain form of employment, as well as the environment of the territory. On the other hand, on empowerment, by developing capabilities at the territorial level to create and implement projects. These two elements lead to several recommendations concerning public policies, set out in the conclusion of this chapter.

Conclusion and Recommendations

The capability approach measures the effectiveness of development strategies at the local level against the yardstick of the territorial capabilities that these strategies will develop. Reasoning in terms of collective capabilities, defined as capabilities accessible to all individuals at the territorial level, is particularly relevant. This is because the capability approach makes it possible to reflect on the development dimensions to study in a given context. For example, concerning rural marginality, the definition of significant development dimensions has resulted in a thought process on the notion of marginality and its involvement in the framework of rurality.

The indicators are interesting because they address issues that are overlooked by territorial diagnostics, such as the presence of certain skills, job insecurity or access to housing. They also contribute to the development of the territorial project in several ways. First of all, they provide material for debate, for example on the place of stakeholders, on the significant dimensions of development, and on the means of developing them. Thus, secondly, the capability approach helps to prioritise development issues.

Lastly, the creation of these indicators may be an incentive to create territorial databases, in particular at a very local level. Indeed, this represents a significant limitation in the framework of the capability approach. Existing databases, at least those available in France, are not sufficient to assess all the development dimensions at very local levels. And yet, it appears important to have an excellent knowledge of the territory when drawing up policies. Creating more comprehensive databases is therefore a fundamental recommendation.

With respect to the link between tourism and the development of capabilities, it appears critical to establish real support for tourism development in a given territory and to create a network of stakeholders around this project. It is this involvement that will determine whether or not the tourism-oriented development strategy will be a success.

To conclude, by placing freedom, and, by extension, the creation of individual opportunities, at the heart of the analysis, this work sheds new light on the link between tourism and territorial development. However, it also opens up many theoretical and empirical perspectives, in which the capability approach plays a central role.

References

Alkire, S. 2005. Why the capability approach? *Journal of Human Development*, 6(1), 115–33.

—. 2008. Using the capability approach: prospective and evaluative analyses, in *The Capability Approach: Concepts, Measures and Applications*, edited by F. Comim et al. Cambridge: Cambridge University Press, 26–49.

Arnsperger, C. and Van Parijs, P. 2003. *Ethique Economique et Sociale*. Paris: La Découverte.

Bensahel, L., Donsimoni, M. 1999. Tourisme et développement, in *Le Tourisme, Facteur de Développement Local*, edited by L. Bensahel and M. Donsimoni. Grenoble: Presses Universitaires de Grenoble, 13–34.

Colletis, G. and Pecqueur, B. 2005. Révélation des ressources spécifiques et coordination située. *Economie et Institutions*, (6–7), 51–74.

Courlet, C. 2008. *L'Economie Territoriale*. Grenoble: Presses Universitaires de Grenoble.

Davezies, L. 2008. *La République et ses Territoires*. Paris: Seuil.

Deneulin, S. 2008. Beyond individual freedom and agency: structures of living together in the capability approach, in *The Capability Approach: Concepts, Measures and Applications*, edited by F. Comim et al. Cambridge: Cambridge University Press, 105–24.

Dubois, J.-L., Brouillet, A.-S., Bakhshi, P. and Duray-Soundron, C. 2008. *Repenser l'Action Collective: une Approche par les Capabilités*. Paris: L'Harmattan.

Dutta, S. 2009. Disparities in human development and economic development: the case of Assam, in *Human Development: Dimensions and Strategies*, edited by H.S. Rout and P.K. Panda. New Delhi: New Century Publications, 374–85.

Ibrahim, S. 2006. From individual to collective capabilities: the capability approach as a conceptual framework for self-help. *Journal of Human Development*, 7(3), 397–416.

Joye, J.-F. 2007. La production des politiques de développement territorial et le droit administratif: regard sur les moyens d'action des collectivités décentralisées françaises, in *Eléments d'Analyse sur le Développement Territorial: Aspects Théoriques et Empiriques*, edited by J. Lapèze et al. Paris: L'Harmattan, 29–58.

Kanbur, R. and Venables, A.J. 2005. *Rising Spatial Disparities and Development*. UNU-WIDER, UNU Policy Brief n. 3.

Loubet, F., Dissart, J.-C. and Lallau, B. 2011. Contribution de l'approche par les capacités à l'évaluation du développement territorial. *Revue d'Economie Régionale et Urbaine*, (4), 681–703.

Perret, B. 2002. *Indicateurs Sociaux: Etat des Lieux et Perspectives*. Conseil de l'Emploi, des Revenus et de la Cohésion Sociale, Les Papiers du CERC n. 2002–01.

Robeyns, I. 2003. *The Capability Approach: an Interdisciplinary Introduction*. Training course preceding the 3rd International Conference on the Capability Approach, Pavia, Italy, 6 September.

—. 2005. The Capability Approach: a theoretical survey. *Journal of Human Development*, 6(1), 93–117.

—. 2006. The capability approach in practice. *The Journal of Political Philosophy*, 14(3), 351–76.

Sen, A. 1993. Capability and well-being, in *The Quality of Life*, edited by M. Nussbaum and A. Sen. Oxford: Clarendon Press, 30–53.

Chapter 12

What Contribution Do Environmental Amenities Make to Territorial Development?

Amédée Mollard and Dominique Vollet

Introduction

The question of environmental amenities lies at the heart of current discussions on the dynamics of rural development. When the value of these amenities is suitably enhanced, they supposedly create jobs and increase revenue. The question to consider is whether this assertion, often put forward by local stakeholders, can be confirmed in scientific terms. Is it merely an assumption, or a proven, enduring lever for development?

In reality, the ways in which amenities contribute to these dynamics are poorly understood, since the term 'amenities', which evokes 'a nice place', is itself difficult to grasp. This term emerged in the 1990s when the OECD presented the second pillar of the Common Agricultural Policy (CAP) as a vector for promoting the environment in rural areas.

This chapter seeks to show that the contribution of environmental amenities to territorial development can only be effective if these amenities are jointly promoted by 'produits de qualité terroir'[1] (local quality products) and tourist services. The analysis is based on the example of two massifs in France: Bauges (Savoie) and Sancy (Auvergne). It is organised into three successive parts: 1) amenities (definitions, concepts and methods, fields of observation); 2) the promotion of local quality products and amenities through tourism; and 3) rural tourism as an operating service for enhancing the value of amenities.

We will conclude this analysis with an overview of the results obtained in methodological terms, the actual or potential development of amenities through local quality products and tourist services, and the forms of governance best suited to the development of rural areas.

---

1   'Produits de qualité terroir' are products that benefit from an official sign of quality ('Signe Officiel de Qualité' – SOQ), i.e. a label that guarantees a level of quality defined by precise specifications in terms of production methods and geographic origin. As a result, these products cost more than their generic counterparts. However, depending on the appellations or labels, these signs of quality are highly diverse, even heterogeneous.

Amenities: Definitions, Concepts and Methods, Fields of Observation

Multiple Definitions of 'Amenities' with the Increasingly Important Role of the Environment

In its Latin root, 'amenity' described a given place or space as having qualities considered to be pleasant. It underscored the perception and actual experience of a given place's 'charm', in the sense of the pleasure and convenience it provided to its users. In the twentieth century, this definition became obsolete and fell from use.

In Anglo-Saxon culture, this term, always written in the plural, refers to the non-market benefits associated with the ownership of an asset or a piece of equipment.[2] The satisfactions resulting from the use of a charming and pleasant 'asset' can thus be seen as having a 'material anchor'. This is a more objective vision that is oriented towards a supply of amenities associated with a right of ownership.

Stemming from two different cultures, these two visions are in fact complementary, and lead to a combined supply/demand analysis of amenities. Both allow us to understand the interest shown in amenities by the fields of regional economies and regional science when the oil shocks of 1973 and 1979 intensified environmental concerns. In the literature, amenities have been defined as the non-market attributes of a place where it is pleasant to live and work, sometimes underscoring the hedonic aspects associated with the natural and cultural attributes of rural areas (Marcouiller et al. 2002). Today, following research by the OECD (1999) which focuses on the environmental attributes of rural areas, with a more implicit reference to the experience and appreciation of the quality of these attributes, amenities are usually defined as the 'natural or built attributes associated with an area or territory that differentiate it from other areas or territories in which they are absent'.

Although heterogeneous, these complementary definitions underscore two essential characteristics of amenities: 1) they are localised and specific, thereby contributing to territorial differentiation; and 2) they are usually 'local public goods', the use of and access to which are free, and with a monetary value that is not always established a priori.

Better Understanding Amenities through the Concepts of Public Economics and of Other Disciplines

Enhancing the value of amenities poses an important problem in terms of method, since it not clear whether the amenities in question contribute to the 'stock' of natural capital or whether they represent the 'flow of utilities' resulting from this stock. This 'stock/flow' distinction is important in order to analyse how the

---

2 'The pleasant satisfactions that are received through using rights in real property but that are not received in the form of money. The tangible and intangible benefits generated by a property' Institut canadien des évaluateurs (1975) in *Le Grand Dictionnaire Terminologique,* Office québécois de la langue française.

amenities are developed (for a review of the literature, see Horns and Sandler 1986, Salanié 1998): the area representing the source of amenities is mostly a public area accessible to all, while the flow of utilities that comes about as a result of people visiting this area is a 'positive externality'. Amenities can thus be internalised by local economic activities such as accommodation, catering, shopping, the sale of local products, etc. This is often the case with remarkable sites, even if it is always difficult to evaluate the price attributable to these amenities. In addition, an 'agglomeration effect' may reduce the degree to which amenities are enhanced, and impose regulated access to these sites. With these reservations, it has been demonstrated that the development of amenities represents a real factor for territorial development (Mollard et al. 2005), even if these amenities are not traded on a market. Many authors have analysed different vectors for internalising externalities due to amenities via property prices (Cavailhès et al. 2009, Thorsnes 2002) or local tourism services such as 'gîtes ruraux' (country lodges) (Le Goffe 2000, Mollard et al. 2007). However, not all the vectors of this development have been identified because their evaluation methods are often difficult to analyse.

To overcome these difficulties, we have called on disciplines other than economics.

- Firstly, cognitive sciences (Gibson 1979) and marketing (Filser 1996) allow us to better consider the diverse ways in which amenities are perceived. These disciplines use innovative methodologies such as photo-language, eye-tracking devices and marketing experiments with consumers. We used these methodologies in our field observations to analyse the diverse ways in which amenities attract people and shape consumer preferences. We took into account their cognitive dimension based on sensory aspects and how representations are formed, as well as their global ('gestalt theory') or analytical character. This allowed us to better evaluate the potential for enhancing amenities via the channel of what we call in our analysis 'Territorial Quality Rent' (TQR).[3]
- We then completed these approaches with an ecosystem-based analysis of the amenities. In fact, there are sets of amenities that form systems in a given place. The ecologists with whom we conducted our research delimited these systems based on the ecological habitat concept from which we established a typology of large ecological sets, with landscape component awareness indices, so as to overlay them with the tourist areas (see Figure 12.1).

---

3 A rent is defined as a price surplus in relation to the total production cost (profit included). To highlight the potential rent of a given product on a territory, a comparative statistical analysis must be carried out on series of homogeneous prices of the product or service observed and its generic substitute. Territorial Quality Rent (TQR) occurs when, on a given territory, there is both a complementary supply of quality products and services and a strong demand for goods typical of – and specific to – that territory.

LEGEND

Frequency (of 281 respondants)

- 1 - 8
- 9 - 19
- 20 - 34
- 35 - 62
- 63 - 128

Type of sites and routes

- Mountain passes
- Summits
- Forests
- Valley
- Water, wetlands
- Refuge
- Around the villages

—— Paths

Land use

- Water, wetlands
- Forests
- Shrub vegetation
- Herbaceous vegetation
- Villages and crops
- Bare rocks

N

0 0.5 1   2   3   4
Kilometers

(a) Bauges area

(b) Sancy area

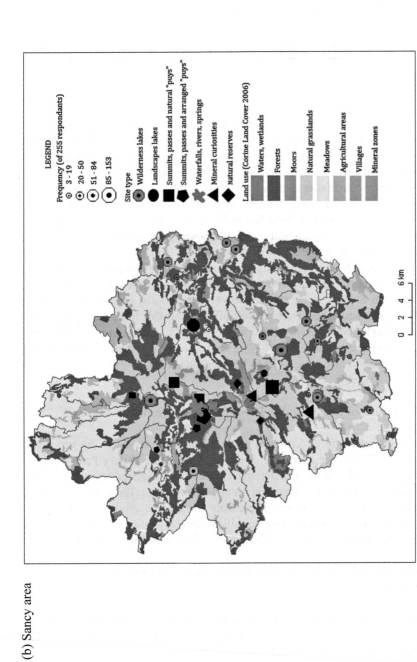

Figure 12.1 Ecological systems, environmental amenities and use of location for tourists. Reproduced by permission of the creators V. Breton, V. Reynal and G. Bretière, all at IRSTEA

- Finally, the legal approach was essential to better know the actual rights of access to – and usage of – the territories endowed with the amenities. This raises the question of the system of rights associated with amenities considered as natural resources: defined either by clearly-identified rights of ownership and usage *(res propria, res communis),* or open as public spaces *(res nullius).* This conditions the ease of access (or not) to the amenities, and therefore their attractiveness and their enhancement potential.

In-Depth Field Observations

For a better understanding of the variables involved in enhancing the value of amenities, i.e. their contribution to territorial development, we made detailed field observations in the Massif des Bauges in Savoie and the Massif du Sancy in Auvergne. These two mountainous territories were chosen since they offer very attractive environmental amenities with considerable development potential. The volcanic Sancy mountain range features open, farmed middle mountain landscapes, while the Bauges Mountains have flower-filled meadows and mountain lakes and a rich biodiversity in the highest areas. Moreover, each territory has a different profile. The Massif des Bauges is very touristic and experiences real estate pressure resulting from its proximity to various urban agglomerations which could deteriorate its remarkable amenities. Although better preserved from urbanisation, the Massif du Sancy can be exposed to very high tourist pressure that is more specific in time and space. Both regions offer remarkable local quality products, many of which benefit from official signs of quality (SOQ: cheeses, mountain honey, Bauges wines and Gentian liqueurs in Le Sancy) and tourist services ('gîtes ruraux', recreation activities, visits to heritage sites, etc.).

The Promotion of Local Quality Products and Amenities by Tourism

Here, the research was underpinned – for comparison purposes – by surveys of four user profiles in the territories of the regional nature parks ('Parcs Naturels Régionaux' – PNR) during the summer vacation: day trippers, tourists (i.e. who stay at least one night), residents and second homeowners. The goal is to analyse the existence of positive price differentials for specific products and services purchased in the Bauges and Sancy massifs in relation to more generic products or services of comparable quality, in the context of summer tourism activities.

*Methodologies Used to Assess the Enhancement of Value of Local
Quality Products*

Our approach was to check whether there was any correlation between the quality of the environment and the high level of prices and/or the Willingness To Pay (WTP) for local quality products. Given difficulties in terms of monetary evaluation in this kind of context, we adopted the hedonic rating method developed by management sciences to reveal buyers' preferences. This concerned local quality products representative of local production (cheeses, wines, honey, aromatic plants, etc.) on the one hand, and a set of multi-attribute environmental variables on the other hand. The task was then to analyse the correlations between these two sets of variables. Ordinal preferences are rated 1 to 7 (Likert scale) depending on their satisfaction, possibly combining compensatory attributes according to Fishbein's model (Fishbein and Ajzen 1975, Moalla and Mollard 2011). We were thus able to evaluate whether there is any synergy between supply and demand for amenities and the territorial rents generated by both local quality products and tourist services: what does an optimal interaction of supply and demand bring to the territorial rents associated with the observed price differentials, compared with more generic products of comparable quality?

The questionnaires on local quality products identified the WTPs for a range of five representative products, as well as the purchases actually made by users during their stay and the actual prices paid. In both study territories, the questionnaires were identical with the same headings:

- Characteristics of respondents: gender, age, socio-professional category, place of residence, etc.;
- Evaluation of the specific environmental amenities in the study territories: hedonic rating of the quality of the environment, number of visits to natural areas, image of the massif;
- Enhancement of amenities by local quality products: consumption, products considered to be representative, rating of the environmental quality associated with the product;
- Enhancement of amenities by tourist services: catering, accommodation, recreation activities, and rating of the environmental quality offered by these services.

A hedonic rating scale was used to mark out the environmental preferences, using exactly the same method for products as for services. We were thus able to compare the unit prices paid for five local quality products considered as 'representative' by local stakeholders (in terms of local identity and volume of products sold), the hedonic ratings of the environmental amenities, and the WTPs declared for these products in relation to more generic products of comparable quality, such as Tome des Bauges cheese (SOQ) versus Tomme de Montagne cheese (no SOQ). A statistical analysis of the results was conducted using Multiple Correspondence Analysis (MCA) and/or Principal Components Analysis (PCA): dispersion of data, profiles of the most frequent users, correlation with the environmental value declared based on preferred photos or most visited areas. By processing the data, we were able to evaluate the effective potential of territorial rents via the unit price of each product purchased compared with the stated WTP, under the classic assumption of equal production costs.

The existence of positive price differentials attributable to the amenities was evaluated through a series of field surveys conducted between 2007 and 2011 in the Massif des Bauges and the Massif du Sancy, with at least one hundred respondents for each.

Local Quality Products, Vectors for Enhancing the Value of Amenities in the Massif des Bauges?

The first field survey carried out in the Massif des Bauges region shows that the WTP of visitors for Tome des Bauges cheese (SOQ, emblematic of the Massif) is 30 per cent higher than the actual in-store price (i.e. €3/kg), and correlates with the quality of the environment.[4] It is also higher than the price of Tomme de Savoie cheese (also with an SOQ label) whose geographic frame of reference is much broader, thereby reducing the image of tradition. However, price differences are highly variable depending on the marketing methods (farms and dairies versus supermarkets and hypermarkets in the Massif region), and cannot easily be attributed to a single type of amenity because amenities are multifaceted (environment, heritage, locality, taste) and they all tie in with one another and with the territory of origin.

An experiment was then performed in the laboratory with 179 consumers for two cheeses from different territories: Tome des Bauges cheese (SOQ) and Tomme de montagne from the Savoyard foreland (non-SOQ). These two cheeses, which have similar sensorial properties, are both produced in 'mountainous areas' (i.e. at an altitude higher than 600 metres) with differences in terms of topography and landscapes. Firstly, the amenities were evaluated, then each of the products. The results show that only consumers who most appreciate the amenities of the Bauges region lend importance to this characteristic of the product, with a WTP that is 14 per cent higher than that of other consumers (Lenglet et al. 2011). By contrast, for the Tomme de montagne cheese, consumers who appreciate the landscapes of the Savoyard foreland do not grant this cheese any higher economic value.

These results must be placed in the context of fairly stiff competition with other SOQ cheeses from the region: Margériaz, Reblochon, Vacherin and Chevrotin des Aravis. Another competing cheese is the 'Tamié de l'Abbaye', the tonnage of which is kept secret, which benefits from the highest level of value enhancement given the remarkable heritage-related amenities of this Cistercian Abbey. Ultimately, despite the positive niche effects for local sales, we can observe a levelling out of prices due to the high concentration of cheese appellations (SOQ) produced nearby, and to competition from other cheeses that prevent the Tome des Bauges cheese from enjoying a higher price differential, whereas its association with the

4   We must nevertheless remain cautious as this high WTP may be partly the result of the considerable disparity in actual prices between dairies and nearby supermarkets and hypermarkets, which may largely account for this high WTP. This was actually revealed in the experimental approach carried out in the laboratory.

region's amenities is proven. In conclusion, while the results of these surveys tend to reveal *real rent potential*, this potential is not always demonstrated given that local and seasonal value enhancement is not enough to stop competition on the national market, with, in particular, a 'Tomme de Savoie' factor, which is an appellation that is better known and more competitive nationally.

Other local quality products (SOQ) in the Massif des Bauges were also investigated: wines from the foothills of the Massif (Chignin and Mondeuse), Savoie apples and pears, honey and wood. However, these products appear less directly related to the heart of the Bauges region. For example, the vineyards face the Chambéry valley rather than the Massif des Bauges; the orchards are situated in the foothills of the Grésivaudan valley at the foot of the massif. Their value enhancement is less than that of Tome des Bauges since they are less associated with the amenities, and are exposed to stiff local competition from the urban periphery. Nevertheless, the correlation between the environment's hedonic ratings and the WTP for four local quality products remains highly significant (see Figure 12.2). Also worthy of note is the case of honey, whose producers ('Rucher des Allobroges') are associated with the pioneering 'flowering meadows' Agri-Environmental Measure (2007) which has strengthened the positive environmental image of products in the Massif.

Unequal Enhancement of the Value of Local Quality Products in the Massif du Sancy

In the Massif du Sancy, the analysis of surveys conducted with tourists (Thimoleon and Vollet 2011) showed a significant statistical correlation between the hedonic rating, the WTP and the levels of expenditure, in particular for farmhouse Saint-Nectaire cheese (SOQ) and to a lesser extent for honey.

Whereas industrial Saint-Nectaire cheese exhibits a low price differential, a series of surveys conducted with producers of farmhouse Saint-Nectaire cheese show a price differential of about €4 (in 2010) compared with its industrial namesake, representing a price/kg of nearly €14, up €2 over the last five years. This differential reaches €6/kg for farmhouse cheeses sold by producers who participate in the 'Route des Fromages' (the cheese trail) and who thereby accept environmental (farm surroundings) and value enhancement (farm tours) constraints. We can thus talk of a true potential of Territorial Quality Rent, especially for farmhouse Saint-Nectaire cheese, which represents the leading product among local purchases (93 per cent of 'gîte' tenants polled). For the moment, this is the highest level of remuneration observed for farmers who agree to protect and enhance the value of the amenities. Consequently, among the cheeses produced in the area, and more widely in the Auvergne Volcano Park, we can observe a split in terms of price differential and potential rent between, on the one hand, farmhouse appellations (SOQ farmhouse Saint-Nectaire and Salers) produced in limited, relatively homogeneous areas that initiate an enhancement of

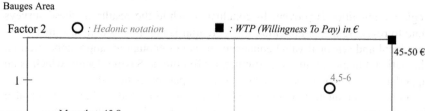

Bauges Area

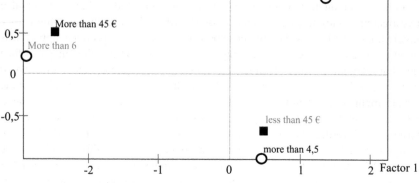

Sancy Area

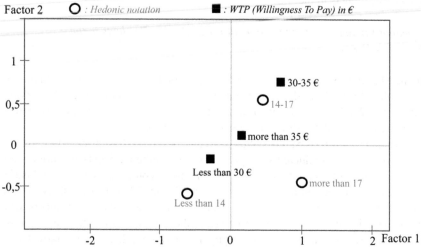

Figure 12.2 Environment hedonic notation and WTP for local quality products in two areas

amenity values, and on the other hand, more generic cheeses (SOQ Cantal, Bleu d'Auvergne) produced over larger areas, and less committed to these issues.

Concerning honey, at the regional level, a quality rent exists for honey produced in 'mountainous' areas. However, it is more difficult to show any Territorial Quality Rent for mountain flower honey produced in the Auvergne Volcano Park (and thus, in part, in the Massif du Sancy). Indeed, on average, between 2005 and

2011, the value of honey bearing the 'Parc Naturel Régional'[5] brand was enhanced considerably better than others, whether sold directly or semi-wholesale, even though comparison test results (Mann-Whitney) are not necessarily significant.

Among other local quality products worthy of mention are Gentian liqueur, which benefits from the 'Parc Naturel Régional' brand and from a definite local connection with a highly specific resource, for which no price differential has been observed, hence the absence of any Territorial Quality Rent (Thimoleon and Vollet 2011). Despite an interesting, significant correlation between hedonic ratings and WTP, honey and Gentian liqueur branded 'Parc des Volcans d'Auvergne' are not associated with territorial amenities, nor are they differentiated from more generic products (especially in the case of liqueur), despite the Park's underscoring of territorial attributes such as volcanoes, open spaces and the gentian flower. In other words, no positive price differential has been found, in particular due to governance problems within the territorialised sectors (honey and Gentian liqueur).

Rural Tourism as an 'Operating Service' for Enhancing the Value of Amenities

The study of rural, summer tourism highlights the significance of tourism practices oriented towards environmental amenities in terms of economic value enhancement: outdoor activities, local heritage visits and gastronomy. This positive link can be found in amenity-rich areas: protected areas, natural parks and rural heritage landscapes. We can also observe substantial interactions between the purchase of local quality products, catering and accommodation. These interactions increase if a particular specificity is displayed (official label of quality, authenticity). Overall, it has been shown that the value of amenities is better enhanced when this is done via tourist services, which promote access to all amenity-enhancing vectors, and therefore optimise the link between amenities and territorial development.

Methods of Analysis of Tourist Services and the Regional Framework of Rural Tourism

The questionnaires about tourist visits included several sections: places visited within the massif, respondents' environmental preferences, tourist services used and respondents' profiles. Respondents were also asked how they had become acquainted with the massif, how often they visited it, for how long and the means

---

5   The 'Parc Naturel Régional' brand is a collective, protected label owned by the State, which transfers its management to each Park. It can be assigned to products, hosting services and know-how that are firmly established in the territories, and in compliance with criteria that reflect the underlying values of the Parks (notably respect for the environment and enhancement of local know-how). Use of the 'Parc' brand is granted to the beneficiary for a three-year period.

of transport used. Environmental preferences were evaluated via hedonic ratings applied to a palette of photos selected by ecologists from hundreds of photos identified and analysed for six different amenity systems:

- predominantly mineral natural areas;
- predominantly hydrologic natural areas;
- forests, wood fringes and logging;
- ecosystems, plant life, wildlife, biodiversity;
- farming areas; and
- built heritage.

For each of these amenity systems, respondents were asked to give three ratings: environmental quality, perceived pleasantness (amenity) and preferred areas to visit. The respondents were also questioned on the massif's overall attractiveness and on their knowledge of protected or regulated areas within the park. The survey on services focused on the nature of the leisure activities pursued, their frequency, their budget and the most visited place of leisure activity (municipality and amenity system as defined above). In the end, using comparable and convergent analysis methods for the surveys on local quality products and tourist services, we were able to compare the results concerning over 500 individuals in each of the two territories observed.

We also evaluated the specificity of the results obtained from these surveys on summertime tourist activities in rural areas by placing them in the context of more general statistical data. These data are provided by TNS Sofres (a market research company) for the Auvergne and Rhône-Alpes regions, as part of its 'Suivi de la Demande Touristique' (tourism demand follow-up) survey conducted in 2003, 2005 and 2007. The results (Bel et al. 2011) show that, contrary to a widely held view, rural tourism is more structured around activities than urban tourism, and each stay generates increased expenditure. Certainly, in rural areas, we can also observe repeat stays that are essentially 'homecomings' that bring about little expenditure given that they are spent with the family, and during which no particular activities are pursued. However, the significance of stays oriented towards the pursuit of outdoor activities and the discovery of the local heritage is noted. These two profiles of stay represent more than half of the summertime stays in rural areas (55 per cent in Auvergne, 62 per cent in Rhône-Alpes). They represent the main vectors of 'modern' rural tourism that effectively enhance the value of the amenities found in these territories: rural/heritage landscapes, parks, seafront hinterland, etc.

Les Bauges and Le Sancy: A Rural, Summertime Tourism that Enhances the Value of Amenities?

Map-based analyses of the Parc des Bauges (Baillet 2010) and the Parc des Volcans d'Auvergne show that tourists opt for 'gîtes ruraux' (country lodges) located in the vicinity of areas of high environmental quality (protected areas or habitat areas for plant and animal life) and major natural sites. In the Massif des Bauges, their price increase over the past 20 years is a result of the enhancement of the value of these amenities. Another survey conducted with 281 users of the Massif des Bauges and 255 users of the Massif du Sancy shows that visitors are particularly drawn to areas of high environmental quality (see Figure 12.1a and b).

In the two surveys conducted with visitors to these two areas (day trippers, tourists, second homeowners), the hedonic ratings for the quality of the environment are positive (mean values of 4.22 to 6.23 depending on the natural area concerned). Visitor profiles differ between those visiting forests, mountain peaks and cliffs, and those visiting rivers, water bodies or even farming areas. In the two massifs, peaks and water are the most highly rated areas (between 5.69 and 6.15) whereas forests garner the lowest ratings: 4.22 for Les Bauges (see Table 12.1). There is also a strong link between the hedonic ratings and the willingness to pay for local quality products (see MCA in Figure 12.2). Thus, the lowest hedonic ratings are clearly linked to the lower WTP amounts, respectively at €30 and €45 in Les Bauges and Le Sancy. Conversely, the highest hedonic ratings are linked to the higher WTP amounts.

Table 12.1   Mean hedonic ratings, from 1 to 7, assigned to the various natural sites in the Massif des Bauges and the Massif du Sancy (all users included)

	Sancy	Bauges
Peaks	6.15	5.69
Water	6.23	5.81
Forest	5.26	4.22
Farming areas	5.54	5.01
Built areas	4.89	5.57

The 'gîtes ruraux' in the Massif des Bauges are often situated on wood fringes, with easy access to summital areas and natural reserves via hiking trails. However, the economic impact is still limited, in particular due to busy camping sites near to water bodies. The prices at 'Gîtes de France' lodges in the Massif des Bauges have increased considerably over the last 10 years, but remain close to the average for the Savoie department (€90 per person and per week in 2009 during the summer). This level remains well below the potential associated with the quality of environmental amenities, as revealed by the existence of WTP amounts 30 per cent higher than current prices.

In the Auvergne Volcano Park, price differentials for 'gîtes ruraux' (in the 'Gîtes de France' listing) differ depending on their location. In particular, the small agricultural region of Les Domes (Massif du Sancy), widely known for its emblematic sites (Sancy summit, spa town of Saint-Nectaire and its namesake cheese), enjoys more value enhancement than the Cézallier and Artense regions (price differential of €20 per person and per week in 2011 for a high quality 'gîte' i.e. 3 'wheat heads' rating). The recreation activities that exist provide access to environmental and heritage amenities (visits to villages and hiking), albeit with a difference between users: tourists account for 58.7 per cent of paid visits, while day trippers account for a mere 3.5 per cent.

Lastly, in addition to the two main types of stay oriented towards amenities (outdoor activities and discovery of the local heritage), the analysis of rural tourism mentioned above highlights the emergence of a culinary tourism that underscores the complementarity between a territory's amenities and cultural heritage. While, as yet, it represents only 5 per cent of all stays, the expenditure per person and per day is significantly higher, notably due to the frequency of meals in restaurants and more comfortable accommodation (e.g. €93.82 per person and per day in Rhône-Alpes, according to data from TNS-Sofres 2003, cf. Bel et al. 2011).

Conclusion

There are three types of results of this research:

- methodological results in relation to the usefulness of an integrated, interdisciplinary approach;
- overall results concerning the territorial development potential of amenities; and
- highlighting of the most appropriate forms of governance to smoothly integrate activities for sustainable territorial development purposes.

From a methodological perspective, the selected interdisciplinary approach proved to be particularly fruitful since it combined objective ecological approaches to describe the richness of the environments with cognitive approaches to reveal consumers' perception and willingness to pay in relation to the systems of amenities representative of these environments, identified in the previous stage of the research. While the 'objective' approaches – based on ecological expertise – revealed different combinations of amenities that all form systems, the fields of experimental economics and environmental economics contributed to the amenity enhancement question by establishing a price not simply for an amenity considered individually (which, in reality, is extremely rare), but for systems or 'packages' of amenities (which is more often the case).

Concerning the results, the research conducted in these two substantially different areas (in terms of their size and location) showed a current level of amenity value enhancement well below the existing potential, given the high quality of the environment and of the amenities inferred by this quality. However, the very substantial development potential observed for both territories means that the positive relations between the quality of local products and that of tourist services must be made clearer and more explicit and, consequently, better enhanced. This will imply consistent territorial development strategies by private and public stakeholders, taking into account the different profiles of tourism demand.

Therefore, we can conclude that the 'systems of amenities' observed in these two territories – both of which benefit from a high environmental value – have a substantial value enhancement potential, provided links are established between the tourist services drawn by the attractiveness of these natural areas, and the supply of local quality products to be found in these areas. From this perspective, the legibility of these products' official signs of quality (SOQ) must converge better with the outdoor and eco-tourism activities available in these territories.

In previous research work, this model of value enhancement was clearly observed in certain areas of Auvergne and Rhône-Alpes when the precise conditions identified here were met, but without an accurate definition of the systems of amenities involved. The resulting territorial development can be maximised when a 'joint, integrated form of economic value enhancement' is implemented based on a set of complementary products and services, in line with the 'basket of goods and services' model (Mollard et al. 2001), consistent with the system of amenities found in a given, clearly-delimited territory. This requires collective management of the amenity value enhancing process by the territory's public and private stakeholders.

Insofar as forms of governance are concerned, all the research carried out thus far clearly shows that the complementarity of relations between the products that make up the basket of goods depends primarily on the private stakeholders. Their key interest is to foster the emergence of complementary quality products and to ensure that the basket reflects the territory by excluding local products that lack specific character. This means that the professional stakeholders must have in mind a strategic vision of development tailored to the production area. Regarding the emergence of new signs of quality, in keeping with the 'basket of goods and services' model, it would be highly desirable for private stakeholders to agree on the perimeter of origin and the specifications' level of requirements, whereas this is often a source of conflict. Indeed, the sustainability of Territorial Quality Rent (TQR) depends on their ability to concur and to stand by the commitments made in the specifications.

Ultimately, two sets of conditions are required if the value enhancement of amenities is to effectively lead to territorial development:

On the one hand, the environmental and heritage amenities of a given territory can represent a substantial economic value enhancement potential, subject to three constraints:

- That the territory's amenities are attractive, renowned and appreciated, thereby establishing a significant reputation capital.
- That the territory is clearly delimited for most of its users, thus allowing them to easily identify its components. This form of identity ties in chiefly with attractive geophysical variables (mountainous terrain, streams and

rivers, etc.), but is also established by history (e.g. the boundaries of a former province).
- That there is 'congruence', i.e. correspondence and harmony between the specific nature of the territory's amenities, and the characteristics of the products and services the value of which is enhanced by stakeholders. This means being able to easily perceive the correspondence between the territory's positive qualities and the nature of its locally-enhanced products and services.

On the other hand, this potential of Territorial Quality Rents can be fully expressed if the local stakeholders establish a common strategy based on four objectives:

- Identifying the most appealing systems of amenities that best represent the attractiveness of a given territory. This is the case with the 'summits-lakes-villages' synergy in the Massif des Bauges, or the structuring importance of the 'flowering meadows' in the heart of this Massif.
- Coordinating the interactions between public and private stakeholders to effectively protect and manage the amenities, following a rationale of sustainable value enhancement. This is the case, for example, when farmers manage their summer pastures in synergy with the actions of the Auvergne Volcano Park. By encouraging farmers to participate in agri-environmental measures, this Park becomes a stakeholder that promotes the integration of environmental constraints in agricultural activities; when, in addition, it facilitates the promotion of agricultural products among tourists, it helps to create new modes of enhancement of local farm products.
- Establishing territorial development trajectories that clearly differentiate the expectations of the different visitor profiles to a given territory (tourists, day trippers, residents, second homeowners, etc.). This serves to improve the interaction between supply and demand for amenities and therefore their value enhancement potential via products and services. The surveys carried out in the Massifs des Bauges and the Massif du Sancy clearly show that tourists and day trippers have very different expectations in relation to amenities. The attractiveness of the systems of amenities incites 'affordance' behaviours that range from inaction and complete passivity to action and interaction with specific territorial resource profiles (Gibson 1979).[6] This translates into a broad diversity of levels and modes of consumption of products and services.
- Ensuring that these beneficial trajectories are maintained in the long term, with no deviations resulting from opportunistic behaviour, which would

---

6   According to James J. Gibson (1979) an 'affordance' is an 'action possibility' latent in all objects on humans (and animals). This affordance generates active or passive forms of behaviour in relation to these objects, depending on the direct perception of their capacity to meet their needs.

merely seek to monopolise the Territorial Quality Rents. Such deviations are always possible, as we have seen in our previous work, for example in the case of Nyons olive oil. Production has multiplied by 2.4 in 10 years, but with increasing stocks and consequently decreasing prices. This has also been the case in the Aubrac region, where the renowned Laguiole knife has had to face competition from knives of highly variable quality made outside the region.

In these extreme cases, it is ultimately the entire development momentum based on TQR and from the related sales of local products and tourist services (basket of goods) that may well collapse. Again, regulating these situations by the public and private stakeholders concerned will prove to be extremely valuable, even critical, to get 'sustainable territorial development', which could also be described as 'eco-development', referring back to the analyses carried out since 1972 by Maurice Strong and Ignacy Sachs under the United Nations Environment Program. This perspective warrants further investigation since it brings with it the idea of an endogenous form of development associated with the rationale of the needs of the population concerned, not that of production as an end in itself, taking account of the ecozones which represent places for effectively regulating the constraints generated by human-nature relations.

Acknowledgements

We gratefully acknowledge the financial support of the PSDR 3 funding programme (INRA, IRSTEA, Aquitaine, Auvergne and Rhône-Alpes regions). We would also like to thank the students who conducted the surveys as part of their Master's thesis: in the Massif des Bauges, Cl. Heinisch (in 2007), G. Le Gars (in 2008), Cl. Durand (in 2009), E. Monnet (in 2009), and B. Baillet (in 2010); in the Massif du Sancy, M. Thimoléon (in 2010) and V. Reynal (in 2011).

References

Baillet, B. 2010. *The Valorisation of Environmental Amenities as a Vector of Territorial Eco-Development: Massif des Bauges Case Study*. Master's thesis, ISARA, UMB Äs-Norway.

Bel, F., Lacroix, A., Lyser, S., Rambolinaza, T. and Turpin N. 2011. Determining the tourist demand for rural areas. *Working Paper*.

Cavailhès, J., Brossard, T., Foltête, J.-C., Hilal, M., Joly, D., Tourneux, F.-P., Tritis, C. and Wavresky, P. 2009. GIS-based hedonic pricing of landscape. *Environmental and Resource Economics*, 44(4), 571–90.

Cornes, R. and Sandler, T. 1986. *The Theory of Externalities, Public Goods and Club Goods*. 2nd edition. Cambridge University Press.

Filser, M. 1996. Vers une consommation plus affective? *Revue Française de Gestion*, 110, 90–99.

Fishbein, M. and Ajzen, I. 1975. *Belief, Attitude, Intention, and Behaviour: an Introduction to Theory and Research*. Reading, MA: Addison-Wesley.

Gibson, J.J. 1979. *The Ecological Approach to Visual Perception*. Boston: Houghton Mifflin.

Le Goffe, P. 2000. Hedonic pricing of agriculture and forestry externalities. *Environmental and Resource Economics*, 15(4), 397–401.

Lenglet, F., Kréziak, D. and Lacroix, A. 2011. La prise en compte des aménités environnementales pour l'évaluation d'un produit de terroir: proposition d'un instrument de mesure. *Working Paper GAEL*.

Marcouiller, D.W., Clendenning, J.G. and Kedzior, R. 2002. Natural amenity-led development and rural planning. *Journal of Planning Literature*, 16, 515–42.

Moalla, M. and Mollard, A. 2011. Le rôle des cognitions environnementales dans la valorisation économique des produits et services touristiques. *Géographie Economie Société*, 13(2), 165–88.

Mollard, A., Boschet, C., Dissart, J.-C., Lacroix, A., Rambonilaza, M. and Vollet, D. 2012. *Les Aménités Environnementales: Valorisation, Gestion et Contribution au Développement Durable des Territoires*. Research report, AMEN project, PSDR 3 funding programme, 15 January 2012.

Mollard, A., Pecqueur, B. and Lacroix, A.J. 2001. A meeting between quality and territorialism: the rent theory reviewed in the context of territorial development, with reference to French examples. *International Journal of Sustainable Development*, 4(4), 368–91.

Mollard, A., Pecqueur, B. and Moalla, M. 2005. Offre de produits et services territorialisés et approche lancastérienne de la demande de biens combinés, in *Proximités et Changements Socio-Economiques dans les Mondes Ruraux*, edited by A. Torre and M. Filippi. Versailles: INRA Editions, Coll. 'Le Point Sur', 73–93.

Mollard, A., Rambolinaza, T. and Vollet, D. 2007. Environmental amenities and territorial anchorage in the recreational-housing rental market: a hedonic approach with French data. *Land Use Policy*, 24(2), 484–93.

OCDE. 1999. *Cultiver les Aménités Rurales: une Perspective de Développement Economique*. Paris: OCDE.

Salanié, B. 1998. *Microéconomie: les Défaillances du Marché*. Coll. 'Economie et statistiques avancées'. Paris: Economica.

Thimoléon, M. and Vollet, D. 2011. *La Valorisation des Aménités Environnementales par les Produits de Terroir et les Gîtes Ruraux Labellisés Gîtes de France: le Cas du PNR des Volcans d'Auvergne*. Research report, October.

Thorsnes, P. 2002. The value of a suburban forest preserve: estimates from sales of vacant residential building lots. *Land Economics*, 78, 426–41.

PART IV
Conclusions

Chapter 13

North American Perspectives on Tourism and Outdoor Recreation

David W. Marcouiller

Introduction

The tourism product in North America represents an increasingly important component of regional economic, social, and cultural development. Widely varying in typology, the tourism product on this continent largely depends on location and regional amenity assets. While travel demands to urban and suburban areas often present confusion to tourism definitions due to the large component of non-leisure based (business) travel, tourism demands within exurban and rural regions of North America are much more clearly defined by leisure-based travel with a strong motivating element of travel for unique and region-specific natural amenity attributes. The component of tourism demands motivated by outdoor recreation in particular provides an interesting focus of discussion.

In this chapter, I provide an overview of natural amenity based tourism and outdoor recreation in North America with a keen eye toward supportive literature, public policy implications, and continuing research needs. My focus is centred on integrative tourism planning elements specific to the developmental role that tourism plays in exurban and rural regions of North America. Given the focus of this book, my discussion will compare and contrast this topic with the European, and specifically, the French context. My intent is to draw upon generic elements of rural tourism to provide a more comprehensive understanding of the phenomena that assists in the integrative tourism planning process.

As way of introducing the topic, it is important to begin with a brief overview of the academic arguments that surround tourism planning as a developmental strategy in North America.[1] Particularly relevant to the vast exurban and rural parts of North America, tourism is viewed as an important economic catalyst; stimulating private sector entrepreneurial activity within retail and service sector business categories (Andereck and Vogt 2000) and providing a host of non-economic benefits (Wang and Pfister 2008).

---

1   For this chapter, I will use the conventional definition of North America that includes Mexico, the United States, and Canada. While some definitions include Central America a part of the North American continent, contextual differences preclude their use here.

This said, rural tourism in North America is not without its set of critics (Rothman 1998) who argue for a more careful approach to stimulating this form of development. For a growing number of academics, tourism is viewed as causal to increased rural income inequality by providing a plethora of low wage, low-skill, seasonal and dead-end jobs (Lacher and Oh 2012) while generating substantial profits for business owners, many of whom are not from the local rural or exurban regions in which they operate for-profit business (McNaughton 2006). This leads to a loss of local hegemony.

From a social class perspective, other research points out problems associated with local planning and public decision-making with respect to tourism. Key elements to this dilemma focus on planning processes being usurped by stakeholders representing merchants, chambers of commerce and local landed elites (Byrd et al 2009) which lead to power and control vested in a disproportionately limited set of local capitalist interests.

From an environmental perspective, still others argue that the natural resources upon which rural tourism is based (lakes, forests, viewsheds) are often irreversibly damaged by tourism (Cater 1995). Further, academics forward significant environmental justice issues with respect to tourism; namely that publicly owned environmental resources, when used for tourism, differentially benefit affluent absentee amenity migrants (short and long-term), are increasingly inaccessible to local residents and indigenous populations, and are reliant on publicly owned common-property resources rife with recreational use conflict and supported by large-scale public subsidies (Bramwell and Lane 2008).

Finally, there is a significant academic debate that underscores the importance of tourism definitions. It is fair to view tourism as unique from the standpoint of economics. Indeed, the questions of how tourism is produced, who produces tourism, whether tourism is an 'industry', and the nature of production are mired in ill-defined structures, lacking theoretical foundation. This is best reflected in the long-standing back and forth between Stephen Smith and the late Neil Leiper (cf. Leiper 2008, Smith 1988 and a host of other writings by these two authors). Ultimately, tourism reflects the activities of a partially industrialised set of business sectors in responding to tourism demands but is fundamentally a jointly produced and experience-based product heavily reliant on a significant set of publicly provided inputs (Ellis and Rossman 2008). To complicate things further, consumers, though classically associated with tourism demand, may also play an active role in the production of the tourism experience, as shown in Frochot's chapter.

These issues raise important implications for tourism within the context of rural development. Tourism and the generic attributes associated with amenity-led development of rural regions can be transformative (Gartner 2005). Transformation occurs along several thematic arenas; notably economic, socio-demographic, and environmental. While public policy makers tend to accept conventional wisdom which precludes in-depth assessment most often leading to a planning approach known as regional tourism boosterism (Hall 2008), academics have made progress in uncovering the complexities associated with this as it relates to rural development.

The specific problems that I will address in this chapter revolve around tourism supply (or production of the tourism product), tourism demands (or travellers and their motivations), and the increasing uniqueness of tourism experience as a driver of rural North American tourism incidence. In particular, I will develop the broader aspects of traveller demand and focus on recreational homeowners as tourists. This allows a focus on land-based natural amenities as central to the construction of (producing) the tourism product. An experience-scape approach to tourism ties together both supply and demand attributes critical to understanding the tourism phenomenon in North America.

Following this introduction, this chapter is organised into three subsequent sections. I will first develop the context for North American tourism that allows both comparison and contrast with tourism in France. This will be followed by a discussion of tourism types including both demand and supply issues. My particular interest in this discussion delves into the future forefront of leisure motivators in an increasingly affluent and multi-functional rural development scenario; that of the recreational homeowner and leisure estate elites. Also, I discuss intricacies and complexities associated with the tourism product and outline a broader, more comprehensive approach to tourism supply. I conclude this chapter with a section that outlines public policy and integrative tourism planning issues associated with rural tourism and further research needs to more formally develop a comparative assessment of tourism in North America relative to France.

North American Tourism

While there are many distinctions that can be made about tourism in North America relative to elsewhere across the globe, it is important to note the importance of geographic and demographic scale that make country comparisons difficult. North American tourism is largely about domestic travel of varying durations within North America. This is important due to the overall reliance on demands for travel and hospitality sectors, the context of travel, and the over-riding importance of sub-continent, and sub-national regional contexts for travel with respect to both the incidence of and reliance on tourism.

To support these statements, let us examine broader statistics on inbound visitation using the data summarised in Table 13.1 that are drawn from a variety of sources (OECD 2012, CTC 2012, USDC 2013, Ruggles-Brise and Aimable 2012). Despite data comparison issues and some issues associated with double counting, simple arithmetic to net out intra-continental travel is illuminating. Note that of the 67 million or so inbound visits to the United States, more than half (55 per cent) are North American (roughly 37 million arrive from Canada and Mexico). This leaves fewer than 30 million inbound visits to the United States from non-North American originations. The picture is more pronounced when looking at Canadian

**Table 13.1   North American inbound travel and tourism by nation relative
to France (in individual visits and representative of 2012 with
minor exception)**

Travel to:	Annual inbound visitation				
	Total inbound	From United States	From Canada	From Mexico	From France
United States	67,000,000	—	22,700,000	14,510,000	1,460,000
Canada	15,580,000	11,470,000	—	120,000	420,000
Mexico	22,680,000	16,790,000	1,460,000	—	190,000
France	77,150,000				

Sources: OECD (2012), CTC (2012), USDC (2013), Ruggles-Brise and Aimable (2012).

and Mexican inbound visits. Of the almost 16 million Canadian inbound visits,
only 4 million (or 25 per cent) originate from outside of North America. Only
about 20 per cent (or 4.5 million) of inbound visits to Mexico originate outside
of North America. In a net sense, North America receives only about 38 million
inbound visits from outside of North America.

Compare this to the over 77 million inbound visits to France. Indeed, there is
much more of a chance for the 65 million or so French to find non-French within
their midst as compared to 38 million or so non-North Americans to be encountered
amongst the almost 500 million North Americans. This becomes even further
pronounced when examining the sub-continental nations of Canada and Mexico.

Further, examination of inbound visits at the national and continental level is
not done to discount the importance of tourism, writ large, within each of these
regional contexts. Indeed travel and hospitality sectors within all three North
American countries provide significant components of each country's national
economic structure.[2] Certainly, there is dramatic variation that exists within each
of these countries with respect to the incidence of tourism and regional dependency
on travel and hospitality sectors for jobs, income, and household sustenance. This
brings forward the context within which we can examine tourism as a sub-national,
or regional set of heterogeneities. Again, wide variation exists as we adapt to
alternative regional scales that bring to the front the ill-defined nature of travel and
tourism. The inbound context is a key to examining the net effects of tourism.

To be sure, regional scale matters. This is true for geographic, demographic,
and economic scales which affect issues related to density, inflows and outflows,
dependency, and specifically who is a 'tourist'. As a tourism tautology, the finer

---

2   While comparisons and definitions do vary among countries, using OECD data
(OECD 2012), traveller expenditures account for roughly 2.8 per cent of U.S. GDP, 1.92 per
cent of Canadian GDP, and 8.00 per cent of Mexican GDP. This compares to roughly 7.10
per cent of French GDP.

the geographic scale, the more apt one is to be classified as 'tourist'. Also, as one moves along the urban to rural continuum, population density declines as does economic diversity; tourism has a relatively larger influence on regional economic and social structure as one moves toward more rural locales.

With respect to broader comparisons, there are both similarities and unique elements associated with the approaches taken in tourism planning in North America (OECD 2012). In all cases, a national presence only reflects a small portion of overall tourism planning with local, regional, and state/provincial efforts acting to reflect and speak to the domestic travel markets; again, domestic markets dominate North American tourism. For instance, the United States is marked by a highly decentralised travel and tourism framework; heavily influenced by the boosterism approach to tourism planning that focuses primarily on marketing and promotion. The federal government does not regulate travel and tourism as a distinct industry with the Department of Commerce serving as a facilitator between private and public with respect to policy coordination. States play a large role in tourism promotion, spending nearly $800 million in mostly public funds (92.5 per cent in 2006–2007) to promote tourism within their borders (TIAA 2007). Regional and local chambers of commerce likewise spend vast sums of public money to promote local tourism. Indeed, very little effort is placed in the United States within what most academics refer to as integrative tourism planning (Hall 2008).

In Canada, government plays a more focused role with a fairly well-coordinated federal, provincial/territorial, and municipality role in supporting tourism. While tourism promotion is still a dominant activity in Canada, there does appear to be a more integrative approach to examining how tourism can be best matched to overall regional development through coordination and collaboration (Canada 2013). In Mexico, attraction of foreign currency and a relatively less developed (as compared to both Canada and the U.S.) macro-economic context place tourism as a key sector within the larger national economy. This said, planning for tourism in Mexico focuses largely on marketing with a Ministry of Tourism coordinating the National Fund to Promote Tourism (FONATUR) and the Mexican Tourism Board (OECD 2012: 236–41). With the exception of specific regional efforts, North American tourism planning is decidedly non-integrative, highly decentralised, and dominated by regional boosterism. This may be compared with current trends furthering a decentralised organisation in France (despite its strong tradition of State intervention), as shown in previous chapters by Vlès and by Marsat. In the latter, the evolution towards more local governance is far from being obvious.

Tourism Types

Locational factors are central to regional comparative advantage with respect to tourism, regional incidence of non-local visitation, and activities pertinent to travel and hospitality sectors' local presence (Christaller 1964). In large part, amenities broadly defined serve as key motivators for travel and tourism. There has been a long-held academic understanding of the conceptual importance of amenity factors in regional development (Ullman 1954) and, increasingly, empirical research tests and provides confirmation of this theoretical element (Isserman et al. 2009). In particular, amenity influence in North American rural development plays itself out through both an alternative form of agglomeration based on migration and tourism attractiveness.[3] These two elements are not mutually exclusive but are often found to be highly related and transitional.

A Broad View of Tourism Demands

Most tourism planning venues focus myopically on attracting short-term destination travellers (demands of day-trippers and short-term 1–3 overnight stay visitors). Curiously, most North American tourism planning neglects to examine and provide insights into one of the most important local travel and tourism demands. Here, I refer to the recreational homeowner (also often referred to as 'the summer people', 'cabin dwellers', and the 'second-home owner'). These are individuals and household units who are increasingly affluent, typically living permanently in urban areas 1 to 6 hours from their recreational homes, and do indeed travel to high amenity rural locales to spend time in leisure pursuits and outdoor recreation endeavours (Hall 2011). As pointed to by Godbey and Bevins (1987), they are known to experience transitions that begin with short term destination travel and end in retirement. Often, there is a family heritage component and estate transfer interest to their motivations as well. Their economic impacts locally are wide-ranging; from travel and hospitality related sectors, to local amusement businesses, to real estate and construction sectors, and also including banking, insurance, and home related expenses.

To substantiate these statements, let us examine the tourism demand type known as recreational homes in the three Lake States of the United States: Minnesota, Wisconsin, and Michigan.[4] The natural amenity endowments of the Lake States are alluded to in their title; lakes, rivers, and forests dominate the northern portions of these three states. With some exceptions, the vast majority of this region is

---

3   Here, I adapt the agglomeration term for application to tourism. In particular, this reinforces the concepts drawn forward in the classic treatise on French tourism elaborated upon by Christaller (1964) and turns the term on its head. Note that Christaller sees tourism as avoiding the 'central place and agglomerations of industries' (p. 95) which reflects his insights that indeed, tourism 'clusters' in the periphery (exurban and rural) and reflects locational agglomeration based on demands.

4   Note that the Lake States reflect one of several North American regions that possess high levels of natural amenities and subsequently high levels of tourism demand. In North America, other regions include the vast Canadian lakes region spanning the provinces of Saskatchewan, Manitoba, Ontario and Quebec, the entire Pacific Coast (Alaska, British Columbia and Southward through California and Mexico), the intermountain West (Canada, US, and Mexico), the Northeastern US, and the Coastal regions of the Eastern Seaboard, Gulf Coast, and Mexico.

characteristically rural. Indeed, these three states possess nearly 60,000 miles of freshwater lake and river shoreline spatially distributed as shown in Figure 13.1.

Spatially correlated with these water resources, it is interesting to note the widespread residential developments as tracked by recreational homeowners. This is spatially outlined by minor civil division in Figure 13.2. In addition to waterfront private lands, important local attributes that correlate water frontage and recreational homes include infrastructure for access and specific services that cater to residential development. In the Lake States during the most recent decennial census (2010), there were roughly 600,000 recreational homes which is roughly 12.5 per cent of the total number in the entire United States (roughly 5 million in total). In areas with higher densities of these homes, they strongly dominate local housing markets with recreational homes comprising often more than 50 per cent of the total local housing stock.

To give perspective of recreational homeowner demands and their relative economic value, a conservative average property value ($200,000) would place an estimate of the total market value of these homes in the three Lake States at roughly $120 billion (2010 USD). Annual spending by recreational homeowners is an elusive statistic but one recent applied research project (Berard and Trechter 2007) randomly sampled a large number (1,265) of recreational homeowners in Northern Wisconsin and identified an average recreational home expenditure level of $17,571 (2007 USD) per year spent locally (within the county where the second home exists) and $56,136 (2007 USD) in total. This annual expenditure when expanded to all of the recreational homes in the Lake States reflects an annual amount of total recreational home spending of $10.3 billion (2007 USD) locally (within the county in which the second home exists) and $32.9 billion (2007 USD) in total for all items spent for their recreational properties.

For comparative purposes, this amount of spending can be compared to all other forms of tourism generally considered in tourism planning venues (most often defined as more than 50 miles of travel for day-tripping, short-term destination travel, and business travel). Note that the recreational homeowner is rarely, if ever, considered in these assessments. Further, as alluded to above, business travel is largely focused in urban areas.[5] It is important to note that according to state departments of tourism in the three Lake States, this combined total spending of all non-recreational home tourists in 2010 amounted to roughly $35.6 billion USD (Minnesota = $11.3 billion; Michigan = $15.1 billion; Wisconsin = $9.2 billion).[6] Thus, in this very cursory comparison, recreational homeowners spend roughly as much as all other tourists combined. Further, the recreational homeowner

---

5   In another chapter of this book, Cortés Jimenez and Anton Clavé underline this point for the Spanish case.

6   To be sure, statewide comparisons are rife with empirical difficulty. The sources for these numbers are from state tourism agencies; all are for 2010 with the exception of Michigan (which reflects 2008). There is a wide variation in research methods, their rigor, and basic elements that involve how tourists are defined and spending levels are measured.

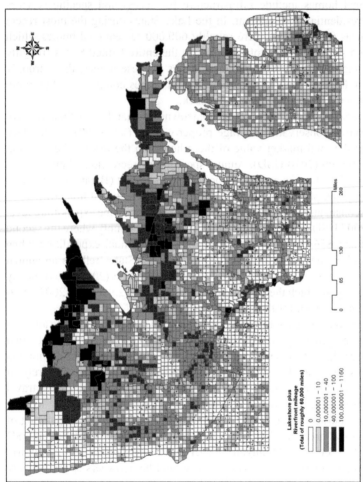

Lakeshore plus
Riverfront mileage
(Total of roughly 60,000 miles)

0
0.000001 – 10
10.000001 – 40
40.000001 – 100
100.000001 – 1160

Miles
0   65   130   260

Source: Respective state department of natural resources files combined by author's graduate student shape file.

Figure 13.1   Lake States (US) water frontage in miles by minor civil division

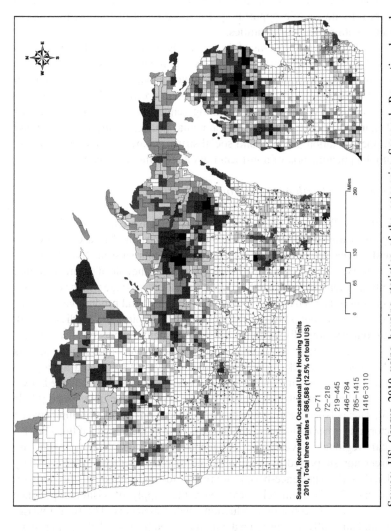

Seasonal, Recreational, Occasional Use Housing Units
2010, Total three states = 586,588 (12.5% of total US)

0–71
72–218
219–445
446–784
785–1415
1416–3110

0   65   130   260
Miles

Source: US Census 2010 using housing statistics of the categories Seasonal, Recreational, and Occasional Use.

Figure 13.2   Lake States (US) distribution of recreational homes by minor civil division

is spending these sums for recreational property located often far-distant from urban regions thus exacerbating the importance of local impacts felt within the high amenity rural regions in which these homes exist. This exists in addition to other non-monetary impacts associated with the presence of this type of tourist. Good examples of such non-monetary impacts can be found in Loubet and Perrin-Bensahel's chapter. Certainly, time spent in these receiving regions by recreational homeowners provides ample opportunity for these types of tourists to connect with residents within local communities.

The developmental implications of this are fairly straightforward. 'Tourism' as conventionally defined only partially explains the impact of leisure-based travel on local communities. In addition to the sole involvement of tourism agencies in marketing and promotion, recreational homeowners create a widely varying set of issues for inclusion within tourism planning venues. With this broader view of tourism demands, land use change, environmental justice, business retention and expansion, local taxation policies, and social structure now become more clearly in-line with the phenomenon of non-local travellers within rural communities.

A Perspective on the North American Tourism Product

Since the 1950s, affluence in disposable incomes and leisure time combined with vastly improved transportation infrastructure has contributed to a dramatic rise in retail and service sector activity considered to be tourism-sensitive (Eugenio-Martin et al. 2008). Changes have also been noticeable in the role of natural resource endowments as amenities. This is reflective of development stage which some refer to as post-productivist (Wilson and Rigg 2003) viewing rural productive activities as within the broader context of multi-functionality (Barbieri and Valdivia 2010). Building on our previous discussion, rural development impacts of leisure travel extend beyond traditionally defined tourism sensitive retail and service sectors particularly when we include recreational homes and their associated linkages to rural land, real estate, construction/remodelling, and financial services. Indeed, if we do so, the rural development attributes of leisure travel become quite broad (Gude et al. 2006). This perspective is consistent with a focus on the relationship between tourist sectors and other non-tourist stakeholders (one of the threads of this book).

Practical regional development concepts associated with tourism are neither direct nor supported by an abundance of relevant theory. This partially industrialised and experience-based approach to understanding the tourism product (Leiper 2008) ultimately deals with the supply of visitor experience and resulting regional economic production-related elements. The rural tourism product is fundamentally a co-produced output marked by a decidedly joint private and public process. Experience-based tourism product outcomes depend on a variety of public and private interactions, as well as the tourist's own contribution (including auto-construction and co-construction mechanisms within the tourism experience, as shown in Frochot's chapter). Leisure based non-local travellers (tourists) are combined with local consumers (non-tourists) to contribute to the receipt base of private sector firms (restaurants, hotels, amusements, etc.), most of which are involved in the personal service and retail sectors of the regional economy. The tourism component of this demand (non-locals) are drawn to the area because of bucolic rural landscapes that are multi-functional; land which jointly produces agriculture, forestry, and mineral commodities and their forward-linked processing outputs (food, wood products, and processed minerals). Public outdoor recreation providers and private non-tourism actors play prominent and indispensable roles in producing a sustainable tourism product (Font and Tribe 2000). This is consistent with the discussion found in Marsat's chapter on the organisation between various types of actors from a management perspective.

These joint producers ultimately provide un-priced amenity-based subsidies to those private firms involved in retail and service sector businesses. Once again, this is consistent with the thinking described earlier in this book by Vollet and Mollard which reflects the economic rent associated with the presence of rural amenities. This amenity subsidy comes in the form of non-local leisure travel demand stimulation to these for-profit firms involved in transportation, overnight accommodations, eating and drinking, amusements, and local retailers. Further, if we extend tourism definitions to include recreational homeowners and other amenity migrants such as retirees (indeed, these involve leisure travel), a significant amount of additional non-local contribution to receipts fall within finance, insurance, real estate, and other related sectors (e.g. construction and remodelling, arts and crafts, and recreational toys such as boats and their docking equipment). Indeed, empirical evidence increasingly suggests that amenities serve as primary motivators behind in-migration to rural regions (Isserman et al. 2009).

Restating the obvious, tourists rarely travel to rural regions because these regions possess great hotels or restaurants. Instead, they are motivated to travel to rural regions because these regions possess unique natural resource assets. Lakes, coastlines, mountains, forests, and bucolic rural landscapes are driving inputs to the production of the rural tourism product. A large portion of the overall demand for rural travel and the rural tourism product is motivated by natural amenities accessed by recreational sites, often publicly owned and managed. Effectiveness of growing the rural tourism product depends on how well tourism mediators develop the underlying experience of leisure travellers. The tourism product is a coproduced and joint public and private set of goods and services; ultimately serving the experience-base of non-local leisure travellers.

This discussion has focused on natural amenities and tourism. There are readily adaptable discussions that could also focus on other factors that foster tourism and recreation, such as culture (Corneloup et al.'s chapter) or social capital (the chapter by Truchet and Callois) which may be considered complementary resources to natural amenities. These exist beyond the scope of this chapter.

Summary, Conclusions, and Policy Implications

North American tourism continues to play an important role in the development of regions. This is particularly true in exurban and rural regional contexts. Approaches to tourism development vary widely within and among the three nations of Canada, the United States, and Mexico. While specific national frameworks indeed differ dramatically, tourism at the local and regional levels is much more about competition for domestic travellers often pitting one region against others. Boosterism, as a tourism planning approach, dominates with an acceptance of conventional wisdoms that indeed benefits exceed costs of attracting tourists (non-local visitors). These wisdoms are being challenged by academics (good examples of which can be found in earlier chapters of this book by Loubet and Perrin-Bensahel or Cremer-Schulte and Dissart) who argue for increased care and an understanding of the underlying complexities associated with tourism impacts. More integrative and community-based tourism planning approaches are the key to more comprehensive approaches to tourism development. This is particularly true as we move to more rural contexts along the urban to rural continuum.

With reference to this continuum, North America continues to experience rapid counter-urban amenity driven development in regions that possess superior quality natural amenities. While these regions can have large urban agglomerations, the greatest relative impacts to regional economies, cultures, and socio-demographic elements exist in rural counter-urbanising areas due to much lower levels of diversity (economic, cultural, demographic), greater proportional effect, and more rapid change.

For instance, potential policy topics that involve North American integrative tourism planning and the tourism product could include transportation and communications planning that expands physical (roads and service provision) and digital (broadband and wireless) infrastructure further and further into remote amenity-rich regions. This would lead to an enhancement of the tourism experience, stimulation of increased (and new) tourism demands, and further spin-off impacts to local economic activity. Depending upon the proactive-ness and progressive-ness of this public policy and planning effort, there are potential downsides to such an approach. Negative externalities associated with this could easily affect the natural resource bases upon which this form of tourism relies. Examples include increased forest and waterfront parcel fragmentation, increased nutrient loading (and subsequent algal blooms), introduction and exacerbation of non-native invasive species (in the Lake States, these include water milfoil and zebra mussels), and other environmental change.

Another area of potential integrative tourism planning involves the maintenance and enhancements required to stimulate human-made elements of the landscape. Examples of this involve both cultural and built heritage which could require significant protections in accordance with local public policy priorities. For instance, Native American (indigenous peoples) artefacts and culture, could easily serve as an enhancement to local tourism products and experience-scapes if developed appropriately. This requires sensitivity to local cultural attributes if the intent is for sustainable cultural resource use. There is ample opportunity, if done insensitively, to damage or irreparably harm local stakeholder relationships.

There is a need to develop local public policy and fiscal planning to address the significant perception of taxation without representation. This focuses attention on the inability of recreational homeowners to vote in elections within the precincts of their recreational properties (they vote for local issues in the precinct of their permanent, or first, home). Properties that are taxed for local revenues use local property values as the basis upon which tax levels are set. There is a strong perception among recreational homeowners that the services they receive from local governing units are low; disproportionate to the amount they pay locally. Certainly, integrative tourism planning can act to improve service provision to this residential group to enhance their touristic experiences.

And, of course, my discussion about boosterism is not done with the intent to discount the importance of marketing; promoting territorial marketing to 'sell' local assets to tourists and day travellers. The dilemma deals more with the broader need to extend public policy and planning to involve more than just marketing. Further, there is a need to weigh touristic outcomes with alternative development strategies with an eye toward social, economic, and environmental attributes of alternatives and improvement in the rural condition.

Extending a broader definition of who tourists are increases the complexity of pro-active public policy. A definition of tourists that include the recreational homeowner forces public policy and development planning to address the spectrum of local services from a life-cycle perspective. This needs to match the analytical complexity of second homeowner transitions from short-term destination traveller, to recreational homeowner, to retiree. This could extend thinking to involve locally available health care facilities, assisted living opportunities, and nursing care.

In this chapter, I have discussed counter-urban amenity driven development focusing on generic elements reflective of this rapid transition in land use, economic development, and social justice. Substantive issues raised by other authors in this edited volume provide comparative discussion sets that can contrast the French context with elsewhere across the globe. Ultimately, the following questions rise to the fore. What factors contribute to the growth of amenity driven development? How do stakeholders of amenity driven development approach public policy and private decision-making? How does amenity-driven exurban development affect regional economic, social, political, and demographic structures? Where are these regions headed? From an integrative regional planning perspective, this chapter concludes with more substantive public policy and applied research needs than it does answers.

References

Andereck, K.L. and Vogt, C.A. 2000. The relationship between residents' attitudes toward tourism and tourism development options. *Journal of Travel Research*, 30, 27–36.

Barbieri, C. and Valdivia, C. 2010. Recreation and agroforestry: examining new dimensions of multifunctionality in family farms. *Journal of Rural Studies*, 26(4), 465–73.

Berard, D. and Trechter, D. 2007. *Non-resident Property Owners and their Impact on Sawyer County Businesses*. Sawyer County Development Corporation, Hayward, WI: UWEX Sawyer County.

Bramwell, B. and Lane, B. 2008. Priorities in sustainable tourism research. *Journal of Sustainable Tourism*, 16(1), 1–4.

Byrd, E.T., Bosley, H.E. and Dronberger, M.G. 2009. Comparisons of stakeholder perceptions of tourism impacts in rural eastern North Carolina. *Tourism Management*, 30, 693–703.

Canada, Government of. 2013. *Canada's Federal Tourism Strategy: Welcoming the World*. Ottawa, Ontario: Industry Canada. [Online]. Available at: http://www.ic.gc.ca/eic/site/034.nsf/eng/h_00002.html.

Canadian Tourism Commission (CTC). 2012. *Tourism Snapshot 2011 Year-in-Review*. Facts and Figures 6th Edition.

Cater, E. 1995. Environmental contradictions in sustainable tourism. *The Geographical Journal*, 161(1), 21–28.

Christaller, W. 1964. Some considerations of tourism location in Europe: the peripheral regions – underdeveloped countries – recreation areas. *Papers in Regional Science*, 12(1), 95–105.

Ellis, G.D. and Rossman, J.R. 2008. Creating value for participants through experience staging: parks, recreation, and tourism in the experience industry. *Journal of Park and Recreation Administration*, 26(4), 1–20.

Eugenio-Martin, J., Marin-Morales, N., and Sinclair, M.T. 2008. The role of economic development in tourism demand. *Tourism Economics*, 14, 673–90.

Font, X. and Tribe, J. 2000. Recreation, conservation and timber production: a sustainable relationship?, in *Forest Tourism and Recreation: Case Studies in Environmental Management*. New York: CAB International Publishing.

Gartner, W.C. 2005. A perspective on rural tourism development. *Journal of Regional Analysis and Policy*, 35, 33–42.

Godbey, G. and Bevins, M. 1987. The life cycle of second home ownership: a case study. *Journal of Travel Research*, 25(3), 18–22.

Gude, P.H., Hansen, A.J., Rasker, R., and Maxwell, B. 2006. Rates and drivers of rural residential development in Greater Yellowstone. *Landscape and Urban Planning*, 77, 131–51.

Hall, C.M. 2008. *Tourism Planning: Policies, Processes, and Relationships*. 2nd Edition. New York: Pearson Prentice Hall.

—. 2011. Housing tourists: accommodating short-term visitors, in *Rural Housing, Exurbanization, and Amenity-Driven Development: Contrasting the 'Haves' and the 'Have Nots'*, edited by D.W. Marcouiller et al. Farnham, UK: Ashgate Publishing, 113–28.

Isserman, A.M., Feser, E. and Warren, D.E. 2009. Why some rural places prosper and others do not. *International Regional Science Review*, 32, 300–42.

Lacher, R.G. and Oh, C.-O. 2012. Is tourism a low-income industry? Evidence from three coastal regions. *Journal of Travel Research*, 51, 464–72.

Leiper, N. 2008. Partial industrialization in tourism: a new model. *Current Issues in Tourism,* 11, 205–35.

McNaughton, D. 2006. The 'host' as uninvited 'guest': hospitality, violence, and tourism. *Annals of Tourism Research*, 33, 645–65.

Organisation for Economic Cooperation and Development (OECD). 2012. *OECD Tourism Trends and Policies 2012*. OECD Publishing. doi: 10.1787/tour-2012-table128-en

Rothman, H.K. 1998. *Devil's Bargains: Tourism in the Twentieth-Century American West*. Lawrence, KS: University Press of Kansas.

Ruggles-Brise, O. and Aimable, E. 2012. *Travel and Tourism Economic Impact 2012 – Mexico*. London, UK: World Travel and Tourism Council.

Smith, S.L.J. 1988. Defining tourism: a supply-side view. *Annals of Tourism Research*, 15, 179–90.

Travel Industry Association of America (TIAA). 2007. *2006–2007 Survey of U.S. State and Territory Tourism Office Budgets*. Washington, DC: TIAA.

Ullman, E.L. 1954. Amenities as a factor in regional growth. *Geographical Review*, 44(1), 119–32.

US Department of Commerce. 2013. *Top 10 International Markets: 2012 Visitation and Spending*. Washington, DC: International Trade Division, Office of Travel and Tourism Industries.

Wang, A. and Pfister, R.E. 2008. Residents' attitudes toward tourism and perceived personal benefits in a rural community. *Journal of Travel Research*, 47, 84–93.

Wilson, G.A. and Rigg, J. 2003. 'Post-productivist' agricultural regimes and the South: discordant concepts? *Progress in Human Geography*, 27, 681–707.

Chapter 14

Perspectives from the United Kingdom and Ireland

Mary Cawley and Gordon Clark

Introduction

This chapter covers two countries, the United Kingdom and Ireland. The former is about the same size as France in terms of population whereas Ireland is much smaller (about 7–8 per cent their size). Yet Ireland and the UK share island status, a common land border, a legal tradition, the English language and a style of public administration which has endured since Irish independence from the UK in 1921. There are very strong economic and political ties between the two countries; for example, around half the foreign tourists who visit Ireland come from Great Britain or Northern Ireland. Both countries have experienced reduced public expenditure and falling living standards, associated with recession since 2008, which have affected their tourism sectors. This chapter describes the broad features of tourism in the UK and Ireland and the administrative structures within which rural tourism operates, which will contextualise the discussion of the main themes. Similarities and differences with the French experience are then discussed.

National, Regional and Local Contexts of Tourism in the UK and Ireland

In both the UK and Ireland tourism forms a major part of the national economy, accounting for 6–7 per cent of employment and substantial fractions of GDP and export earnings. Attracting non-domestic visitors is the focus of much marketing expenditure. The UK, outside the Eurozone, can use the sterling exchange rates to attract more foreign visitors whereas Ireland cannot. Ireland needs to rely on marketing and quality of visitor experience to maintain its tourism competitiveness. Yet in both countries the recession and austerity of the last seven years have reduced tourism and efforts have been taken to reinstate its economic contributions.

Irish tourism is more heavily dependent on overseas tourists because of the relatively small size of the domestic market. One of the main problems facing the Irish tourism industry currently relates to offsetting the decline in overseas tourist numbers that took place between 2007 and 2011. Emphasis is placed on recapturing lost markets, especially from the UK and USA, and gaining new markets in Asia, the Middle East and Latin America. In the UK the key targets are

China, India and Brazil. In both countries the idea of the 'staycation', meaning holidaying in Britain/Ireland (not necessarily remaining in one's own home, as in general US usage of the term) has been promoted to stop domestic tourists worsening the balance of payments by holidaying abroad (Page et al. 2012). This reflects that around 60 per cent of tourism expenditure in the UK, for example, is made by UK citizens (Department for Culture, Media and Sport 2011).

In both countries the incidence of tourism has always varied considerably regionally and locally. The largest single tourist centres are the capital cities (London and Dublin). During the recession in Ireland, tourism became more concentrated in Dublin and other large towns as distinct from the more rural west and southwest, mainly because of lowered accommodation prices, and the average length of stay shortened. In the UK tourism and leisure investment has been at the heart of urban regeneration in many cities, with public-realm improvements and new or refurbished museums and art galleries in places like Edinburgh, Manchester and Liverpool. The economic value of urban tourism is now widely recognised (for example, see Garcia et al. 2010). The 'city break' is now a major competitor for UK and foreign tourists, a strategy that is followed in Ireland also.

One difference between the two countries lies in the priority accorded to tourism in public policy – lower in the UK than in Ireland. In the UK the free immigration of (especially) EU nationals to work in tourism conflicts with a rising anti-immigration policy. The tightening of the visa system for non-EU nationals (directed at fewer immigrant workers) also reduces tourist inflows from target markets, such as China and India. The English regional development agencies, which were *regional* promoters of tourism, have been disbanded. The budgets and staffing at Visit England and Visit Britain have been reduced, because cutting public expenditure has priority. Because tourism promotion is not a statutory function for UK local authorities, jobs in local tourism agencies have also been severely reduced, with the remaining tourism staff incorporated into general promotional units for regeneration/development. The argument for public intervention in promotion has been weakened by a sense that tourism's economic benefits will occur spontaneously. In Ireland, by contrast, tourism has been assigned a role in regional development and significant investment has taken place in infrastructure since the 1990s. To increase visitor numbers, Ireland introduced a visa waiver programme in 2011 for tourists from certain countries who already hold a visa to visit the UK. An employment investment scheme was also introduced in 2012 to stimulate employment in the tourism sector through investor tax relief.

Tourism has attracted criticism in both countries. The economic effects of tourism and leisure are disputed: UK tourism agencies have stressed tourism's job creation, Gross Value Added and foreign exchange earnings (Department for Communities and Local Government 2006, Visit Britain 2012). Others have criticised tourism's low productivity, low pay and the consequent immigration of foreign workers to fill labour shortages (Department for Culture, Media and Sport 2011). In Ireland weaknesses have included the seasonal nature of employment in tourism and low wages in the less skilled sectors, including among immigrant labour. Some recent investment in tourism infrastructure has resulted in over-supply in the hotel sector and severe price competition (Fáilte Ireland 2012). Nonetheless, even during recession, investment in tourism continued; in 2008, for example, Fáilte Ireland, the national tourism development authority, launched a new €100 million fund to help stimulate public and private investment, with particular reference to providing high-quality activities and attractions. Hotel chains, especially at the budget end of the urban market, have continued to expand in the UK. There is an increasing emphasis by tourist agencies on how tourism can help the nation achieve its central economic goals (Visit Scotland 2010), partly through less regulation of the sector and partly by better staff training (Department for Culture, Media and Sport 2011).

Tourism Structures

At the highest level Tourism Ireland unites tourism promotion internationally for Ireland and Northern Ireland. Within Ireland, Fáilte Ireland is the national tourism development authority. Seven regional tourism authorities, which include members of the tourism trade, play a strategic management role at regional and local scales. This includes providing services for visitors through local tourism information offices, developing products and facilities, improving and monitoring standards and assisting with marketing efforts. The county councils have a tourism planning function and provide amenities such as parks and some finance for marketing and special events. Large hotels and leisure facilities also conduct extensive marketing which indirectly benefits other local businesses in their areas.

In the UK Visit Britain coordinates the overseas promotion while Visit England and its equivalents in Scotland, Wales and Northern Ireland promote those nations through their devolved administrations. In England the next tier down are local or county organisations. As in Scotland the membership includes substantial private-sector representation. Budget cuts have reduced this tier's public funding. There is more emphasis on private companies organising and paying for their area's promotion rather than this being seen as a public good to counteract a highly fragmented industry.

At a local level, development organisations funded through the EU LEADER and national programmes are sources of funding for establishing and marketing, primarily, small tourism businesses. Membership marketing groups exist for both products and areas. Some UK business groups in a locality will offer discounts for repeat visits, if you visit more than one member or if you arrive by public transport. However, in neither the UK nor Ireland do tourism functions reside with an equivalent to the French commune, or community of communes.

Tourism and Leisure: Here and Not Somewhere Else

The reasons why tourism and leisure activities are located differentially across space may be related to the existing local resource base as expressed in terms of natural, social and cultural heritage capital, financial investment, internal and external networking and collaboration.

Local Natural Heritage

Nature has been a focus for tourism and recreation in the UK and Ireland for a long time, whether to hunt it or observe it and its role is increasing. Bird watching on reserves and in the wider countryside has long been a popular pastime and new reserves have been created, mostly in rural areas but also a few in cities (e.g. Barnes in London). Rare species, iconic ones and recent re-introductions often attract many visitors. Similarly, watching whales and dolphins is becoming popular and some mammals (e.g. beavers and otters) may have a similar effect. High-profile television programmes about nature have intensified the public's interest in visiting places to observe nature. The public sector is deeply involved here as they designate and monitor the areas where nature conservation takes priority. Increasingly conservation is taking place within European Union (EU) designations such as Special Areas of Conservation, Special Protected Areas and Natural Heritage Areas as part of Natura 2000 inventories. Measures for conservation and species re-introductions may be contentious with landowners.

Nature is central to the international image of Wales, Ireland and Scotland and to the activity holidays that are promoted there. 2013 was the 'Year of Natural Scotland'. Maintaining the quality of the environment is therefore a key concern and obtaining and retaining Blue Flag status is particularly important in coastal areas. Fishery boards in Ireland are vigilant in opposing new housing developments and improper disposal of farm waste near angling lakes and rivers. The location of wind turbines has recently become a major source of controversy in landscape terms. The Royal Society for the Protection of Birds (2002) has calculated the considerable economic benefits of conservation and bird reserves in the UK. Their larger reserves promote not only conservation but also development through employment in a shop, cafe and education centre.

The complexity of land ownership systems in some conserved areas and the implications for balancing the demands of recreationists and tourists against those of nature conservation, illustrated with reference to islands in the Gironde Estuary by Cazals and Lyser's chapter, have emerged from studies in the UK and Ireland also. Examples include the Doey Peninsula in County Donegal where a common landownership system has created a 'tragedy of the commons', where no one has been willing to take responsibility for conservation, resulting in damage to a sensitive dune system (McKenna et al. 2007). In the UK, the lack of control and multiple interests in offshore areas have made marine conservation very difficult to implement.

Tourism and Culture

The promotional material for UK and Irish tourism is steeped in cultural references which involve imagery that often appeals to the expectations of tourists, as identified in market research. In this sense, both countries are constructed as cultural products. The message is multi-dimensional to appeal to as many market segments as possible. The UK is portrayed as polysemic – traditional and modern; peaceful and vibrant; busy and quiet; metropolitan and deeply rural. The images of the modern, creative and exciting are stronger in the promotion of London whereas natural beauty and outdoor sports are more prominent in Welsh and Scottish advertising. At a local level, cultural bases for tourism include classical music festivals (for example, in London and Aldeburgh) and the Beatles (Liverpool), high literature (Wordsworth in the Lake District) and popular literature (James Herriot in the Yorkshire Dales).

Irish tourism promotion draws extensively on culture and heritage with strong rural connotations. Traditional agricultural ways of life, a strong musical tradition, the Irish language along the west coast and friendly welcoming people are promoted as iconic images of Ireland. The literary heritage of the country in the English language is also invoked for tourism purposes (e.g., in literary events held in Sligo and Dublin to honour the poet W.B. Yeats and the author James Joyce, respectively). A vibrant night life, focused on pubs to some extent, and in which both traditional and contemporary Irish music feature, also forms part of the image portrayed and is targeted particularly at younger tourists. The annual Irish traditional music festival, the *Fleadh*, attracts many thousands of participants – Glasgow in Scotland has copied this – and is held in a different town each year. There is also an increasing range of cultural festivals provided in British and Irish cities, towns and villages, which link with local authors and traditional musicians. Cultural and heritage tourism has been identified for specific investment as a new defined product by Fáilte Ireland.

Tourism experiences are also increasingly being co-constructed and reconstructed as part of cultural economies in France, the UK and Ireland (Kneafsey 2001). Corneloup et al. show, in their chapter, how two Alpine ski resorts (Chamonix and Deux Alpes) have responded to changing tourist tastes by facilitating the co-construction of experiences in interactive ways through use of new communication technologies. Some rural destinations in the UK and Ireland have become involved in providing opportunities of this type through devices as diverse as historical re-enactments, gift products redolent of the locality, and interactive websites and social media forums. New or re-modelled cultures for tourism have been created around, for example, seafood in SW England and SW Ireland (via upmarket restaurants, fresh fish sales and smoked fish and farmhouse cheeses in SW Ireland, in particular) and around meats in Scotland, both focusing on a constructed image of quality and distinctiveness outside the global food market (Sage 2003, Everett and Aitchison 2008). National food and tourism organisations and local development programmes are increasingly supporting what were initially private sector initiatives, as part of joint policies to enhance the range of attractions for tourists in rural locations and add value to local products.

Social Capital

'Social capital exists in the relations among persons' (Coleman 1988: S100-S101). Findings from the SPRITE project in the UK, Ireland and France (see chapter by Marsat) identified the role played by horizontal local networks and vertical extra-local networks in, respectively, sharing knowledge and information and attracting financial investment in rural tourism (Clark and Chabrel 2007). Parallels exist in the structures and actions associated with local bonding social capital and external bridging social capital, discussed by Truchet and Callois with reference to growth in rural tourism accommodation in the Pays de Lafayette and the Pays des Combrailles, in Auvergne. However, as these authors illustrate, excessive bonding among long-established providers may serve to exclude newcomers and inhibit innovation, a factor which tourism policy makers need to be aware of.

The capacity of rural tourism providers to capture a local rent from tourism is also influenced by their human capital resources. The enhancement of human capital in the tourism sector through training and educational programmes receives particular attention in the UK and Ireland, not least because of the growth of social media, such as Twitter and Facebook, in moulding and expressing tourists' judgements.

In Ireland, a wide range of degree, certificate and short course training forms part of the professionalisation of the tourism and catering sectors with marked success (Baum and Szlvas 2008). In the UK, the focus has been on streamlining the system of qualifications available to staff in the tourism sector and increasing the proportion of well trained staff in post. People 1st and the National Skills Academy for Hospitality are the new vehicles for improving staff training. Tourism can be a sector with low entry barriers. The difficulty some new entrepreneurs face is their lack of business skills, so raising these has been a major focus of work in both the UK and Ireland (Visit England 2011). During a recession, training is unfortunately one of the first areas of expenditure that employers reduce. Skill shortages in Ireland and the UK have been filled by importing workers, particularly from Eastern Europe and The Philippines, which has reduced the incentive to train local staff. There is also some import of human capital into rural tourism businesses through the return of locals who have gained appropriate skills whilst working elsewhere.

Inter-Area Cooperation and Tourism

Inter-area cooperation in tourism in the UK and Ireland involves both public and private organisations and businesses. However, the redistribution of influence downwards to the comarca in Spain and, potentially, upwards to the communities of communes in France, as documented in Vlès' chapter, is not replicated in either of our countries. In the UK, the slimming down of local authority departments specifically for the promotion of tourism has at least integrated the remaining staff into wider place-promotion organisations, recognising the synergies between promoting places for tourists, inward investment, conferences and locations for films or television programmes. The local-area tourist boards are increasingly bringing together representatives of local tourism businesses so that they can cooperate to promote the area, while relying less on public funding. But the dominant motif is inter-area competition, apart from issues of general tourism concern (e.g. legislation and taxation).

The Regional Tourism Authorities in Ireland are expected to play a role in promoting inter-area cooperation but difficulties can arise in overcoming excessive localism (Cawley and Gillmor 2008). This finding reflects the reluctance that Vlès identified among local tourism providers and communes in France to cede influence to higher levels. Greater integration between rural areas and between rural areas and towns, which act as tourist destinations, is nevertheless recognised as being necessary in order to disperse the benefits of tourism more widely. Thus, 'The Wild Atlantic Way' was launched in April 2013 by Fáilte Ireland as a 2500 km-long touring route along the west coast from County Donegal to County Cork. Local looped routes are designed to encourage tourists to explore rural areas to experience the natural and cultural heritage and a range of recreational and food experiences. Food and walking trails have been developed locally in Ireland and the UK linking small towns and villages together such as Cork's Coastal Food Trails and the Westport Greenway. Bonding and bridging social capital are again involved in facilitating these initiatives.

At the Heart of Destinations: Users and Stakeholders

Tourism and recreation areas include both natural spaces and constructed spaces. The following section discusses national and nature parks as tourism and recreational spaces, the roles played by stakeholders and users in promoting environmental conservation in destination areas, and the management of tourism resorts. There are both similarities and differences between the evidence for the UK, Ireland and France which inform the broader issues that frame the discussion.

National parks are important for conservation in the UK and Ireland but the two countries follow different models. In England, Scotland and Wales, national park land (mostly touristically attractive uplands) is primarily in private ownership and is managed through committees that include representatives of stakeholder groups and locally elected representatives. Their remit includes both conservation and economic and social development, so management creates tensions greater than in ordinary rural areas, as Bramwell (2011) illustrates for the Peak District National Park. A clear primacy for conservation is found only in nature reserves though it has more weight in national parks than in other rural areas. The Regional Nature Park model in Auvergne, discussed in Marsat's chapter, has some broad similarities with UK national parks in its representative governance structure and wide-ranging functions. Both serve strategic management functions relating to tourism at a sub-regional scale and comparative study of both models could provide new insights into the management of rural resources for tourism purposes.

In Ireland the national parks are owned and managed by the State. Their primary role relates to conservation of nature; tourism and recreation are secondary functions. The capacity to control land use is a major benefit but a disadvantage relates to the limited area of the six national parks in meeting the demand for outdoor recreation space. Nine forest parks managed by Coillte (an Irish word meaning 'woods'), which is a commercial company wholly owned by the Irish government, fill the lacuna to some extent. Entry to private land in Ireland for hiking has to be negotiated on an individual basis with landowners and supply of access does not meet demand (Buckley et al. 2009). Some owners allow access on a 'permissive' basis free of charge, whilst others are willing to do so only for payment to maintain the routes, gates and stiles. In England and Wales the Countryside and Rights of Way Act (2000) allowed public access to more private land (a right long enjoyed widely in Scotland) and new long-distance trails have been created in Ireland (e.g. the Great Western Greenway) and the UK (e.g. the West Highland Way). The parallel with the Grandes Randonnées in France is clear.

The numbers of visitors and types of usage in conserved areas can pose threats to the quality of the natural environment through erosion of pathways, damage to flora and interference with fauna, for example. Avoidance of such impacts is of increasing importance in our three countries. Various management strategies exist in the UK and Ireland to avoid, minimise and remediate ecological damage but contravention of regulations may occur because of traditional norms, for example car parking in coastal dune areas (Kindermann and Gormally 2013). In a similar vein, Ginelli's chapter illustrates how existing norms and the expectations of users, with reference to the continuation of hunting, kayaking and sub-aqua diving, impinged on the introduction of more effective policies to protect nature in the Calanques National Park near Marseilles and the Arcachon Bay area of southwest France. Ennerdale in NW England is an example of 're-wilding' where the norm changes to greater biodiversity and enhanced conservation without economic hardship and, if possible, more employment and incomes. The experience here shows that long-term interaction with the resident population and landowners is essential for the norm-changing success of re-wilding.

The UK and Ireland, particularly on the coast, developed in the nineteenth century some of the world's earliest mass tourism resorts. The challenge for these resorts came in the 1960s when cheap package holidays to warmer countries became widely available. Some UK resorts declined (e.g. Morecambe), some carried on in their traditional style with updated attractions (e.g. Blackpool) and others changed their tourism offerings to appeal to new markets, with conference centres (e.g. Bournemouth) or marinas (e.g. Brighton), reflecting varying responses at the stagnation stage in the life cycle model. Inland and coastal resorts have tried to create new attractions – shopping districts, restaurants and exhibitions. In 1995 the Irish Government introduced a tax-efficient investment Resort Renewal Scheme to regenerate 15 coastal resorts (Mottiar and Quinn 2001). Investment took place in self-catering accommodation, refurbishing or building hotels and, in some cases, in providing swimming pools and indoor activities for children to attract back families. Seasonality remains a problem for many of these resorts. Major public-realm investment has occurred in UK resorts such as Blackpool, which often have high seasonal unemployment and much poverty. New resorts have been created around theme parks for the day visitor. The challenge for all resorts is how to find the money (even in a recession) to invest in new or updated facilities to provide visitors with novelty and gain advantage over rival resorts. The upward trend in standards (visitors' expectations of accommodation, food and entertainment) makes reinvestment all the more vital for the resorts' future (Northwest Development Agency 2003).

The evolution of the ski resort of Aviemore in Scotland may be compared with some of the ski resorts in France and Switzerland discussed by Clivaz and George-Marcelpoil. In Scotland, public and private investment in the 1960s needed updating by the 1990s to create a year-round resort with indoor winter and other sports in the face of unpredictable snow cover. Smaller Scottish skiing resorts remained more dependent on the varying fortunes of skiing. More generally, the stagnation of seaside resorts in the UK and Ireland during the 1970s and the 1980s bears some similarities with the recent experience of the ski resorts in Switzerland and France where rejuvenation is required. In both British and Irish resorts the infrastructure that was developed by private as well as public investment during the nineteenth century required reinvestment in the 1970s which was not available or considered financially inappropriate because of the decline in tourist numbers (Agarwal 2002). Hotels and boarding houses became converted to use as nursing homes for elderly people in Bournemouth on the south coast of England or as student accommodation in Morecambe near Lancaster in the northwest. A similar process of decline and reallocation of accommodation took place in Ireland. In the latter case, as Mottiar and Quinn (2001) illustrate, the resort renewal programme of the 1990s contributed to oversupply of investment properties for rent and second homes, which often remain vacant for much of the year, reflecting the evidence presented by Clivaz and George-Marcelpoil.

Tourism and Leisure: Opportunities for Places?

Many social and economic impacts potentially arise from tourism development, both positive and negative, and optimising the positive impacts is an aim for national, regional and local stakeholders. The following discussion addresses the issues of tourism taxes and willingness to pay for outdoor tourism and leisure experiences, the need for an integrated approach to tourism development in rural areas and the relationships between the valorisation of local products and tourism services.

Periodically the idea of a tourism tax emerges, most recently in the UK in Edinburgh. There is a 'polluter pays' argument for this where many tourists impose costs on a small resident population who need to rectify tourism's externalities. There is also the desire to replace declining public expenditure with general income from tourists, and to find a way to fund local improvements for tourism. The barrier to a tourism tax is the argument that in a global tourism market such a tax would make the place uncompetitive. Another approach is a voluntary tourism tax, whereby accommodation providers ask visitors to make voluntary donations to a fund to improve local tourism. The best-known UK example is in the English Lake District. Voluntary payments are often sought in museums, galleries and cathedrals that are free to enter. The extension of this tactic to rural areas is more controversial and perhaps less likely to provide significant amounts, given the scale of tourism's externalities.

A notable feature of many UK and Irish tourism centres is the focus on quality – in products such as clothing, foods, drinks, gifts, services and accommodation. The argument is that fewer, higher-paying tourists will lessen the externalities and be a less price-sensitive market, immune from price competitors elsewhere. The difference from a tourism tax is that the direct benefits (uncertain in scale in a recession) go to the private sector whereas the public sector (locally and nationally) benefits indirectly.

The trend since 2011 in Ireland has been to reduce taxes in the tourism industry (VAT, Value Added Tax; employers' PAYE, Pay As You Earn contributions; and an air travel tax), to stimulate growth in numbers and employment. However, access to forest parks and some private cultural heritage resources incurs charges. Access for walking and hiking is supported by the Exchequer through maintenance payments to landowners and these may be curtailed because of economic recession. Studies have shown that some tourists are Willing To Pay (WTP) for such access (Buckley et al. 2009). Similar to findings by Dehez et al. among recreationists in the Gironde Estuary, there is some evidence of willingness among recreationists to pay for non-use value, in terms of scenic landscape qualities, as well as use-value public goods in Ireland (Yadav and O'Neill 2013). WTP studies in the UK have shown similar results but their sensitivity to the research methods used has limited their practical application and policy impact.

Rural tourism destinations in the UK and Ireland include iconic sites that attract large numbers of tourists (e.g. Stonehenge, the Lake District, Hadrian's Wall in England and Newgrange, the Lakes of Killarney and Inis Mór on the Aran Islands in Ireland). In general, however, much rural tourism consists of small and medium-sized businesses that are widely distributed and these can be greatly assisted by flagship developments (Sharpley 2007). Overcoming geographical and business fragmentation is, however, often viewed as problematic.

A more integrated approach between tourism and other sectors of the economy is recognised as necessary in the UK and Ireland, as a way of contributing to regional development (Cawley and Gillmor 2008). There is a growing realisation of how tourism interacts not only with general economic development but also with many other aspects of public policy – for example, immigration policy and landscape protection. The agri-environmental Rural Environmental Protection

Scheme has served to maintain scenic landscapes in remoter Ireland since the mid-1990s. In the UK perhaps more than in Ireland, tourism's needs are usually less important than other policy goals such as revenue raising, immigration control or landscape protection.

Saxena et al. (2007), Clark and Chabrel (2007) and Bramwell (2011) have shown how one can analyse and measure the all-round effects of tourism on the various stakeholders and how one can identify forms of tourism that will maximise (or at least increase) the total benefit among all the stakeholders. These studies illustrate that the personal and community social capital of entrepreneurs are influential in moulding their capacities to use local resources sustainably to promote tourism and contribute to local and regional development. Loubet and Bensahel draw on Amartya Sen's work to study the impact of mutually reinforcing personal and community capacities with reference to tourism within a territorial framework, in the Rhône-Alpes region. Their results illustrate that tourism capacity is affected by several factors including cultural economy, social relationships, the scale of touristic resources and the resilience of local identity. It must be remembered also that tourism is never free from conflict, nor is any other type of development, rural or urban. Conflicts around tourism are inevitable in part because of the sector's many stakeholders – the residents, tourists, businesses and public agencies – whose perceptions of, and interests in, tourism do not always coincide.

Increasingly in the UK and Ireland links between food and tourism are being promoted, especially through food trails which incorporate both local food producers and restaurants, as a way of embedding tourism more fully in the locality and contributing to local economies (Sims 2009). Such embedding formed part of the philosophy behind Fáilte Ireland's National Food Implementation Framework 2011–2013. An association with place is present but the concept of *terroir* is less well developed than in France. Mollard and Vollet's comparative research in Savoy and Auvergne is instructive in illustrating that the potential for local amenities to contribute to the valorisation of food and tourism depends on: (i) their being attractive, known and appreciated; (ii) clear delineation of the territory; and (iii) congruence between the amenities and the products or services. A strategic approach is required that coordinates public and private actions to preserve amenities, differentiates the profiles of the potential target populations and maintains a long-term perspective instead of short-term gain.

Summary and Conclusion

Tourism makes important contributions to the economies of France, the UK and Ireland. The UK and Ireland have features in common in terms of their tourism resources but there are also differences. Interesting perspectives on rural tourism emerge from the experience of the three countries. Geography is not deterministic but certainly influences some of the dominant types of tourism present; thus, sun resorts are of particular importance in southern France but sunshine and high temperatures are less predictable around the coasts of the UK and Ireland. The high elevation of the Rhône-Alpes region and the Pyrenees gives France winter tourism resorts – the UK has only one equivalent. The administrative context for tourism differs between the three countries, with the county, district or equivalent being the lowest administrative level in the UK and Ireland with significant tourism functions. The UK and Ireland also differ from France in the more severe impacts of economic recession on their tourism industries.

Natural, cultural and social resources are key assets for tourism in all three countries and measures are in place to protect the first two and support the third. All three countries are subject to EU legislation for environmental protection. The working out of conservation measures on the ground differs, to some extent, because of differing institutional frameworks and inherited norms. Some rural areas in all countries have experienced a loss of human capital through outmigration. Innovative tourism enterprises have been established, however, through individual effort and social networking. It is clear that local personal and territorial capacities are important in generating small-scale tourism development in all three countries and these deserve support from public agencies. Tourism stakeholders in the UK and Ireland are also seeking to follow the established French model of capturing a rent (both for the location and for the quality) from food and tourism products based on a wide range of local natural and cultural amenities.

To some extent the absence in the UK and Ireland of a tourism function at a level equivalent to the French commune, or community of communes, weakens the capacities of local communities to undertake collaborative tourism activities. Exceptions include a growing number of locally organised food trails and festivals in both countries. The UK has also experienced a weakening of regional support for tourism. The creation of a western coastal touring route in Ireland reflects an increased commitment by the national tourism authority to contributing to local and regional economies through tourism.

Some of the most marked differences between the three countries arise in the context of national and regional parks and their governance. French regional nature parks and the UK's national parks follow a participative-management model which involves a range of goals (conservation and development) and of public and private stakeholders. In contrast the Irish national parks are in state ownership. Given the importance of such parks for nature conservation and tourism, further insights should be gained from comparative study.

All three countries experienced the phenomenon of seaside resort development in the nineteenth century. The Mediterranean coastal resorts of France have continued to expand since the 1930s and have become areas of marked in-migration, whereas the seaside resorts of the UK and Ireland have generally suffered decline since the 1970s followed by re-investment and restructuring. France also developed winter tourism resorts during the twentieth century which contributed to regional development in marginal locations. Some problems are emerging associated with a need for reinvestment and competition from newer destinations which have parallels with the fate of the coastal resorts in the UK and Ireland during the 1970s.

The French experience illustrates that new communication technologies provide scope to find innovative solutions to attracting tourists.

Finding ways of increasing the contribution of tourism to regional and local incomes and development is receiving increased attention in all three countries, using a range of different mechanisms. The capacities to raise taxes from tourism at a commune, or community of communes, scale in France are absent in the UK or Ireland. There is also a reluctance to introduce such taxes during the current recession in case it depresses tourist numbers further. The willingness of recreationists to pay for recreational use of the countryside and protection of landscapes as public goods is being investigated in all three countries as a way of offsetting tourism's externality costs. It is likely that the costs as well as the benefits of tourism for rural and regional economies will receive increased attention in future discussion.

References

Agarwal, S. 2002. Restructuring seaside tourism: the resort lifecycle. *Annals of Tourism Research*, 29(1), 25–55.

Baum, T. and Szivas, E. 2008. HRD in tourism: a role for government? *Tourism Management*, 29(4), 783–94.

Bramwell, B. 2011. Governance, the state and sustainable tourism: a political economy approach. *Journal of Sustainable Tourism*, 19(4–5), 459–77.

Buckley, C., van Rensburg, T. and Hynes, S. 2009. Recreational demand for farm commonage in Ireland: a contingent valuation assessment. *Land Use Policy*, 26(3), 846–54.

Cawley, M. and Gillmor, D.A. 2008. Integrated rural tourism: concepts and practice. *Annals of Tourism Research*, 35(2), 316–37.

Clark, G. and Chabrel, M. 2007. Measuring integrated rural tourism. *Tourism Geographies*, 9(4), 371–86.

Coleman, J.S. 1988. Social capital in the creation of human capital. *American Journal of Sociology*, 94, Supplement S95-S120.

Department for Communities and Local Government. 2006. *Good Practice Guide on Planning for Tourism*. [Online]. Available at: https://www.gov.uk/ government/uploads/system/uploads/attachment_data/file/7725/151753.pdf [accessed: 23 April 2013].

Department for Culture, Media and Sport. 2011. *Government Tourism Policy*. [Online]. Available at: https://www.gov.uk/government/uploads/system/ uploads/attachment_data/file/78416/Government2_Tourism_Policy_2011.pdf [accessed: 23 April 2013].

Everett, S. and Aitchison, C. 2008. The role of food tourism in sustaining regional identity: a case study of Cornwall, South West England. *Journal of Sustainable Tourism*, 16(2), 150–67.

Fáilte Ireland. 2012. *Tourism Barometer*. [Online] Available at: http://www.
    failteireland.i.e./FailteIreland/media/WebsiteStructure/Documents/3_
    Research_Insights/3_General_SurveysReports/REPORT_Failte_Ireland_
    Barometer_Dec_2012-1.pdf?ext=.pdf [accessed: 20 April 2013].

Garcia, B., Melville, R. and Cox, T. 2010. *Creating an Impact: Liverpool's
    Experience as European Capital of Culture*. [Online]. Available at: http://
    www.liv.ac.uk/impacts08/Papers/Creating_an_Impact_-_web.pdf [accessed:
    23 April 2013].

Kindermann, G. and Gormally, M.J. 2013. Stakeholder perceptions of recreational
    and management impacts on protected coastal dune systems: a comparison of
    three European countries. *Land Use Policy*, 31, 472–85.

Kneafsey, M. 2001. Rural cultural economy: tourism and social relations. *Annals
    of Tourism Research*, 28(3), 762–83.

McKenna, J., O'Hagan, A.M., Power, J., McLeod, M. and Cooper, A. 2007. Coastal
    dune conservation on an Irish commonage: community based management or
    tragedy of the commons? *The Geographical Journal*, 173(2), 157–69.

Mottiar, Z. and Quinn, B. 2001. The economic and social effects of the Seaside
    Resort Areas Scheme. *Administration*, 49(3), 68–87.

Northwest Development Agency. 2003. *A New Vision for North West Coastal
    Resorts*. [Online]. Available at: http://www.coastalcommunities.co.uk/library/
    published_research/A_new_vision_for_Northwest_coastal_resorts.pdf
    [accessed. 23 April 2013].

Page, S., Song, H. and Wu, D.C. 2012. Assessing the impacts of the global
    economic crisis and swine flu on inbound tourism demand in the United
    Kingdom. *Journal of Travel Research*, 5(2), 142–53.

Royal Society for the Protection of Birds. 2002. *RSPB Reserves and Local
    Economies*. [Online]. Available at: http://www.rspb.org.uk/Images/
    Reserves%20and%20Local%20Economies_tcm9-133069.pdf [accessed: 23
    April 2013].

Sage, C. 2003. Social embeddedness and relations of regard: alternative 'good
    food' networks in south-west Ireland. *Journal of Rural Studies*, 19(1), 47–60.

Saxena, G., Clark, G., Oliver, T. and Ilbery, B. 2007. Conceptualising integrated
    rural tourism. *Tourism Geographies*, 9(4), 347–70.

Sharpley, R. 2007. Flagship attractions and sustainable rural tourism development:
    the case of Alnwick Garden, England. *Journal of Sustainable Tourism*,
    15(2), 125–43.

Sims, R. 2009. Food, place and authenticity: local food and the sustainable tourism
    experience. *Journal of Sustainable Tourism*, 17(3), 321–36.

Visit Britain. 2012. *Annual Review 2011–12*. [Online]. Available at: http://www.
    visitbritainannualreview2011–2012.org/ [accessed: 23 April 2013].

Visit England. 2011. *A Strategic Framework for Tourism 2010–2020*. [Online].
    Available at: http://www.visitengland.org/Images/Strategic%20Framework%20
    main%20document_tcm30-33240.pdf [accessed: 23 April 2013].

Visit Scotland. 2010. *Visit Scotland Corporate Plan 2013/2016*. [Online]. Available at: http://www.visitscotland.org/pdf/Corporate%20Plan%2013-16.pdf [accessed: 23 April 2013].

Yadav, L.P. and O'Neill, S. 2013. Is there agreement between beneficiaries on who should bear the costs of conserving farm landscapes? *Tourism Management*, 39(1), 62–70.

Chapter 15

Tourism in Spain:
Southern European Perspectives

Isabel Cortés Jiménez and Salvador Anton Clavé

Introduction

The Spanish tourism sector has attracted the attention of scholars and policymakers given the unfaltering expansion of tourism since the 1960s. Like France, Spain is one of the leading countries worldwide in inbound tourism and this notably determined the geographic location of leisure activities. Tourism mobility in Europe has traditionally responded to flows of tourists from the northern countries to the southern destinations in the search of sea, sun, and sand (3-S tourism). The development of beach tourism in southern Europe is therefore not surprising, with Spain as one of the main recipients of mass tourism, and the subsequent spread of tourist resorts all along the Spanish Mediterranean coast and the Balearic and Canary Islands.

However, the particularity of Spain from a research viewpoint lies in its ability to take advantage of the expansion of tourism, also seen as a major source of foreign currency, for the development of the country. Likewise, from a geographical distribution perspective, it is essential to examine the recent development of strategies to renovate coastal mature destinations as well as the emergence of urban tourism and the spread of tourism along rural and natural interest areas, often via the development of new specific products.

This chapter analyses the factors that determine the current map of tourism in Spain from an economic and geographical perspective, the basics of the Spanish tourism model of development and recent changes in the geographic scope of the activity and economic performance. It is important to understand the new paradigm and the recent economic events that influence tourism and leisure such as low-cost carriers, short and frequent holidays throughout the year, and emerging (and competing) destinations. We will begin with a comparative overview of the tourism sector in Spain and France.

Overview of the Current Tourism Sector in Spain

Spain has, together with France, been one of the world's top tourist destinations and this privileged position has remained up to date. According to the latest UN World

Tourism Organization (UNWTO) figures, France is the world's top destination while Spain ranks fourth[1] in terms of international tourist arrivals. In terms of international tourism receipts Spain ranks second while France occupies the third position. Regarding the geographical distribution of international tourists in Spain, the regions that received the largest number of tourists in order are Catalonia, the Canary Islands, the Balearic Islands and Andalusia (IET 2011).

Domestic tourism in Spain and France is not to be overlooked. The proportion of this category is the same in Spain and France. For trips of four or more nights, 83.3 per cent of Spanish tourists choose a Spanish destination while 82.1 per cent of French tourists choose a French destination (IET 2011). According to the same source, in 2011, Spanish residents did 160.8 million trips, 91.7 per cent of which were in Spain, and their main destinations were, in order of importance, Andalusia, Catalonia, Castile-Leon and the Valencian Community. With the exception of Castile-Leon, the rest of the regions are distributed all along the Mediterranean coast.

From a general perspective, there are a number of similarities in the main factors contributing to the success of tourism in France and Spain, following the list of factors presented by Boniface and Cooper (2009). France and Spain are the largest and second largest countries in Western Europe, respectively. Both countries have a variety of climates and landscape features that allow for different types of tourism, from beach tourism to ski tourism. French and Spanish are two of the most widely spoken languages in the world. Even if the culture of 'spending the summer in the south' has benefited the development of a specific type of tourism in these two countries, each one has a specific cultural heritage that makes it unique. France is reputed for fashion, haute couture and fine cuisine whereas Spain is identified with the flamenco folklore tradition, festivities and pilgrimages, and bullfighting, although this image is evolving. After the Spanish transition, the autonomous communities have tried to develop an image linked to their own identity (Fernández Cifuentes 2007). Both countries stand out in worldwide recognised contributions to literature and the arts. While the French Mediterranean coast is related to luxury and high spenders, e.g. the French Riviera (Marbella or Ibiza in Spain), the Spanish Mediterranean coast is more generally related to mass tourism and holiday package tourists, which is also the case of the Languedoc-Roussillon French coastal region. These features have contributed to constant efforts to attract other types of tourists over the decades with some success although Spain continues to be associated most with the 3-S tourist group.

Other differences in the tourism development process are the time scale of events and the difference in vision about the planning of the activity from the time tourism emerged as a true economic driver in the 1960s. Firstly, a review of certain historical facts shows that France is ahead of Spain. For example, Paris

---

1 In 2011, France received 79.5 million tourist arrivals and US$ 53.8 billion tourism receipts whereas Spain received 56.7 million tourist arrivals and US$ 59.9 billion tourism receipts.

held the Olympic Games for the first time in 1900 (also in 1924) while in Spain the tourism sector flourished as from the 1960s and Barcelona held the Olympic Games in 1992. Secondly, although Spain showed early signs of official attention to tourism with the first national commission of tourism created in 1905 (Barke and Towner 1996) and France set up a national tourism office for the first time in 1910 (Boniface and Cooper 2009), the Franco dictatorial regime following the civil war deteriorated not only the potential attraction of tourists into Spanish territory but also conditioned the process of emergence of the activity in the 1960s. Thus, while in France the mass tourism development process has been linked to the implementation of major planning projects such as those in the Languedoc-Roussillon and Aquitaine coasts since the 1960s, the starting process in Spain was without any planning direction and rather fragmented, spontaneous and financially speculative. Also, from the very beginning, it included the development of the real estate industry rather than purely touristic activity.

Tourism Expansion in Spain: An Economic Perspective

During the seventeenth and eighteenth centuries, Spain remained an unknown destination which was not part of the Grand Tour; Italy and France were the most popular destinations in Europe (Barke and Towner 1996). In the nineteenth century, timid attempts to attract tourists occurred, often related to health resorts, but the poor transport infrastructure and scarce and mostly low-quality accommodation and catering services did not motivate tourism. In the first half of the twentieth century there was official interest for the tourism sector, however the country suffered dictatorships and a civil war. The turning point for Spain can be dated to the 1960s, achieving in a relatively short time span an enormous growth of the tourism sector, which 'with the balance of payments, receipts from tourism have played a far greater role in Spain than in virtually any other industrialised economy' (Bote Gómez and Sinclair 1996: 89).

In 1958 Spain joined the OECD and in 1959 Spain joined the IMF and The World Bank. In 1959, the Spanish government launched the Stabilisation Plan whose main objectives were to achieve economic stability, equilibrium of the balance of payments and to strengthen the currency. That plan implied the opening of the country to outside trade (after a post-war period of autarchy) and consisted of a series of initiatives. Significant examples are the cutting of import tariffs and the freedom to import raw materials and capital goods, which proved to be necessary for industrialisation. This plan allowed foreigners to invest freely in Spain as long as foreign ownership did not exceed 50 per cent (this was progressively relaxed later), and the borders were opened to foreign tourists. The impact of these measures was immediate. International tourism receipts increased in one year (1960–1961) more than five million pesetas (1960–1961) and in 1963–64 these figures tripled. We can draw on the study by Cortés Jiménez (2007) of the annual evolution of tourism receipts in Spain from 1960 and look at the ten-year period from 1960 to

2000 (see Table 15.1). In the 1960s, tourism receipts increased by 416 per cent, whereas the 1970s and 1980s exceeded growth rates of 250 per cent. Such a huge expansion allowed Spain to become a strong emerging destination with a robust consolidation in the 1990s, and still one of the world's top four destinations.

Table 15.1   Economic features of Spain, 1960–2000

	1960	1970	1980	1990	2000
Real GDP per capita (€)	1,107	2,729	6,446	12,525	19,037
Labour force (million people)	11.7	12.7	13.9	15.7	17.8
Investment share of real GDP (%)	22.6	30.2	25.8	27.4	25.5
Exports of goods and services (% GDP)	8.4	12.6	14.8	16.3	30.1
International tourism receipts (million €)	107	707	3,003	11,390	33,750
Over previous decade: Growth rate of international tourism receipts (%)		416	270	283	161

Source: Adapted from Cortés Jiménez (2007).

With the volume and growth of these figures, it is not a surprise that receipts from tourism, as Bote Gómez and Sinclair (1996) pointed out, served to alleviate the balance of payments. During the 1960s, foreign currency receipts from tourism dominated receipts from the uncompetitive agricultural and manufacturing sectors, and continued to offset deficits of the balance of trade in the 1970s and 1980s.

The development process of Spain has not followed the traditional path of an agricultural-based economy into an industry-based one with the last stage of the service sector expansion. As Bote Gómez and Sinclair (1996) explain, Spain had an alternative development model moving from agriculture into services, in this case the tourism sector, which played a role by financing the industrialisation process via the imports of the necessary capital goods. According to these authors, in 1955, the value of production was broken down into 20 per cent from agriculture, 38 per cent from industry, and 42 per cent from services (6 per cent of which correspond to construction). According to World Development Indicators, in 1970, agriculture accounted for only 10 per cent of GDP while the industry sector was 40 per cent and services 50 per cent. In 2010, agriculture was only 3 per cent of GDP, industry 26 per cent and services 71 per cent. Currently, the tourism sector, both domestic and international, contributes to the Spanish national accounts by representing more than 10 per cent of the GDP and generating more than 2 million jobs (INE 2011).

In the literature, Spain is often referred as an archetypal example of an economy that made an optimal use of its tourism advantages in achieving the industrialisation process. This unique experience has promoted a large body of literature and it receives a theoretical treatment known as the Tourism-Led

Growth (TLG) hypothesis that assumes that the expansion of inbound tourism serves as a mechanism to achieve long-run economic growth. Proponents of the TLG hypothesis emphasize that international tourism can bring foreign exchange, generate employment, spur local investments, exploit economies of scale, and diffuse technical knowledge.

The first econometric study for Spain was presented by Balaguer and Cantavella-Jordá (2002) who derived the TLG hypothesis from the largely studied export-led growth hypothesis while understanding tourism as a particular type of export where it is the consumer who moves rather than the good. This study has been followed by other authors interested in demonstrating the soundness of the Spanish development model (Cortés Jiménez and Pulina 2010, Nowak et al. 2007). They empirically demonstrate the importance of tourism to the long-run economic growth via financing capital goods imports (machinery and technology) necessary for industrialisation and subsequently the country's growth. It is what Nowak et al. (2007) call the TKIG (tourism-capital goods imports-growth) hypothesis or what, according to Cortés Jiménez and Pulina (2010), is in complement with the expansion of human and physical capital. Recently there has been a proliferation of research studies to try to understand whether the TLG hypothesis is valid for other countries but so far the success of this hypothesis cannot be generalized. For future possible investigation, it might be interesting to consider the very diverse natures of these economic impacts, similarly to Cremer-Schulte and Dissart's or Loubet and Bensahel's chapters of this book.

However, the tourism industry is unevenly distributed across Spain. In 2011, six regions (out of 17) concentrated 72.6 per cent of people employed in the tourism sector (IET 2012). These regions are: Catalonia, Andalusia, the Community of Madrid, the Valencian Community, the Canary Islands and the Balearic Islands. With respect to the relative importance of tourism by region, the Canary Islands and the Balearic Islands stand out with 25.5 per cent and 25.4 per cent of total tourism sector employees respectively, whilst the national average was 11.8 per cent. When employment opportunities are limited, the tourism industry is perceived as a potential generator of jobs. In fact, there is an increase of tourism infrastructure (hotel and catering services) in Spanish regions that are not tourism-specialised but are trying to develop tourism. Spanish regions rely on territorial assets in terms of culture, environment and heritage in order to exploit the potential of tourism.

In terms of future investigation, there is no doubt of the contribution of tourism to economic growth in Spain so new lines of research can be developed towards the contribution of tourism to human development, understood as the process of enlarging people's choices and opportunities. For example, these studies may adopt the capability approach as the driving methodology like in Loubet and Bensahel's work. In any case, further analyses on the effects of tourism in Spain should take into account issues of well-being and quality of life, for example, in terms of income, stable employment, access to services, decent housing conditions, environmentally-friendly activities, education, health, among others. These, in turn, can benefit both the local community and visitors.

Tourism Expansion in Spain: Geographical Insights

The most obvious result of the described tourism development is at the geographical level. A fundamental characteristic of the existing model is its strong association with certain resources and/or with some cultural features and the development of specific tourist areas and spots. As a starting point, let us examine the current geographical distribution of tourism in Spain (see Figures 15.1 and 15.2) ranking the destinations with the highest number of hotel overnights in 2012.

As it can be observed, the two most important tourism markets are urban and beach tourism, the former is still expanding while the latter has levelled off. There are wide disparities in the spatial distribution of the activity, with large territories of internal and northern regions lacking any outstanding tourism destination. Spain lags behind France, where generalised rural tourism, nature-related tourism and cultural and heritage medium city tourism have a longer tradition (as shown in several chapters of this book such as Cazals and Lyser's, Ginelli's, Dehez et al.'s or Mollard and Vollet's).

Figure 15.1 shows the 15 top urban destinations in Spain. Barcelona and Madrid are the most important ones, with a substantial higher number of overnights than the rest of cities and tourist profiles that combine tourism business and leisure travel with multiple motivations. They have also a very powerful hotel industry and, in most cases, a higher level of prices. Compared to France, while Madrid has 9.7 international visitors and Barcelona 7.5 million in 2012, Paris has about 16 million of international arrivals per year.

Among the other Spanish cities with significant tourism activity there are heritage cities such as Salamanca, Santiago de Compostela and the Andalusian cities, regional hubs such as Pamplona, Valencia or Zaragoza, cities in beach tourism regions such as Alicante, Palma de Mallorca and Las Palmas de Gran Canaria and the two largest metropolitan areas in the Basque Country. The development of cultural amenities is a key feature in the recent emergence of cities as culture-oriented attractions. This is the case of Barcelona and Bilbao with attractions like the Sagrada Familia and the Guggenheim museum as main icons of this process. A very fragile path of development that is dependent in many cases on the celebration of events (Zaragoza) or on image building through architecture, global sports or cultural facilities (Valencia) is also observed.

Although heritage and cultural icons are part of the landscape of most Spanish cities, there are only a few specialised art and culture cities among the top 15 urban destinations in Spain. This is a clear difference not only with France but also with other Southern countries such as Italy, where art cities with urban heritage tourism is highly significant. A noteworthy example is the role of Santiago de Compostela linked to the cultural project of the Route to Santiago. Otherwise, beyond its characteristics, the tourism attractiveness of each city has to do especially with its external connectivity. In this sense, Vera and Ivars (2009) demonstrate the relationship between the recent growth of tourism in selected cities and the expansion of low-cost airlines. For the Spanish case indeed, accessibility features

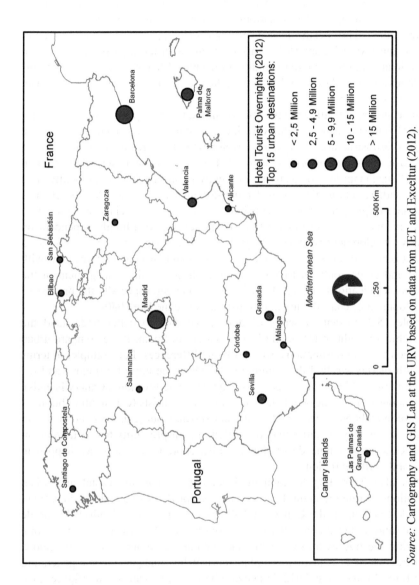

Source: Cartography and GIS Lab at the URV based on data from IET and Exceltur (2012).

Figure 15.1   Top Spanish urban destinations in 2012

of this type must be fully taken into account in addition to traditional access modes like motorway or distance to urban centres (similarly to Cremer-Schulte and Dissart).

When we analyse the top 25 beach tourism destinations, we observe that the largest number of top beach destinations is concentrated in the Balearic and Canary Islands, followed by specific coastal spots in Catalonia, the Valencian Community and Andalusia (see Figure 15.2). This is in line with the high presence of both international and domestic tourism along the entire Mediterranean coastline plus the islands and is the key to understanding the role of Spain among the top tourism receivers in the world.

Since the second half of the twentieth century, the multiplication of elementary forms of tourism such as holiday residences, golf courses, campsites, resorts, transport infrastructures and hotel development has created complex and in some cases chaotic territorial systems. It has brought about new challenges in terms of sustainability, connectivity, productivity and territorial competitiveness in line with results explained by Cremer-Schulte and Dissart. Moreover, it is important to highlight that besides the hotel and other commercial accommodation developments, the Spanish beach tourism model has been highly dependent on property development with very huge levels of growth since the 1990s. So a relevant issue to discuss about beach tourism in Spain, in a comparative view with France and other Southern Mediterranean countries, is the management of the territorial implications of coastal tourism development, especially the process of redevelopment of coastal tourism destinations since the late 1980s.

Table 15.2 presents a series of descriptive data to better understand the geographical weight of urban and beach tourism in Spain. If we compare urban and beach tourism destinations, we find large differences. For example, in terms of length of stay we find the minimum of 1.69 in the city of Zaragoza and the maximum of 9.03 in the municipality of Pájara (in Fuerteventura, Canary Islands). This responds to the seasonal behaviour of coastal tourists (e.g. summer holidays of approximately one week) and the city tourist behaviour (e.g. weekend visits). In general, longer stays in cities may be related to their proximity to coastal tourism dynamics such as Palma de Mallorca, whilst shorter stays in cities happen in inland and northern regions.

It is also interesting to compare income per room in coastal and urban destinations. While the highest earners are, except Barcelona and San Sebastián, beach destinations in the Canary and Balearic Islands, only Madrid, Palma de Mallorca and Bilbao among urban destinations achieve figures up to €45 per room. Observing the figures on overnights and income per room between Barcelona and Zaragoza, it is evident that urban tourism has unequal income-generating capabilities. Moreover, in 2012 Zaragoza achieved significantly lower figures than any of the top 25 coastal destinations, despite the strong seasonal character of beach tourism. This is a clear indicator of the low profitability of tourism in such cities and, secondly, of the importance of reducing seasonality (Canary Islands) and having a clear destination image attracting high-spending segments (such

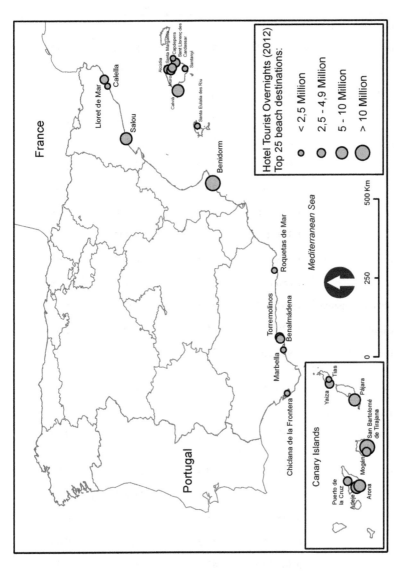

Source: Cartography and GIS Lab at the URV based on data from IET and Exceltur (2012).

Figure 15.2   Top Spanish beach destinations in 2012

Table 15.2   Top urban and beach destinations in Spain in 2012

Destinations	Hotel tourist overnights	Hotel RevPAR (€)	Maximum hotel beds in destination	Length of stay (nights)
Top urban destinations				
Barcelona	16,184,168	78.3	68,939	2.47
Madrid	15,454,314	52.9	80,656	1.95
Palma de Mallorca	7,871,367	50.5	41,425	4.62
Sevilla	3,581,089	42.2	19,041	1.91
Valencia	3,203,091	38.7	17,542	2.03
Granada	2,608,439	34.0	13,509	1.79
Málaga	1,813,017	39.5	9,413	1.91
Bilbao	1,468,736	47.6	7,350	1.85
Alicante	1,371,885	31.4	8,205	2.31
Zaragoza	1,308,940	21.3	10,604	1.69
Córdoba	1,286,049	33.6	6,849	1.58
Santiago de Compostela	1,064,961	27.5	7,955	1.97
San Sebastián	1,028,661	65.5	4,908	1.97
Las Palmas de Gran Canaria	982,852	35.2	5,691	3.25
Salamanca	910,890	25.6	5,724	1.56
Top beach destinations				
San Bartolomé de Tirajana	10,695,389	68.2	40,025	7.99
Benidorm	10,418,343	44.4	40,719	5.82
Adeje	9,742,233	67.4	34,991	7.83
Calvià	8,718,592	48.7	50,000	6.72
Pájara	6,720,985	56.3	29,222	9.03
Salou	5,483,249	47.0	33,092	5.24
Arona	5,316,537	58.5	18,468	7.99
Lloret de Mar	4,919,809	35.9	31,534	4.97

Destinations	Hotel tourist overnights	Hotel RevPAR (€)	Maximum hotel beds in destination	Length of stay (nights)
Torremolinos	4,626,603	44.0	20,617	5.12
Yaiza	4,166,811	43.0	16,254	7.56
Sant Llorenç des Cardassar	3,824,723	49.3	23,414	7.26
Puerto de la Cruz	3,740,495	37.6	15,187	7.52
Mogán	3,320,844	54.4	12,256	8.04
Alcúdia	3,174,912	49.5	19,658	7.53
Muro	2,981,544	63.5	16,471	7.76
Benalmádena	2,554,902	46.6	12,875	5.89
Santa Margalida	2,508,840	41.5	14,065	7.98
Marbella	2,444,773	67.8	16,433	4.33
Tías	2,426,278	59.7	9,486	8.51
Capdepera	2,303,337	47.7	15,355	7.30
Roquetas de Mar	1,999,566	35.3	14,811	5.81
Calella	1,998,546	31.9	11,896	4.90
Santa Eulalia des Riu	1,942,712	58.8	15,484	6.88
Chiclana de la Frontera	1,868,903	68.0	12,160	4.38
Santanyí	1,852,388	68.2	11,702	7.09

Note: RevPAR is the revenue per available room. A performance metric in the hotel industry, it is calculated by multiplying a hotel's average daily room rate by its occupancy rate.

Source: Authors, based on data from IET and Exceltur (2012).

as Ibiza, some Mallorca destinations or Marbella) as key factors to increase the economic impact of tourism in coastal destinations.

Moreover, the table includes the maximum number of hotel beds per destination, showing that two urban destinations have more than 60,000 hotel beds (Madrid and Barcelona) and five coastal destinations more than 30,000 hotel beds (Calvià, Benidorm, San Bartolomé de Tirajana, Adeje, Salou and Lloret de Mar). In addition to property vacational supply in the form of second homes or part time residences and apartments, it is worth noting that peninsular beach destinations such as Benidorm, Salou and Lloret de Mar have also an important supply of campground facilities ranging from 12,582 tourist places in Benidorm to 9,658 in Salou and 5,241 in Lloret de Mar.

A key feature of the tourism dynamics in Spain is the discussion about the need to redevelop beach destinations and the creation of specific policy tools to achieve this challenge. Since the late 1980s, Spanish mass beach destinations have been faced with new challenges. These include:

- growing competition among destinations;
- the transformation of tourist profiles;
- the transformation of systems of intermediation;
- increased awareness of the environmental and social impacts related to the development of the activity; and
- the role of the new technologies as providers of information and in terms of positioning destinations among others (Anton Clavé 2012a).

Finally, many of these transformations (intermediation, new technologies, etc.) refer to the process of the co-construction of tourist services as described by Frochot in this book.

In response to these changes, since the late 1980s, the destinations have undergone reactive processes of adaptation and improvement, innovative dynamics associated with the gradual integration of specific products and transitional situations where the tourist aspect has given way to the urban and metropolitan aspect. Thus, three types of destinations – reactive, creative and transitive – have been distinguished on the Spanish coast based on the results of the decisions taken by their stakeholders (see Anton Clavé 2012b). For example, while reactive destinations such as Benidorm have adopted measures of adjustment fundamentally aimed at maintaining the activity, innovative destinations such as Salou have proposed new development strategies based on the development of new products aimed at capturing new visitors, and transitive destinations (most of them not in the top of the beach destination ranking) such as Benicàssim or Fuengirola are intensifying urban residential functions before other recreational and tourism linked developments. Such activities may have social impacts aside from the possible economic benefits for tourism and the local industry.

Parallel to this, new focuses of planning are now being applied in beach tourist destinations in addition to the traditional systems of urban planning. The first initiative was the launching of the *Framework Plan for the Competitiveness of Spanish Tourism, Futures* (1992–1995) in the early 1990s (see Ivars 2004). In the new millennium, the *Horizon 2020 Spanish Tourism Plan* and related provisions for the short and medium term have been drafted and enacted (see Vera Rebollo et al. 2011). This includes programmes to boost tourist products, initiatives to rehabilitate amenities and urban and natural environments such as the *Tourism Infrastructures Modernisation Fund* (FOMIT); the *Plan Renove*, a renewal plan dedicated to modernising the supply of tourism accommodation, catering and leisure facilities; the *Plan FuturE*, which aimed to implement eco-efficiency criteria in tourist facilities; and especially the *Special Reassessment Plans for Mature Destinations* (including specific urban and strategic actions in Palma de

Mallorca, Costa del Sol, Gran Canaria and Tenerife), aimed at the modernisation of supply and the overall improvement of the quality of the environment and landscape of destinations (see also Beas Secall 2012). Along the same lines, the *21st Century Coastal Tourism Plan* was approved in 2011.

It is without question that Spain has developed and implemented a constructive long-term policy over the last 20 years with the aim of maintaining the competitiveness of its beach destinations. The results have been mixed at the local level because the success of the implementation in each destination depends on the local strategic management and resort organisation. This is in line with the chapters presented by Marsat and Vlès in this book.

In addition to urban tourism and beach tourism spots, ski destinations are relatively important in Spain, even though they have very low figures of arrivals compared to those of the top urban and beach destinations. Those ski resorts located in the Pyrenees are among the most visited and had the highest number of hotel tourist overnights in 2012 (372,363 overnights) in the municipality of Vielha. This figure not only includes winter sports visitors but also people attracted by the development of year-round recreational facilities. This is a relatively small activity resulting from the 6 million or so ski passes sold by Spanish resorts early in the 2010 decade while 55 million ski passes were sold in France. Tourist demand in this ski destination is mainly domestic.

Otherwise, effects of other tourism activities in Spain are not comparable to those observed in France. This is the case of the 3.5 million of visitors to a theme park such as Port Aventura located 100 km south of Barcelona (the Disneyland resort in Paris attracts about 16 million visits yearly) and, in general, the magnitude of theme and leisure parks tourism activity in France compared to Spain or, inversely, the role of Barcelona as a leading cruise ship port with more than 2.6 million passengers in 2011.

The Challenge of Low-Cost Carriers from the Perspective of Southern European Destinations: the Spanish Case

The tourism industry faces constant challenges, requires constant processes of innovation, and necessitates understanding changes in consumer behaviour, tastes and decision-making processes. This is particularly important in a highly competitive environment where consolidated destinations such as Spain compete with other consolidated destinations across the entire Mediterranean (France, Italy, Greece or Malta) with strong emerging destinations such as Croatia and Turkey, which currently ranks 6th in number of international arrivals in the UNWTO's latest world's top destinations classification. In recent years, the tourism sector has witnessed a series of transformations. The main ones are Low-Cost Carriers (LCCs) versus traditional carriers, independent trip organisation via online booking versus physical travel agencies, short-break tourists versus residential second-home coastal tourists, and the enormous influence of the critical mass of online tourist reviews (after visiting a destination) versus catalogues in the decision process for a destination or specific accommodation. In the following we pay special attention to review the influence of LCCs as drivers for consumer change.

The spread of low-cost flights is the most important aspect explaining the increase in the number of international tourists recorded in six coastal regions of Mediterranean Europe, notably Malta, Croatia, Cyprus, Greece, Italy and Spain. Boniface and Cooper (2009) explain that almost 75 per cent of tourists arrive by air; the inclusive tour market ensures a constant supply of tourists arriving mainly on charter airlines, owned in most cases by the major North European tour operators. Nevertheless, their share of the holiday market is being eroded by the LCCs that can offer greater flexibility in travel arrangements for the increasing numbers of visitors staying in second homes, or in rented apartments and villas. According to Vera and Ivars (2009), from 2000 to 2005 low-cost carrier traffic in Spanish airports rose by 26.9 per cent, while traditional companies decreased by 0.7 per cent. In 2010, the number of passengers using traditional airline companies rose for the first time (1.1 per cent) since 2001. For example, in 2000 Alicante airport had 60 per cent charter traffic and only 10 per cent low-cost carrier traffic but by 2006 LCCs provided 53 per cent and charter airlines 19 per cent (although this was partly due to the re-branding of charter companies that had started operating as LCCs).

According to the IET, in 2011 Spain received 63.5 million of international arrivals, more than a half (56.9 per cent) of which used LCCs. Six regions concentrated 96 per cent of all arrivals by LCC, namely the Balearic Islands, Catalonia, the Canary Islands, Andalusia, the Valencian Community and the Community of Madrid. The Balearic Islands were in the same year the principal destination of the international passengers of LCCs, with a share of 21.6 per cent and an annual growth of 11 per cent, the main markets being Germany and the United Kingdom. Although Madrid and Barcelona are important gateways, most North European holidaymakers fly to one of the regional airports serving a particular holiday area (Boniface and Cooper 2009). The main LCC airports were Palma de Mallorca, Barcelona and Malaga, which altogether received 42.9 per cent of all arrivals in 2011.

Tourists that arrive in Spain via LCCs have the following general profile (IET 2011). There are two main age groups: 15–24 or 65+ years. A remarkable feature is the loyalty of these tourists given that 81.9 per cent were repeat visitors; interestingly 36.3 per cent had already been in Spain at least ten times. These tourists are characterised by an intense use of the Internet (77.3 per cent) and organise their trip individually while only 30 per cent of the tourists using LCCs had contracted a holiday package. An example of the stronger implication of the consumer in the service co-construction process (see Frochot), this category diverges from the category of tourists who travel with traditional carriers. The main motivation for visiting Spain was leisure. Interestingly most of them used owned homes or rented homes while a smaller proportion stayed in hotels. The average expenditure by European tourists travelling to Spain by LCCs (not contracting holiday packages) was lower (€802.40) than that of tourists arriving to Spain by traditional carriers (€1027.40).

However, Vera and Ivars (2009) state that the effects of low-cost carrier operations go beyond the context of the tourism sector and affect land-use and infrastructure planning policies, gradually shaping a new scenario where the specialisation of tourism in real estate along the Spanish Mediterranean coast becomes reinforced. In fact, the development of LCCs to develop new routes usually includes the financial support of institutions and business-oriented associations in the destination area. However, research is needed to understand if LCCs in a mature destination serve effectively as carriers of a new brand of tourists or as carriers of the same tourists reconverted into LCC travellers (from charter all-inclusive packages). Moreover, future investigation on development issues, and more specifically in terms of Loubet and Bensahel's territorial capabilities, might consider the possible impact of LCCs on territorial economic dynamics.

In the case of France, the LCCs have also had a considerable impact in providing business for regional airports, encouraging the foreign ownership of second homes in rural areas, and also allowing the French population to have a wider choice of destinations (Boniface and Cooper 2009). A well-known example is the large presence of British investing in villages near airports where LCCs with routes between the United Kingdom and France operate such as in Dordogne or Gers with the subsequent potential generation of new activities for local businesses. However, little is known of the profile of tourists travelling with LCCs to France; this would be a promising object of future research.

Final Remarks

Spain is a mature destination and one of the most important world tourism destinations. After the huge expansion of tourism in the 1960s, characterised by a lack of planning, the predominance of spontaneity and permissive sector legislation and municipal town planning, followed by consolidation in the 1980s and 1990s, it is currently in a phase of continuous reinvention, diversification and adaptation to new challenges. Today, parallel to major transformations in some of the most important Spanish mass coastal destinations, new tourism modalities have gained significant value since the 1990s including the consolidation of cities as prime tourist destinations.

Nevertheless, over and above tourist emergence in cities and the recent transformation at a small scale in rural areas, the Spanish tourism model is basically still a legacy of the successful tourism development of the 1960s, when the Spanish coast started to become one of the most important leisure peripheries for European tourists. After the 1970s and 1980s, the Spanish demand markets progressively embraced this process, strengthening the model and extending the second-home phenomenon across the entire country. It was during the 1990s that the environment, heritage, culture, cities, sports, entertainment and other assets started to be included in the model, creating a new ability to produce new experiences and emotions.

Spain is perceived as an archetypal example given the huge expansion of tourism in a relatively short time span, which generated a significant influx of foreign currency that contributed to the industrialisation process. Five decades on, Spain is a country specialised in tourism, which is a sector still perceived as bringing opportunities in terms of creation of employment and boosting local economic activity with direct, indirect and induced multiplier effects. Nevertheless, the economic benefits of tourism are somewhat blunted by the extremely uneven distribution of tourism across the country: the Mediterranean coast and the islands continue to be the most important destinations with the largest number of tourists. We therefore need to reconsider what may be perceived as 'benefits' by introducing various economic and social indicators. Once again, the prospect of 'blending perspectives', which is at the heart of this book, will be of great help.

From a more general southern European perspective, the flow of tourists continues to be from North to South in search of warm temperatures; and the LCCs contribute to the ease in reaching new and established destinations alike. However, new challenges constantly appear. For example, it is now, more than ever, crucial for destinations to understand tourist motives and ensure high tourist satisfaction (very quickly transmitted on-line through Web 2.0 technology). Simultaneously, other Mediterranean countries like Portugal, Italy or Greece also have an important share of beach tourism and make constant efforts to attract new tourists, or even attempt to turn away loyal tourists to Spain or France for example, by offering a similar product at very competitive prices. Altogether, they encourage the constant development of new strategies to ensure the loyalty of tourists and to attract new visitors.

References

Anton Clavé, S. 2012a. The change of tourism model and the competitiveness of consolidated destinations. The case of Vila-seca, in *10 Lessons on Tourism. The Challenge of Reinventing Destinations*, edited by S. Anton Clavé. Barcelona: Planeta, 253–67.

—. 2012b. Rethinking mass tourism, space and place, in *Routledge Handbook of Tourism Geographies. New Perspectives on Space, Place and Tourism*, edited by J. Wilson. Oxford: Routledge, 217–24.

Balaguer, J. and Cantavella-Jordá, M. 2002. Tourism as a long-run economic growth factor: the Spanish case. *Applied Economics*, 34, 877–84.

Barke, M. and Towner, J. 1996. Exploring the history of leisure and tourism in Spain, in *Tourism in Spain. Critical Issues*, edited by M. Barke et al. Oxon: CAB International, 3–34.

Beas Secall, L. 2012. Effects of the implementation of tourism excellence plans (1992–2006) in Spain. The case of the Catalan coast. *Journal of Policy Research in Tourism, Leisure and Events*, 4(1), 84–104.

Boniface, B. and Cooper, C. 2009. *Worldwide Destinations Casebook. The Geography of Travel and Tourism*. 2nd Edition. Oxford: BH-Elsevier.

Bote Gómez, V. and Sinclair, M.T. 1996. Tourism, the Spanish economy and the balance of payments, in *Tourism in Spain. Critical Issues*, edited by M. Barke et al. Oxon: CAB International, 89–117.

Cortés Jiménez, I. 2007. *Essays on Tourism and Economic Growth: Spain and Italy Revisited*. PhD Thesis, Universitat de Barcelona.

Cortés Jiménez, I. and Pulina, M. 2010. Inbound tourism and long-run economic growth. *Current Issues in Tourism*, 13(1), 61–74.

Exceltur. 2012. *Barómetro de la Rentabilidad y el Empleo de los Destinos Turísticos Españoles. Balance de 2012*. Madrid: Exceltur.

Fernández Cifuentes, L. 2007. Southern exposure: early tourism and Spanish national identity. *Journal of Iberian and Latin American Studies*, 13(2), 133–48.

IET (Instituto de Estudios Turisticos). [online]. Available at: http://www.iet. tourspain.es/ [accessed: 28 March 2013].

Ivars, J.A. 2004. Tourism planning in Spain: evolution and perspectives. *Annals of Tourism Research*, 31(2), 313–33.

Nowak, J., Sahli, M. and Cortés Jiménez, I. 2007. Tourism, capital goods imports and economic growth: theory and evidence for Spain. *Tourism Economics*, 13(4), 515–36.

UN World Tourism Organisation. [online]. Available at: http://www.unwto.org/ [accessed: 28 March 2013].

Vera Rebollo, J.F. (coord.), López Palomeque, F., Marchena, M.J. and Anton Clavé, S. 2011. *Análisis Territorial del Turismo y Planificación de Destinos Turísticos*. València: Tirant lo Blanch.

Vera, J.F. and Ivars, J. 2009. Spread of low-cost carriers: tourism and regional policy effects in Spain. *Regional Studies*, 43, 559–70.

Index